D1005994

Yes, Lord,
I'm Comin' Home!

DOUBLEDAY

New York   London   Toronto   Sydney   Auckland

Yes, Lord,

COUNTRY MUSIC STARS

I'm Comin'

SHARE THEIR STORIES

Home!

OF KNOWING GOD

Lesley Sussman

PUBLISHED BY DOUBLEDAY
a division of Bantam Doubleday Dell Publishing Group, Inc.
1540 Broadway, New York, New York 10036

DOUBLEDAY and the portrayal of an anchor with a dolphin are trademarks
of Doubleday, a division of Bantam Doubleday Dell Publishing Group, Inc.

The lyrics of "Swingin' Bridge" used by permission of Jim Rice and
Benson Records.

Book Design by Richard Oriolo

ISBN 0-385-48445-3
Copyright © 1997 by Lesley Sussman

Printed in the United States of America

Special Book Club Edition

14 · 1186G

To Patricia A. Leone,

a very special and spiritual friend,

whose encouragement rescued me

from my own misgivings,

and to the Almighty,

the true author

of this book.

ACKNOWLEDGMENTS

Thanks to . . .

Edwin Benson, executive director of the Country Music Association for all his association's help, and Gene Higgins, executive director of the Christian Country Music Association, for steering me in the right direction. Also, the Gospel Music Association for suggesting performers with inspiring stories to tell about faith and renewal.

Special appreciation to Leanne Hardy at Sparrow Records and Lisa Bily at New Haven Records, who seem to know which performers are walking the path, and April Hefner, managing editor of Christian Country Music Magazine.

There's a talented army of personal managers and publicists behind each performer, and not enough space to thank each and every one for their generous support and cooperation. Here are a few names that stand for a bunch more:

Richard Davis of Tater-Patch Records, who went out of his way to help; Judi Turner at Turner and Company; Michael Smith & Associates; Lisa Wysocky of White Horse Enterprises; Bridget Dolan Little of Little Horn Communications; Kathy Gangwisch; Norma Morris at The Press Office; Jill Wylly; Kathy Allmand; Kami Thomas at Media West. And a very special thanks to Jackie Monaghan at Morning Star Public Relations, who also served as something of a spiritual mentor.

Finally, thanks to Claire Gerus, my agent and friend, and Mark J. H. Fretz, Ph.D., senior editor of Religious Publishing at Doubleday, who had faith in this project. Much thanks to Maura Nolan for her excellent transcription skills and comments, Robert Cutarella, who said it could be done.

CONTENTS

PHOTO CREDITS

Naomi Judd	PETER NASH
Barbara Mandrell	DICK ZIMMERMAN
Louise Mandrell	DICK ZIMMERMAN
B.J. Thomas	PETER NASH
Charlie Daniels	DENNIS KEELEY 8/95A
Donna Fargo	MARK TUCKER
George Hamilton IV	COURTESY OF NELSON–WORD (U.K. LIMITED)
Penny DeHaven	DENNIS CARNEY
Doug Stone	GWENDOLEN CATES
Rick Trevino	RANDEE ST. NICHOLAS
John Berry	MARK TUCKER
Marty Raybon (Shenandoah)	MARK TUCKER 8/94E
Toby Keith	DEAN DIXON 6/94
Mark Collie	MARK TUCKER
Ricky Lynn Gregg	MARK TUCKER 5/94B
Susie Luchsinger	PAUL YATES
Paul Overstreet	BEN PEARSON
Kent Humphrey (MidSouth)	PETER NASH 0994B
Jim Rice (Brush Arbor)	VERN EVANS PHOTOGRAPHY
Joy Lynn White	E. J. CAMP
Lisa Stewart	RANDEE ST. NICHOLAS
Brian Barrett	RUSS HARRINGTON

AUTHOR'S NOTE

There comes a time in each of our lives when we yearn to have a closer connection to our Creator. I experienced such a feeling while writing my previous book, *Miracles Can Happen*.

The intensity of faith expressed by those I interviewed for that book—everyday people who had experienced miracles in their lives—was, for me, a spiritual eye-opener. It made me want to shore up my own faith in God.

The problem was in not knowing exactly where to begin. So as any writer worth his salt might do, I decided to commence my own spiritual renewal by writing about the subject of faith and renewal.

When my good friend and agent, Claire Gerus, suggested that I interview Country music stars as part of my research for the book it seemed a good idea.

After all, I knew that many Country music performers were deeply rooted in religion as well as music, and that many of them had strayed from the spiritual path only to find their way back again. They would certainly have important spiritual insights to offer me as well as my readers.

So while some pilgrims might begin their spiritual quest by planning a trip to Jerusalem or some other holy site, my journey would lead me to a city called Nashville.

Little did I realize at the time what a spiritual center that city is, and what a positive effect getting to know members of Nashville's Country music community would have on my own spiritual quest.

As the interviews for the book progressed, and I listened to many Country music artists openly talk about the heartaches, personal tragedies, and spiritual struggles that ultimately led to their spiritual renewal, I became deeply moved by these tales of rediscovered faith.

I also felt inspired by those performers who, despite having faced severe trials and tribulations in their lives, barely faltered in their spiritual walk.

I soon came to realize that no matter how long the detour, and regardless of how many roadblocks there are to faith, there is no such thing as a spiritual dead end if one is truly intent on reaching his or her destination.

With each succeeding interview for the book, my own stumbling gait along the spiritual path gradually became a much more confident stride. I was slowly becoming empowered by these inspirational accounts of faith and renewal that I was writing about.

Instead of just being a listener and a recorder of stories, it was as if something deep inside me was actually being touched by the very spirit of the storyteller. I felt as if some energy vortex within my body had been shifted from the negative to the positive side of my spiritual battery.

This was particularly true during conversations I had with stars such as Donna Fargo, who took the long way back to God, and other performers—like B.J. Thomas, Ricky Lynn Gregg, Louise Mandrell, and Penny DeHaven—whose sensitive and moving accounts of faith and renewal were quite inspirational.

Although today I still feel that I am at the beginning rather than at the end of my spiritual odyssey, I feel blessed that I have been given the opportunity to begin that rewarding journey.

And now that you have been divinely guided to read this uplifting book, I hope that the stories contained within touch your soul as much as they have touched mine, and that together we can continue our journey toward the light . . .

LESLEY SUSSMAN
New York City,
February 19, 1996

Faith is the substance of things
hoped for, the evidence of things
not seen.

—*Hebrews 11:1*

Man has not invented God,
he has developed faith to
meet a God already there.

—*Edna St. Vincent Millay*

Naomi Judd

She was named Diana Ellen Judd when she was born on January 11, 1946, the first child of Polly and Glen Judd of Ashland, Kentucky—a baby who quickly grew into a pretty little girl who townsfolk would describe as a "perfect China doll."

It was here in this fertile central Kentucky horse country not far from the coal mining towns of West Virginia that Diana—who later would change her name to Naomi—learned her lessons about the power of faith from her God-fearing parents and Sunday school teachers.

For Naomi, it is a faith that has been sorely tested over the years, but one which always remained steadfast. She has experienced several dark nights of the soul, including the tragic death of her younger brother from cancer, a bitter divorce, a struggle as a single parent to support her growing family, and, most recently, her life-threatening illness—one which abruptly brought to an end eight glorious years of living the American dream.

Any one of these events might have plummeted another woman deep into the depths of despair. But not Naomi. She has always been a strong and determined woman, one who has created miracles in her life before.

Today Naomi Judd continues to be an inspiring figure who strongly believes in the power of faith—a power, she says, that has built a bridge to healing in her own life . . .

It was 1990 and The Judds, a sensational mother-daughter Country music act considered by many to be the greatest female duo of all time, were at the pinnacle of their success.

They had arrived on the Country music scene in 1983, capturing the public imagination with their vocal harmonies and sharply contrasting stage personalities. They also impressed critics with their free-flowing, "back-to-their roots" sound and optimistic, down-home lyrics.

The Judds returned to California for a while, where Naomi finished her nursing degree and did some secretarial work to support her family.

For Naomi Judd, it was a time of personal triumph. She could look back to her days of hardship in 1979 with a sense of accomplishment—remembering how she and her two small daughters had arrived in Nashville from California, penniless, jobless, and homeless, and the long hours she worked as a county nurse to support her family as a single parent.

Today, life was very different for The Judds, and Naomi, an ambitious, hardworking woman, had been primarily responsible for their astonishing success.

Through all their hard times Naomi Judd never lost faith in her dream of someday establishing herself as a Country music performer. When she recognized that Wynonna, even at age twelve, was blessed with a beautiful voice, Naomi's plan to perform with her daughter began to take shape.

When they returned with their earnings a second time to Nashville, Naomi began making demo tapes on an inexpensive home tape recorder. She haunted the city's Music Row, doing her best to get those tapes into the hands of people in the music business.

And her efforts paid off. She and Wynonna were now, in 1990, at the top of the charts, and the reigning duo of Country music. They were The Judds. In the seven years that mother and daughter had performed together, they had achieved a first for a female harmony group —recording more than a dozen number-one hits (eight of them consecutively), and selling more than 15 million records. *Billboard* even proclaimed them, "the Number Five Top Artist of the Decade."

The sky seemed to be the limit for The Judds. It was a clear blue sky, one that appeared to extend to the very ends of the world. But suddenly, without any warning, ominous clouds appeared on the horizon. And for Naomi Judd, a hard rain would soon begin to fall . . .

Naomi says she will never forget that January 12—the day after her forty-fourth birthday. And how could she? On that day her Cinderella existence would come to an end.

In her best-selling autobiography, *Love Can Build a Bridge,* she recalls awakening that morning in her Franklin, Tennessee, home feeling unwell. It wasn't the first time in recent months that she had listlessly gotten out of bed. Maybe it was from too much work, she thought, reflecting on The Judds' exhaustive concert schedule over the past couple of months.

Naomi writes that she tried to ignore her own discomfort. Right now it was twenty-one-year-old Ashley whom she was worried about. Her young daughter had come down with a bad case of the flu just before returning to college, and Naomi was taking her to the doctor for a blood test.

Seated in the doctor's office waiting for Ashley, Naomi decided that she would have her own blood count checked. As a trained nurse, she knew that the test would give her a better inkling as to why she had been feeling so run-down the past year.

She writes that when she returned for the results the following Monday, the news that greeted her was unnerving. Naomi recalls how her doctor "cleared his throat and folded his arms across his chest" before addressing her. What he had to say was short and to the point. "Naomi, you're a very sick woman."

Naomi discovered that she was suffering from chronic active hepatitis, an often fatal liver disease. Her doctor suspected she had contracted the virus while working as a nurse. Naomi couldn't believe it.

Her concern, she recalls, grew when she was informed that, regrettably, there was no cure for her illness—in fact, there wasn't even any medication or therapy that could permanently relieve her symptoms.

In her book, she relates how the doctor explained that, much like the viruses which cause AIDS and cancer, hers also had the potential to kill—it could destroy her liver and eventually take her life. For Naomi, it felt as if she were living with a time bomb. One that could end her life at any moment.

She further reveals that her next thought was the fear that she might be contagious. "My mind flashed on all the times Wynonna and I accidentally shared the same glass of water onstage." Her doctor didn't think this was a cause for concern.

But he agreed that more tests would have to be taken before he was absolutely certain. More tests? She bridled. Didn't the man realize he was speaking to Naomi Judd, part of the hottest show-business act in Country music? The Judds had a full schedule of concerts ahead of them, and they couldn't disappoint their millions of fans because a doctor wanted to conduct some more tests on Naomi.

"I told him, 'I'm sorry, but we leave early in the morning for our 1990 tour, so I'll have to call you after we get back,' " Naomi recollects. She writes that her doctor had other ideas. He insisted, "Naomi, listen to me. You're not going anywhere except home to bed. You're not gonna feel like putting on panty hose, let alone travel. I've seen the amount of energy you put out onstage, and you're not gonna be able to stand up long enough to sing a single song."

As Naomi left his office, her mind was "whirring," and she was sick with dread. "I felt a huge question mark hanging over my head. Before I had walked into the doctor's office, all I had were symptoms. Now I had a life-threatening disease."

. . .

The symptoms of hepatitis include fever, weakness, nausea, vomiting, muscle aches, lethargy, headaches, and abdominal discomfort. Naomi experienced them all, and recalls them in her book.

"I was so terribly sick, I could barely get out of bed. I felt like I had the world's worst case of flu for months." To Naomi, it was simply incomprehensible that all this was happening to her at a time when The Judds were having their greatest year and things were going well for her personally, as well.

"Wy and I had healed our relationship. I was putting Ashley through college. Larry, my Prince Charming, and I were happily married, and we had even found our dream farm. And now this . . ."

Despite feeling ill, Naomi performed with Wynonna at a couple of concerts. There were moments during those performances that Naomi was so overcome with fatigue, she could hardly go on. But it was just like Naomi to push herself beyond her limits.

Upon returning to Nashville, Naomi paid a visit to yet another specialist. To her shock, this doctor coldly told her that her disease was so deadly, he wasn't certain if she would die first from liver cancer or from complications of her liver "shutting down."

When the physician asked to see her in a week, Naomi writes that she mustered up enough energy to tell the doctor off. "Nope. You've just shoved me out of an airplane at thirty-five thousand feet without offering anything to break my fall. I'm going to find a doctor who will give me a parachute. It's called *hope.*"

She also recalls that in those days after her diagnosis, "I hardly knew myself anymore. There were two Naomis now. The one I had been before, and the stranger to which I found myself chained."

But there was another Naomi Judd, as well—one who over the years had faced other challenges in her life by relying on her faith that things would work out. Once again, Naomi would be called upon to draw from that reservoir of faith.

"I've never had to renew my faith—even after my diagnosis," she testifies. "I've had some very dear friends who have had some really severe valleys of the shadow, but I have *never* not believed. My trials have always come from the world, but I've never had a period in my life where I've questioned God.

"I'm so grateful for that because even though I've been knocked down so many times and have really been kicked in the teeth, I've always known that if I didn't have anything else but God, I was still going to be okay."

In the weeks to come, there were more medical tests along with healing prayer sessions. The only good news was a medical report informing Naomi that she was not contagious, after all.

Always an open-minded woman, Naomi began to look into natural approaches to curing illness. She began to devour books about nutrition and nutritional healing, and even changed her diet.

Naomi had launched a quest for self-healing that continues even to this very day. She sought ways to "incorporate God's promises with modern medicine and psychology." She believed—as she still does—that such a cooperative approach would be the winning formula to beat her disease. She even aroused the ire of members of a Georgia Baptist church by offering this approach to her audience.

"It was a Sunday morning, and I used the term that after I was given my fatal diagnosis, 'I stepped out in faith and determined to become a co-creator with God in my healing.' And I got a lot of flack. The pastor called me and said a couple of people in the church were concerned that I might be going New Age."

Even today, the annoyance in her voice is clear as she recalls that incident. "Now, I was raised Southern Baptist," she pointedly asserts, establishing her religious credentials. "In fact, I was the guest speaker at my hometown church—The First Baptist Church of Ashland, Kentucky—last month."

"So I had this wonderful conversation with the pastor, who said he completely got it—he knew I was only talking about accepting responsibility for doing my part. But some people have this religious indignation, this self-righteousness. God is the Creator." She continues:

"All I was telling these folks—and this stems from me being an RN and having the heart of a teacher—is that it's important for people to become involved in improving their own health."

Naomi also relied upon her sense of humor to remain well. "It's almost as if every time something disastrous comes into my life, I have this wry sense of humor and say, 'Okay, kiddo, this sure is a drag but I know I'm going to go to a higher level of awareness because of this acid test.' "

In addition, she promised herself not to allow any negative thoughts about her illness to enter her mind. "When one textbook said that I might only have as little as three years to live, I knocked this book out of my lap like it was on fire and got down on my face on the rug beside my bed."

Then she offered up the following prayer:

"Father, by whom all things are made,
I love medicine but realize I've been
treating these books as if they were
a bible and looking to doctors as if
they were gods. I'm asking to join
into a partnership with you so that I
may be co-creator with you in my healing.
I know your desire is for me to be well
and happy. I realize you're a supernatural
being and that the universe runs on spiritual
laws. I'm stickin' with you!"

It was from that moment on that Naomi says she began "putting all of my thought processes and all of my resources and all of my energy into my spiritual walk. I had come to discover that security is not in a lab report, CAT scan, X ray, or biopsy . . . it came from within. Control is an illusion. We only have control over ourselves."

Prayer became Naomi's priority—from personal prayer in her private sanctuary located in the valley which she and Wynonna own, to healing sessions with elders of her church. She also put aside all the medical texts she had been reading and has not looked at them since.

"I'm an RN and a member of the mainstream medical community, and I love medicine," Naomi emphasizes. "I would've gone on and gotten my MD had Wynonna and I not taken that detour into singing because of her need.

"But despite my love of medicine I really had to acknowledge that it was so limited. So when you're unable to look to the outside world—to medicine or science or people or institutions for help—because they all have their limitations, then you have to go within."

It was this inner road that Naomi traveled, drawing primarily upon the spiritual lessons of her Sunday school childhood in Ashland, Kentucky, for support.

"I remembered that in the Bible it says that nobody can predict the future. Yet some of these doctors in white lab coats were telling me that I only had X amount of years to live."

She even chewed out one doctor who dared to speculate on her chances of survival. "I challenged, 'Wait a cotton-pickin' minute. Nobody but my God can tell me when my earthly time is over with.'"

Naomi's faith was in for another test when she arrived about two months later at the Mayo Clinic in Rochester, Minnesota, for a liver biopsy. The pathology report on her liver condition was discouraging.

Naomi again turned to prayer, this time even asking the doctors and nurses who were preparing her for her first injection of interferon, a drug used to kill cancerous cells, to join her.

"This was the second time in my life I had ever petitioned strangers to pray with me," Naomi recollects. "The first time had been as I lay on the operating room table earlier that day before the liver biopsy . . . I was pleased to discover that not only did they not mind, but they appreciated my praying for them as well."

The side effects of the interferon injection were devastating. "My body's reaction to the shot exaggerated my discomfort almost beyond my ability to withstand it," Naomi recalls, wincing at the memory. But there were sweet memories as well. She recalls how supportive her family and friends were, including her husband, Larry, who never left her side. "One of my greatest comforts came from him rubbing my back as we listened to our church choir tapes."

Several weeks later, Naomi was back on the surgery table for another biopsy—this time for a lump that had been discovered in her breast. Before her surgery, Naomi prayed the entire One Hundred and Twenty-first Psalm out loud. She believes her prayers were answered, because the lump was benign.

There were days that followed during which Naomi felt deathly ill. She admits that on the worst days she sometimes succumbed to feelings of fear and despair. Those feelings, however, did not last too long.

"I suddenly realized that this fear and darkness came from Satan himself. God doesn't send sickness and trials. Satan does. The devil was trying to make me give up." That very night, Naomi arranged for a prayer healing by the elders of her church.

"I prayed that I might live. I decided that all my physical symptoms were temporary, so I focused on the restoration of my health.

Hope is a gift we give ourselves and remains when all else is gone. From that night on, hope was my constant companion."

Naomi Judd, singer, has today become Naomi Judd, private investigator, of sorts. She is seeking answers to her healing in an unusual area, given her fundamentalist Christian background. Naomi is exploring how the powers of the mind, combined with faith, can be used to help heal the body. "We're at a crossroads, today, where medicine, science, and spirituality are coming together as a new force for healing. We're spiritual beings in a physical body."

Her approach seems to be working. It has been more than seven years since she was diagnosed with chronic active hepatitis, and Naomi's disease remains in complete remission. There are even days, she adds, when she feels completely normal.

Naomi recalls how her research into the spirit/mind/body connection energized her during the early days of her illness. "I became enthused because, first of all, I felt there was something I could do—personal improvement. It also gave me a sense of purpose—I wanted to share this knowledge with others. It helped keep my mind off my aches and pains and the dismal prognosis. I guess I'm just one of those people who can turn a lemon into lemonade."

Nowadays, Naomi is eager to share what she has learned, but sometimes finds that doing so is not that easy. "It gets kind of frustrating because I go out and speak to a couple of thousand people, and afterward people tell me that they don't have anyplace that they can go to and find out about the spirit/mind/body connection. I leave them literature and give them resource material, but I need to continue to reach them in a broader way."

Faith is always on Naomi's mind. These days, in fact, she has just completed writing a song for Wynonna, called "Steppin' in the Light," that sums up her feelings about faith.

*Many paths but only one journey
to find the seat of your soul,
so many questions yet faith holds
the answer, and peace of mind
is the goal.*

Besides keeping one's faith firm, Naomi has some other advice for people who are ill. She urges them to keep a positive outlook and to seek the support of family and friends. To illustrate this, she again relates an incident from her days as a nurse.

"When I was working in the Intensive Care Unit, I could tell you who was going to make it and who wasn't. I would take care of a patient for ten straight hours and I would get to know their attitudes. Those with faith, family support, and positive attitudes fared better."

Positive thinking is nothing new to Naomi since even before her ordeal. "When something awful happens to me—like when I was diagnosed with hepatitis—I just go off alone and say to myself, 'Okay, there's another way of looking at this.'

"Instead of giving into the fear, I recognize that there's going to be some valuable learning experience in it for me. I resist fear. I just really have a lot of trust and faith."

She is also an advocate of support groups. "I was recently the keynote speaker at the Wellness Institute," she relates. "We had fifteen hundred healers from all fifty states converge. The sense of knowing, the sense of community that I felt was so uplifting.

"It's a very special gift to have someone who's been where you've been, whether it's me talking to someone who has chronic active hepatitis, or another single working mother. It's the same sense of connection that I have when I go to church. There's that sense of being on the same level, if you will."

For anyone whose faith may be lagging, Naomi believes that all it takes to reach God is the simple desire to do so.

"I'm not some magical human being," she insists. "There's nothing special or different about Naomi Judd. I have the same insecurities, the same self-doubts, the same challenges that everyone has. What I simply do when something awful comes my way, I remind myself that God is a heck of a lot smarter than I am."

During such trying moments, Naomi retreats to her special meditation place in the woods. "I have a guardian angel statue there. When I've got a need, that's where I go. There's a bit of a ceremony about it, so that I can really be in the moment. I believe in rituals and ceremonies. And I have a special prayer taken from Hebrews:

*"Let us come boldly before
the throne of grace to obtain
mercy and help in the time of
need."*

Naomi believes that the Creator responds to such prayers because people have a "legal binding contract with God." This "contract" was "written and sealed by the blood of Jesus at Calvary to stand before that throne of grace, to lay down our petitions, to talk to God as His child."

And Naomi isn't shy about asking God for good health. "I've already started the healing process by just realizing there is Someone I can turn to for help—that it's not a hopeless situation."

She points out that the choice of words used in a prayer is vitally important. "One of the things I learned during my illness was so simple I can't believe that it hadn't occurred to me before."

She received the powerful insight while consulting a Christian therapist shortly after becoming ill. "I had a teacher who told me to *always pray the answer*. Never pray the problem." Naomi lets the importance of that statement sink in before continuing.

"I had to reorganize my thinking. The Bible says 'in the beginning was the Word, and the Word was with God and the Word was God.'

"Words are the expressions of our thoughts. First, we have to get in touch with and take control over our thoughts. And then we have to be responsible for giving them energy. Before I had said, 'Father by whom all things are made, please be with me because I feel like I have the flu.' " She laughs at the memory.

"All I was doing was reinforcing that I thought I had the flu. I wasn't using the right words. So, I changed my prayer to say instead:

*"Gracious Heavenly Father, God of might
and Lord of Love, I thank you that my
body is a miracle. I thank you for your
bountiless promises that offer me the world
of goodness. I thank you that I'm starting
to feel better. I thank you that when I*

*awaken tomorrow, I'm going to feel much
improved."*

Naomi professes that from the moment she began praying in this manner, "It changed my life."

Her voyage of self-discovery has led her on a journey to wholeness. These days she keeps her life simple—rarely wearing makeup, raising her own vegetables, and experiencing nature for entertainment. She practices life-centered, present-moment awareness and makes time with her family a priority.

Above all, she keeps the faith that she is being sustained through her love for God and His love for her.

"Nothing beats love," she declares. "Love is the greatest healing power there is. Nothing else even comes close! Not ancient cures, modern medicines and technologies, nor interesting books we read or wise things we say and think.

"My knowledge that God is the deepest source of my identity has helped me conquer all the battles of my life. Most recently it has even spared me from the dark night of the soul . . ."

Barbara Mandrell

Ever since her early childhood when Barbara Mandrell's musically talented parents would invite people over to their house on Sunday afternoons for a Gospel music sing-along, religion has always played an important role in her life.

But in 1984, a severe concussion which Barbara suffered as a result of a near-fatal automobile accident changed that. Not only did Barbara begin to neglect her spiritual life, she also experienced a bizarre personality disorder.

It would take an encounter with an evangelist in a downtown Nashville coffee shop to help restore the Country music queen of the mid-seventies and early eighties to the woman that she is today—

one who is again filled with joy, the spirit of God, and the kind of tremendous faith that touches everyone's heart . . .

Barbara Mandrell's last clear memory before the automobile accident that so dramatically changed her life is stopping at a red light on Gallatin Road just outside of Hendersonville, Tennessee.

The superstar was returning home from an antique store where she had just purchased some items for a house that Ken Dudley, her husband, was building for his grandmother. In the car with her at the time were her two children, Matthew, then fourteen, and his sister Jamie, eight.

"We'd gone maybe a block, and at a light we saw this station wagon with its tailgate down," Barbara recalls. "There were some little children in the back. I was thinking that if the driver slammed on the brakes those kids could have been thrown out into the roadway. It was a very dangerous sight."

Barbara was not the type of driver who liked to wear seat belts— in fact, she detested doing so. But the sight of those endangered kids in the back of the station wagon sent chills down her spine. "Looking at Matthew and Jamie I just felt this moment of great discomfort and concern."

There was another reason why Barbara felt compelled to buckle up. As she waited for the light to change, she remembers a silent voice urging her to do so. That voice whispering to the talented entertainer belonged to her younger sister, Louise.

"It was Louise that whenever we rode with her, she would insist we put on the seat belts. I used to argue that 'It'll wrinkle my outfit,' or 'If there's a wreck, I want to be able to get out'—you know, all the excuses. But she wouldn't listen to any of them."

As she continued to wait for the light to change, Barbara finally heeded that silent voice. "I said to myself, 'Well, let's put on our seat belts, and then we'll be okay.'" It was a decision that would prove instrumental in saving her life as well as the lives of her two children.

Barbara still remembers that when she instructed Matthew and Jamie to fasten their seat belts, they looked at her as if she had suddenly lost her marbles.

Matthew and Jamie knew all too well that their mother never

cared whether or not they buckled up. In fact, she never even bothered to wear a seat belt herself. But the tone in their mother's voice convinced them that this time she meant business.

"Buckle up. I mean it," Barbara ordered, fastening her own seat belt to set an example. Despite grumbled protests, Matthew and Jamie did as they were told.

Those words were the last that Barbara would remember speaking until she later awoke in a hospital bed with orthopedic surgeon David Jones standing by her bedside and looking down at her with a worried expression on his face.

Jumbled memories played through her mind—how, as the traffic light turned green, she stepped on the gas pedal. And how, suddenly, with little warning, a car crossed through the turning lane and began to head directly into oncoming traffic.

In bits and pieces she also recalled how a pickup truck directly in front of her swerved to get out of the way. Barbara wasn't so lucky. Before she could take any evasive action, the oncoming car had smashed head-on into her silver Jaguar.

Police later reported they had no explanation as to why nineteen-year-old Lebanon, Tennessee, college student Mark White had driven his 1981 Subaru so erratically. Tests conducted on his body indicated no evidence of drugs or alcohol. Whatever his reason for doing so, White paid dearly for his action—with his life!

Barbara and her children survived the crash. While the front of her car was completely crushed in the collision, and the hood smashed into the windshield, miraculously, no one in her car suffered any fatal injury. Barbara was seriously injured, but Jamie and Matthew escaped with only minor cuts and bruises.

Today, Barbara exclaims that "without God's help and those belts we would have been tossed and broken like cheap toys. We would have all three become missiles and there was no way we would have lived. God knew what was ahead for us, and God brought us through it.

"I had a broken thigh bone, broken ribs, a broken ankle, broken toes, cuts on my knees and my left arm, bruises on my face, and I had cuts inside my mouth from hitting the steering wheel. I also had a concussion. But I was alive."

Although Barbara would eventually recover from her painful injuries, her life would be changed forever. She would never fully recover from the emotional trauma she suffered as a result of that accident, or from the side effects of the traumatic blow to her head.

Even today, the still-popular instrumentalist and vocalist sometimes experiences mood swings which are in complete counterpoint to her usually positive outlook on life. At such moments, Barbara tries to keep in mind that what she is experiencing is a residue of her old head injury.

Despite such flashbacks, Barbara remains grateful to still be alive, and for her ability to continue performing her highly galvanized stage act. "Sure there was great suffering in coming back. But the great physician, Jesus, brought me through things.

"They weren't sure I'd ever be able to perform again. They weren't even sure if I would ever in my life be able to wear any sort of heel. And look what God's letting me do. I don't know of another woman—especially in my field—who has such a physical show, except, maybe, for my sister Louise. I do it in my heels despite all the injuries I had."

Born in Texas but raised in Southern California, Barbara at age five was already able to read music and play the accordion. Her first taste of performing in public took place at the church where her uncle was pastor, and from that moment on nothing could stop her desire to exhibit her obvious musical talents.

"When I was five, Momma taught me the accordion, the bass, and how to read music. She just put this accordion in my hands, placed my fingers where the notes were, and told me to squeeze.

"I don't want to brag, but music came as naturally to me as painting does to some people, or writing, or mathematics. I could just do it."

Her parents, Irby and Mary Ellen Mandrell, were musically inclined themselves and Barbara began playing with the family band while still a youngster. Although adept at a number of instruments, it was the difficult-to-master pedal steel guitar that she excelled at.

"I was just a kid—maybe ten—but I had this gift of music that was given to me by God. Today Mamma thinks I was probably a child prodigy, but we didn't think about it in those terms back then."

By the time Barbara had reached her eleventh birthday, the pretty blond-haired little girl was so proficient with the pedal steel guitar that, while performing at a convention in Chicago, she caught the attention of guitarists Chet Atkins and Joe Maphis. Before the convention was over, the young girl had a contract to perform at Maphis's Showboat club in Las Vegas. "It was no different from getting up in front of a church," she asserts. "They called my name and I came out and played."

Two years later, the talented teenager was invited by Johnny Cash to join him on a tour of military bases in Vietnam and Korea.

Her career got a major boost in 1969, after her family relocated from California to Nashville. Barbara was signed by Columbia Records, and then, in the mid-seventies, changed labels to ABC/Dot records. Several hit songs followed, establishing Barbara as a major star well into the early eighties.

By 1983, the year before her accident, Barbara was so popular that she even hosted her own television program—"Barbara Mandrell and the Mandrell Sisters." Even at this point in her career, her interest in spirituality did not flag. Barbara would make it a point to close each show with a Gospel tune.

In addition to her television success, she was also featured in her own Las Vegas stage show, "The Lady Is a Champ," at the MGM Grand Hotel.

All this success would come to an abrupt halt after her automobile accident. Now it wasn't television cameras or adoring audiences that the superstar found herself facing, but rows of glum-faced doctors who had doubts about her ability to ever fully recover from her injuries.

Barbara still cannot recall whether it was hours or days that she lay in Nashville's Baptist Hospital's Intensive Care Unit before fully being able to comprehend the world around her.

What she mostly remembers is the agonizing pain from her multiple injuries, and a sea of doctors' faces peering at her and trying to explain things to her that she could not quite fully comprehend.

Sedated and still in shock, Barbara remembers looking up at those faces and feeling as if she were in "outer space" where aliens from a different planet were trying to communicate with her.

"The first memory I had since driving along Gallatin Road two weeks earlier was my doctor asking me if it would be all right to switch from Demerol and Valium to Tylenol. I said, 'Of course.' "

Today, more painful than her memories of the accident are Barbara's recollections of the bizarre personality change which she underwent—a transformation which she compares to Dr. Jekyll and Mr. Hyde.

"I was out of my mind, ranting and raving and getting worse." The doctors later told me that it was absolutely normal for somebody to lash out after an accident from any kind of pain. I was moody with them and even the nurses.

"I was cooperative at times, mean at other times. With Ken I was consistent. Consistently miserable. All the pain I felt, all the anger, all the loss of control, I took out on this big, strong, intelligent man who was coordinating everything."

In Barbara's best-selling autobiography, *Getting to the Heart,* Ken recollects that at one point during his wife's recovery Barbara's emotional state was so unstable that he once had to physically restrain her from pummeling a night nurse who had approached Barbara simply to calm her down.

Barbara characterizes her moods as a "runaway tornado," regretting most of all the cursing that accompanied those moods. "It was bad stuff, the kind you hear out in the street . . . really heavyweight cussing. I was just a totally, totally different person.

"I had always prided myself on keeping some control, and my language is something that as a Christian and an adult I believed I could control. So I still haven't gotten over the fact that I was cursing in front of everyone—my doctors and even my parents and sister Louise.

"My mouth became very foul. But there's one thing that amazed the doctors. I'm told that I never once took God's name in vain. If I had, I want to add that's because this can happen to people who have head injuries—it means nothing. There are even ministers who suffer head injuries whose mouths became very foul."

She recollects that after being released from the hospital, "It wasn't the old peppy Barbara who returned home. I was in serious pain —particularly my tail bone—and it was not only physical pain. I was depressed. At times I ached so badly that I wanted to be put out of my misery. I didn't want to die, but I also didn't want to live."

Meanwhile, her vicious temper tantrums continued. "I don't know if you've ever had anyone close to you that's had a brain injury, but things that I once felt very strongly about, I was now totally on the other side of the coin. It was just too strange.

"And I continued to have huge mood swings. Maybe I'd start to cry over nothing or yell and scream at my husband because he set a glass down on my end table or something. It was ridiculous—not even human.

"I stayed in the bedroom for months and months. We had blackout shades, you know. I didn't want any light. I didn't want the drapes open—it was just pretty awful."

When buses filled with her fans would show up outside her Nashville home to show their support for the star, Barbara recalls feeling resentment toward them. "I just wanted the world to go away and leave me alone."

What saddens her the most about that tumultuous period of her life was losing touch with her spiritual roots. "When I was a kid they used to call our family pew jumpers. Holy Rollers. We went to Pentecostal-style churches in Texas and Arkansas and Illinois and California where people believe in celebrating the Lord in music.

"After the accident I never lost my faith, but it distresses me to realize that I did not ask God's help at that terrible time in my life. I still wonder why I did not pray. I just had no feelings one way or another. I didn't care about it. I didn't miss it. It was weird—another result of the head injury. I used to always think of Jesus as my friend.

"Even if I was alone, taking a bath, combing my hair, driving a car, out of the blue, when something would go through my mind, I would say, 'Thank you, Jesus,' and I would talk to Him in passing. We had a relationship, a real relationship.

"And I always believed in the power of prayer. When my father had open-heart surgery, I got down on my knees and I prayed for one solid hour for his recovery. But now in my time of trouble, I did not pray for a long time—although millions of people were praying for me."

Barbara recollects that even when she was visited by her minister, Mike Nelson, the prayers she said with him did not come from her heart. "Although I might pray with Mike or members of my family, in my private moments I just didn't feel that God was with me."

All that would begin to change one afternoon while Barbara was at home switching channels on her television set. She remembers pausing at one station where a preacher was talking about the Word of God. Barbara paid attention. For the first time in months, those words struck a responsive chord in her heart.

"Just hearing him talk about prayer reminded me that I had not prayed for the healing of my pain. I guess my mind was starting to heal at that point."

Soon afterward, Barbara was approached by a friend who asked if the entertainer wanted to meet with an evangelist who planned to visit Nashville. Barbara remembered once seeing that preacher on television, and had enjoyed hearing what he had to say. So she agreed to do so.

"There was no tent meeting, no fire and brimstone. We met at the coffee shop of the Hyatt—JoAnn, my friend, Ken, the preacher, and I. I really don't have a good memory of this—I still can't even remember his name. He was a pleasant-looking man without the flashiness of a public preacher. I remember loving everything he was saying to me."

It was a conversation that would last for more than an hour, while Ken and JoAnn listened in. By the time Barbara and the evangelist parted, she remembers feeling ready to pray for the first time in more than three years.

"I don't think I ever lost my faith, but this man helped me renew it. I now knew I needed healing and I just knew God not only could—but would do it for me. I just needed to look to God to do it.

"This preacher had talked to me about Jesus and he said 'Just start thanking Him. Even if you're hurting, you know He's gonna heal you. But thank Him. Just start thanking God.' I liked his attitude. He didn't make me feel guilty that I hadn't been down on my knees praying.

"We all prayed for a few minutes before I left, and although I was still in some pain when I walked out of that coffee shop, I knew the pain would go away in God's time, and I thanked God for it. When I left the preacher I realized that I was in God's hands."

These days, Barbara may not be recording the number of records that she once did, but she is as popular as ever with fans, regularly doing live performances. It is no surprise that the crowds are large and filled with people happy to see Barbara in person.

Reflecting on her continued success, Barbara gives God the credit for it, adding that "there seems to be an angel in my arms."

Barbara discloses that she often expresses her gratitude through prayer. "I pray with Louise on the phone, and with my mother. I'm growing as a Christian. My faith is growing just as my marriage of thirty years is growing. And I pray everywhere I can.

"I pray driving down the road, I pray putting on my makeup or taking a bath. I certainly pray on my knees when I can. Anywhere I can I just talk to God. And when I begin to thank Him, and praise Him, it makes for the longest prayer of all.

"I pray for health and for my career and for my family and friends. I'm always asking and asking and asking, and He gives me everything.

"I have so many material possessions, all of which came from God. He lets us use them. We have a beautiful home all because God lets us. It belongs to God and I'm just thankful He's letting us use it. He gives me so much, that I sometimes feel that I give Him nothing really in return."

The glamorous star, who was the first artist ever to win the Country Music Association's Entertainer of the Year award for two consecutive years, illustrates the power of prayer by relating a story about a healing in her life.

"I had tendinitis for a couple of years. Even cortisone injections didn't always help it was so painful. This had nothing to do with the wreck—it's something that happened since then.

"I was on the road with my band, the Do-Rites, and it had been about six months since my last cortisone injection. All eight members of my band are Christians. I was complaining about my elbow—I could hardly lift the mike stand. I said, 'Well, when we get home, I've gotta call my doctor and get some more cortisone injections.' "

Two of her band members, however, offered Barbara another suggestion. "They said, 'Could we pray for you?' And I said, 'Would you?' And so the three of us prayed together. When we finished, my arm still hurt. Nothing got immediately better. But I woke up the next morning totally well—totally healed. My elbow hasn't bothered me since."

Barbara advises anyone lacking faith to understand that "God is real. He's the only reason we're here. He created our lives. All you have to do is love Him and then tell Him: 'I'm a sinner. Please forgive me for all the bad things I've done.'

"All you have to do to return to God is acknowledge Him—not just with your mouth—but with your heart and mind as well. Ask for His forgiveness or, as I like to say it, beg for His forgiveness and He'll give it. Through God all things are possible—I know that from my own experience . . ."

Glen Campbell

here was no bigger Country music star in the sixties and early seventies than the apple-cheeked, sweet-voiced Glen Campbell, born the seventh son and one of twelve children of a sharecropper father in Billstown, Arkansas, in 1936.

But the five-time Grammy Award winner, who began his music career when his father ordered a five-dollar guitar from a Sears Roebuck catalog when he was four, was also a man who harbored a dark secret—one that he constantly feared would be discovered and destroy all that he had struggled to attain.

Behind the wholesome public image that helped catapult Glen to megastardom in those heyday years, the country boy from Arkansas was living a turbulent lifestyle of excessive drinking and cocaine usage.

It would take a religious reawakening and an unconditionally loving marriage to turn things around for Glen—and none too soon. The legendary singer and songwriter, who at the height of his career sold some 45 million records, believes if he hadn't found the strength then to straighten his life out, he might not be alive today.

Since the "Rhinestone Cowboy" 's spiritual renewal in the late 1980s, Glen has shaken off the handicaps of reliance on alcohol and drugs. Today, he is in recovery and no longer living life in the fast lane. Instead, Glen is a devout Baptist who makes frequent appearances on the evangelical Christian music circuit.

"I'm the new, improved Glen Campbell," he proclaims proudly. "God has forgiven me, and I have forgiven myself. With faith and fortitude you can overcome anything . . ."

There was one particular night in Las Vegas that Glen Campbell admits he would rather forget.

It was sometime in the 1970s—he can't remember the exact date —a period of his life which the veteran entertainer sarcastically refers to as his "days of wine and roses. I was drunk almost every day, and the cocaine had become a regular thing, too."

As was often the case in those heyday years, this evening while he was onstage impressing his audience with his sweet voice and boy-next-door charm, Glen's mind was elsewhere.

In his bestselling autobiography, *Rhinestone Cowboy,* Glen recalls being anxious to finish his last number so that he could take off for a party where plenty of booze and drugs were available.

"Later that night I woke up on the couch of this place and everybody had long gone home. And I was laying there all alone. It was just pretty bad. I was a mess. It was at this moment that I felt that I had reached the end of the trail."

Alone in the darkness and feeling miserable, Glen remembers praying for hours for the strength to turn his life around. "I kept saying to myself over and over again, 'You know, Glen, you shouldn't be doing this.' I said, 'Lord, just help me.'

"But I couldn't deal with it. It was just incredible. I was taking this stuff and feeling at the same time that I had reached the end of the trail. It was the circle in L.A. that I hung with, and the people that always were giving me stuff. Looking back, I plead temporary insanity during those days because I was crazy for about six or seven years."

As his alcohol and cocaine consumption intensified in direct proportion to his soaring popularity, Glen remembers reflecting that all his childhood dreams of success had become nothing less than a nightmare. Here he was a superstar with millions of adoring fans around the world, but he lived in fear that those very same fans would discover his ugly secret.

When he speaks of those times, his voice still registers some of the self-loathing that he felt back then. "I was a lost soul. I had no time for drinking during those busy days in the wake of my popularity explosion. But I took the time, anyway. I can hardly remember things from the 1970s. There were times I was too drunk to recall what I did or with whom I did it."

Glen recollects that his cocaine habit took a worse toll on him than his excessive alcohol consumption. "That addiction is psychological. You get to a place after a few days where you think the only time you can feel rested and happy is when you're using cocaine. It's a vicious cycle that quickly becomes a nightmare."

Although his life had become a bad dream of "mad spending, multiple marriages, absentee fatherhood, and abusive, public affairs with other men's wives," Glen remains proud of one thing—that he never lost his faith in God.

In *Rhinestone Cowboy,* Glen recollects that "the curious thing about all my addictions is that they never lessened my spiritual appetite. God was on my mind a great deal.

"I realize now that God's emissary, the Holy Spirit, was dealing with me. I could run but I couldn't hide from a God who wanted to bless me and assure eternal salvation whether I wanted it or not."

Glen credits his strong faith to the religious upbringing he had as a child growing up in the Arkansas backwoods. Raised in abject poverty, Glen recalls in his book that "when my father and I weren't in the cotton fields picking cotton to support the family, me and my brothers and sisters would be listening to my dad read the Bible at home.

"My mother was also religious. She would take us to church services that sometimes lasted all day. God and music were my spiritual mainstays, and the Campbells were spiritual people."

It was at Billstown's Church of Christ that Glen recollects first being introduced to the world of music. He remembers it as a backwoods church where singing was permitted but no musical instruments were allowed. He writes:

"The congregation sang alone. My dad and mom took all of us to church and we sat together in one row. I first learned to sing harmony inside that country sanctuary.

"There was also a black church a few miles away in which the members sang fast music with heavy rhythms. I would hike over there, stand outside the window, rise on my bare tiptoes, and peek inside at the black folks rolling on the floor and running up the aisles.

"They were caught up in the spirit and the music, and it was my first experience seeing how moving music could be to people. I also listened to Gospel music on a battery-operated console radio."

Since most members of Glen's family played one instrument or another, he remembers as a youngster always being encouraged to perform. By the time he was age four, Glen was already learning how to play the guitar.

"My dad ordered a five-dollar guitar from a Sears Roebuck catalog for me," he recalls in his book. I was only four but I walked two miles to the mailbox every day to see if it had arrived. When it finally did you couldn't get it out of my hands."

Glen was so gifted at playing the guitar, that before he even reached his tenth birthday the child prodigy was already performing with his uncle's Western swing band in Albuquerque, New Mexico. By his teens, Glen had already quit school and was touring the Southwest with his own band, the Western Wranglers.

Glen was just twenty-four in 1960 when he decided to move to Los Angeles. He had three hundred dollars in his wallet and a pocketful of dreams. Once in L.A., he quickly found work as a session guitarist. He went on to join the Champs, an L.A. band that had a hit song called "Tequila," but left that group a year later to write songs and do demo work for a music publishing company.

During those years Glen was also involved with several Beach Boys hits, touring with them for a while. For a country boy from

Arkansas and a high school dropout, the talented young performer was doing quite well.

The year 1967 brought him his first hit as a pop crooner, and Glen was soon signed as a solo artist by Capitol Records. It was the launch of a career that has spanned more than three decades, earning him many honors along the way including ten gold albums, fourteen gold single records, and five Grammy Awards.

At the height of his career Glen was not only hosting his own television variety show, but also had major roles in movies like *True Grit*. But unknown to his millions of fans, the entertainer was paying a harsh price for his rags-to-riches story, living a turbulent life among the decadence and destructive trappings of fame.

"I was terribly unhappy. You know, the money, the fame—everything—didn't bring happiness." Compounding the superstar's unhappiness was his empty spiritual life.

"There's a place in us where God belongs. If He's not there in it, you're an unhappy cat. I just had that sense—that something was missing in my life. So I'd get high and talk about spiritual things. If people didn't want to talk about it, I'd start preaching to them.

"Can you imagine someone wasted out of their mind telling other people what was wrong with their life and how to find Jesus? It turned off a lot of people who have still not forgiven me. My head was in worse shape than I realized."

As Glen's cocaine dependence mounted, he became less able to conceal the effects of his drug habit from his adoring fans. "I really thought I was going to die. Even my fans were beginning to notice that something was wrong with their idol.

"I was doing television shows and people were sending me letters. They were writing things like, 'Glen, I've been praying for you. There's something happening in your life. We know that there's something wrong in your life. I can see it when you're on TV.' People had faith in me that I could be healed. They had more faith in me than I had in myself."

Glen is convinced that it was those prayers for his recovery from his fans that helped enable him to break free of his addictions.

"It was entirely possible for me to overdose the way I was drinking and doing drugs. It was the unified prayer of people that I never met that possibly saved my life."

While Glen's devoted fans continued to offer up their prayers for his recovery, it was the faith of one woman that Glen submits did the most to turn his life around—Kimberly Woolen, his wife of more than a decade.

It was love at first sight when Glen and Kimberly—a dancer at Radio City Music Hall—first met in New York City in 1982. But their marriage was a stormy one that was always on the brink of dissolving because of Glen's addictive lifestyle.

"I was holding out against God. I was still doing cocaine and drinking, and smoking pot. Even after we had our first child, Cal. I was holding out against the will of God."

Matters between Glen and Kimberly worsened in late 1983, when Kimberly, weary of her husband's behavior, warned that she was preparing to leave him.

Feeling devastated by that warning, Glen remembers how he then and there vowed to try and change his life. "I fell on my knees and I prayed and promised God that I would stop using drugs." It was a promise that Glen has not broken.

Although the superstar was no longer taking drugs, Glen's drinking problems continued unabated. It wasn't until 1986, after performing at a concert in Hawaii and awakening the next morning with "a really bad hangover," that Glen was able to break that habit.

"It was the last straw. I prayed that morning. I prayed, 'Lord, get me off this stuff. Help me find a way to get away from this sin.'"

Glen remembers having uttered the very same prayer many times before, but this day it had a different result. He simply quit drinking. "That's a strangely wonderful thing about God," Glen professes. "He's not always on time, but He's never late."

Now there was one final matter that needed attending to. "I decided that I wanted Kim and I to be baptized together. We made a commitment to have Christ in our lives, have Christ in our family, and to go to church and to raise our children as Christians.

"From that moment the Lord, Jesus, came into my life and He delivered me from everything—even cigarettes. I don't want any. If I get around smoke, now, I get ill. I was a lost soul and I was hoping that God would accept me. And He did.

"I learned that no matter how dire the circumstances, with faith and fortitude you can overcome them. That's what happened to me. I was a Rhinestone Cowboy whose sparkle was fading fast, but who rose to live again, and lived to tell about it."

Today, the "Rhinestone Cowboy" is free of all his chemical addictions. He is happily married and continues to make frequent appearances on the evangelical Christian music circuit performing songs with deeply spiritual lyrics.

"I once performed with a band, but today it's the band and the Holy Spirit. I can feel it when I'm onstage, I can hear it in recorded playbacks, and I can sense it in audience responses.

"When audiences leave my shows, I not only want them to feel entertained, I want them to feel like better people for having attended. I want them to be inspired, uplifted, and blessed."

But Glen is singing more than just contemporary Christian hits. The versatile and popular performer also continues his secular career, performing summers at Branson's Grand Palace, touring, and remaining a headline attraction in the world's largest show rooms in Las Vegas.

"Some people in the Christian community expect me to abandon my secular repertoire and all the hits upon which I built my career. But the audience gets both and the format goes over well everywhere.

"I don't perform only Christian music in the wake of my salvation, because it would only attract Christians to my concerts. I don't want to spend my life and career espousing Christ to people who already know Him. I want to expose Christ to people who don't."

Glen's personal life remains filled with the Bible, faith, and prayer. "I read the Bible because if you don't read it you don't grow," he declares. "And I've learned that you must totally trust God—you must totally have faith in Him and He will guide you. If you don't, if there are any doubts creeping into your mind, you can run amuck again."

Although one of his favorite prayers is "The Lord's Prayer," Glen also confides that he enjoys having one-on-one conversations with his Maker. "I just talk to God, basically, like I'm talking to you. Only I'm asking the questions."

He is a true believer in the healing power of prayer. "No matter how dire the circumstances, with faith, fortitude, and prayer you can overcome them," he declares.

"It was in a moment of prayer that God saved me. It was His faith in me just as much as my faith in Him. Anyone can experience this kind of salvation through faith and prayer.

"I think that what I've been through and where I am now should be an inspiration. I left God for a while but He never left me. I've never been happier than I am now. I'm the new, improved Glen Campbell, a guy who feels an internal glow that glistens . . ."

Louise Mandrell

Louise Mandrell's childhood was every young girl's dream. Not only was the youngster with beautiful black hair and blue eyes doted upon by two loving parents, but also by her older sister, Barbara, who, at age five and a half, became a second mother to the new addition to the Mandrell household.

With this type of pampered existence, it is not surprising that when a sequence of personal misfortunes struck—including her mother's diagnosis of cancer, the breakup of her fairy-tale marriage, and the death of a beloved uncle—Louise was not prepared to cope with it. As a result, she would temporarily lose her faith.

Louise would regain her faith one evening at a rural Midwestern truck stop where the forty-three-year-old Corpus Christi native experienced what she believes was an encounter with her guardian angel.

Since then, the multifaceted entertainer, writer, and actress, who has the distinction of performing on every major Country music television show—as well as starring in her own TV special—has encountered other difficulties in her life.

But she has met those obstacles head-on without abandoning her faith. That's because Louise now knows that no matter how tough things may become for her, somewhere out there is someone who is watching over her . . .

For the fiddle-and-bass-playing kid sister of pop chanteuse Barbara Mandrell, growing up in Southern California was a storybook kind of life.

In addition to a loving home life, Louise's career was an almost effortless climb. While still a junior in high school, she was already playing bass guitar with her sister Barbara's band—the Do-Rites—touring with the group throughout the United States and Europe.

Also while still in her teens, the attractive young performer made her first television appearance as a guest on the Ralph Emery television show. That appearance led to a job singing with former Nashville crooner Stu Phillips, where Louise got her first opportunity to sing onstage on the "Grand Ole Opry."

Her career got another boost when Country music star Merle Haggard became impressed enough with the teenager's voice to offer her a job as a singer in his backup group, Strangers.

Later, Louise garnered major public attention as a result of her sister's successful NBC-TV series, "Barbara Mandrell and the Mandrell Sisters." This would launch her solo career, and the talented singer and instrumentalist would go on to sign a contract with Epic Records.

At the moment, however, what sixteen-year-old Louise, who was still playing with her sister's band, wanted more than a successful career, was a storybook marriage.

When, in 1970 she met and fell in love with Ronny (Note: Louise declines to give his last name), a handsome and talented young entertainer who had joined the Do-Rites after winning a musical talent contest, and who later became the musical director for the "Mandrell Sisters" TV show, Louise believed it was the real thing.

"I'd convinced everyone—including Ronny and myself—that we were in love. At sixteen my visions were a bit romantic and very unrealistic. I just believed life went the way it did in the movies."

It soon became apparent to Louise that her marriage was not going to turn out like a Hollywood movie. Things simply weren't working out between the young couple, and their marriage became marred by constant bickering and a slew of other personal problems.

Although Louise recalls working hard to try and salvage the relationship, it became a futile effort when she discovered that Ronny was already in love with someone else.

That discovery shocked her, and for the first time in Louise's young life she experienced the pain of rejection. "There was no such word in my family as divorce. I came from a family that was very strong.

"So I wanted it to work and I felt I was supposed to be in a good marriage. I just wasn't ready to accept that there was anything other than we would work it out.

"I was taught religiously by my parents that when you want something to work out, and you feel that, it is what is supposed to happen. I just didn't understand any other concept.

"So I wasn't prepared emotionally for the shock, and my pride and confidence were shattered. I was the first one in my family to get a divorce. I had never hurt as much or felt as low, and I also lost some of my faith."

Still recoiling from that traumatic experience, Louise suffered another blow when she learned that her mother had just been diagnosed with cancer. The young entertainer's depression deepened.

"Mom being ill scared me. She was my role model and is still my best friend. I had never thought about losing her before. Just the realization that it could happen had made me want to be closer to her."

Already feeling emotionally overloaded, Louise received a phone call that exacerbated her mental condition. She learned that one of her favorite uncles had just passed away.

"My uncle Ralph was a minister who had always been to me the ideal man of God. He stood for everything that I believed was important in life, the very things on which I based my spiritual faith.

"Now, in the dark of the night, when it seemed my entire world had already come crashing down, a voice on the phone told me that Uncle Ralph had passed away."

When it came to her faith, this was the straw that broke the camel's back. "One of the things that I remember so strongly is that, as a Christian, I was taught not to question whether or not God existed. But now I did.

"I was just pushed to the point that I needed to know there was still something that you could count on and believe in. I grew up never questioning God. I can't remember a time in my life that I didn't believe.

"My entire life I never had questioned Him—I had always had a prayer life. I always knew God was there. This was the first time in my life I ever doubted Him. I guess I was frightened."

Distraught over her uncle's death, Louise remembers hastily packing some clothes and, in the middle of the night, driving off from Nashville. She hoped to be in Illinois by morning, where her uncle's funeral was to be held.

As she watched her house disappear through the rearview mirror of her car, Louise can still remember that her soul that evening felt as dark as the Tennessee night.

"My emotions were frayed, my physical condition weak, and my faith in God, man, and myself, destroyed. Not only did I not have any answers, but I had also run out of questions."

Driving through the late night darkness, memories of brighter days flickered like candles through her head. Louise happily recalled scenes of being seated around the dinner table with her parents, Barbara, and the latest addition to the Mandrell household—her new baby sister, Irlene.

As memories of those times flashed by, a smile creased her face. Louise remembered how those dinnertime discussions inevitably would turn to a subject of great interest to her parents—the efficacy of faith and prayer.

"Mom and Dad would talk about Him and with Him in prayer, causing all of us to accept the Lord as a member of our family. Dad raised his children to understand that God was first, the family second."

Other pleasant memories drifted through her mind as the miles passed by—images of dressing up for church on Sunday mornings, and song-filled church services. Even today those memories remain among her fondest recollections of growing up in Southern California.

"Church was the one central scheduled event that held us together as a family," Louise recollects. "Growing up in the Mandrell family meant growing up with the priorities of God, family, and music —in that order. That wasn't difficult to do, especially if you liked to sing in church with your family, which we did."

She sadly reflected that now it wasn't church and Gospel music which helped to sustain her, but Valium.

Glancing at her reflection in the rearview mirror, Louise thought that the face which peered back at her seemed tired—even scared. She also recalls thinking how lonely she felt. Her gas tank was filled, but that night her soul was running on empty.

The night was dark, the road unfamiliar, and the absence of traffic was disorienting. A sudden flash of lights in her rearview mirror further confused Louise, who stepped hard on the brakes and found herself fighting to control her car as it nearly veered off the road.

Her heart beating rapidly, Louise remembers pulling over to the side of the road in order to collect herself. Lost and on the verge of tears, she recalls uttering a small prayer. "God, if you really exist, please show me a sign." An answer to her prayer came almost immediately.

"Suddenly, a light flashed ahead of me down the road. It was probably just a distant headlight, but I began to believe just a little bit again. Then I saw the lights of an almost-deserted twenty-four-hour truck stop, and I decided to stop there."

Thinking about that truck stop, there is nothing particularly special that she can remember about it—just the usual array of gas pumps lined up in front of a cheaply constructed building made of concrete blocks.

Louise remembers parking the car and entering a small restaurant located in the truck stop, where she approached a waitress and asked directions. The waitress, she recalls, looked at her curiously but did not reply.

"It was then that I noticed a rugged, tall, and muscular man with dark eyes staring at me. He was practically looking through me. I was terrified. He made me feel very uncomfortable because at this point I wasn't really crazy about men. I had lost my pride because of one man.

"I did everything I could to avoid this man, including going into the ladies' room and getting something to drink. Everything I could. He continued to stare, and I felt very alone and very weak.

"I finished my coffee, got up from my chair, looked at the stranger, and said: 'I'm lost, and I'm alone. I just have to get back for my uncle's funeral.' "

Louise still finds it hard to believe that she so easily revealed her predicament to a total stranger—particularly one who so frightened her. "I said to myself, 'Boy, did I leave myself open for this guy to come on to me.' " Yet, for some reason, Louise remembers feeling compelled to be honest with this stranger.

"I put my guard down for another second and I said, 'I guess I don't trust myself in finding my way.' " Long moments passed as the stranger silently continued to appraise her with his intense eyes.

When the man finally spoke, Louise recollects that his eyes took on a warm glow. She also remembers that there was a strong, yet gentle, quality to his voice which appealed to her.

Although what the stranger had to say was short and to the point, Louise asserts that she has never forgotten his words: "Young lady, you're on the right road, and if you just put your trust in the Lord He'll take care of you.' "

Louise recollects that upon hearing those words, she broke out into a broad grin. "It was just so wonderful—it was a great feeling. I turned away and then I thought, 'I want to say something to him again.' "

But the man had mysteriously vanished!

"I turned back and he was gone. I mean, no one will ever convince me that he wasn't an angel—my angel. I do believe he was heaven-sent. He came into my life when I needed him and just when I had asked the Lord to prove He was real.

"I do believe in miracles and that the Lord is real. It was a miracle that this man was there at a time in my life when I really needed to hear those words.

"His words not only helped me through the rest of my drive, but they continued to help me through the next few days. Looking back, I'm able to see that the entire trip was designed to renew my faith.

"I now knew the reality of death for the first time, and I also realized how much I needed God in my life. In the midst of my grief I felt renewed. I was anxiously awaiting a new day."

Louise offers another valuable lesson which she learned that evening—that "everybody needs a best friend when they're going through a problem"—even if it's a complete stranger.

Since then, despite encountering other hardships in her life, Louise declares that she has never again lost her faith. "God is not here to make things perfect. He's here to help us through the bad times. I've lost friends to AIDS, cancer, and heart disease. While it shakes me up, it doesn't shake my faith.

"A little boy in my daughter Nichole's class has cancer. When I think of that I just almost become angry. Why does this happen? And I think of a little boy that was attacked by a dog here in Nashville. He lost a limb. I mean, I just think why? It's so needless and stupid.

"But that doesn't shake my faith. It certainly makes me turn to God more and to prayer. I ask Him to be with these people and help them through it."

When Louise's father, Irby, a retired police officer, recently underwent his third heart surgery, Louise had the opportunity to put her renewed faith to a test.

"It was almost three years ago, and when he went into the hospital I told Barbara and Irlene, 'We need to pray for Daddy that God's will be done.' And Barbara said, 'I'm praying that he gets well.'

"And I said, 'No, we're not. We're praying that if it's God's will then He'll just bless the doctors and help them to use their talent. But only if it's His will and that's what's best for Dad.' "

When Barbara continued to object, Louise recalls trying to explain to her sister her reasons for praying in such a manner. "I said, 'Barbara, we don't know what's going to happen to one of us tomorrow that Dad's going to have to live through.

" 'And we don't know what might happen that he doesn't want to face. Or what illness may come upon him next. If this is God's time, then I want Him to take Daddy. If Daddy's going to suffer, I want him to take Daddy.'

"It was a major discussion, but I don't think she ever came around to this way of praying. Her outlook all the way through the surgery was totally different. It turned out to be a really rough surgery and they lost him a couple of times on the table and brought him back.

"And he is still with us and it's been several years and my prayer to this day is not, 'Please give us Daddy tomorrow,' my prayer is still, 'God, let your will be done but thank you for today that I have him.' " She chuckles: "I'm sure Barbara is still praying, 'Leave him with us tomorrow.'

"I guess what's most important is that people have their own personal relationship with God. God knows their heart and God knows my heart. I feel it's like couples who have lived together for so many years. You know what the other one is thinking.

"That's why I don't feel the need to change Barbara's way of thinking or for her to change mine. What matters the most is that you pray and keep Him in mind."

Despite a busy schedule, which includes touring, performing at Walt Disney World and Opryland, and writing a series of children's books, Louise offers that she always makes time for prayer.

"I don't have a set time of day that I pray because my day is different every single day. I'm grateful to the Lord for that—that I live such an exciting life. But it doesn't matter when you pray as long as you pray.

"But one thing I do feel strongly about is that prayer be part of your family life. One of the things we do in our family is the same thing that every other family does—when we sit down at a meal we pray. And that's wonderful and something everybody should do."

The multifaceted performer discloses that one of her favorite places to pray is at a special location on her farm just outside of Nashville. "It's called Sunrise Point and it's mentioned in the Tennessee history books. The Indians named it because they believed the sun came up there.

"We go there—it overlooks the river—for family prayer. Sometimes we'll go up there on Sundays and sometimes we're just out on the farm and we'll all meet there.

"I believe every family has to have a place they can go to—someplace where there's not a phone and there's not any outsiders and there's a private, quiet place you can go and be alone."

She also discloses that the way she prays has changed over the years due to the influence of her younger sister, Irlene. "I used to pray for success, but then my sister changed that prayer for me. I remember one time I asked her, I said, 'Irlene, people keep asking me what are you going to do next? What's next in line for you? What's your next goal?

" 'I really don't even know what to tell them. What do you tell them?' And she said, 'That I can't pray or wish for anything bigger than what God has given me.' And you know, that's really been the truth. God has always taken care of me."

Louise contends that the only time she will pray for material goods is if she truly believes she needs something. Most of her prayers, she explains, are directed at helping others who are in financial need.

"In the last few years I've prayed for material things for the Boy Scouts—finances for them. Even though it's not for me, I'm still praying about finances because I'm really involved in the Boy Scouts and I donate fifteen hours of my week to them.

"If I was really worried about my own finances I would pray about that. I don't hesitate to pray about anything that I would ask my father for—my earthly father—because if you take something to your earthly father as a child, why wouldn't you do the same as an adult with your heavenly father?

"I never hesitate or question is this right or wrong before God. I just do the best I can and pray to God. When I feel I'm wrong, I ask for forgiveness. And I also pray for wisdom in case I'm making mistakes. But I don't hesitate. I think it's a much bigger mistake not to pray about everything than it is to pray too much."

One of Louise's favorite prayer partners is her sister Barbara. "When I talk to Irlene on the phone, we talk about things. But she's got toddlers running around, and so we usually talk about things and I say, 'I'll pray for you.'

"But when I talk to Barbara, we end the phone conversation with, 'Let's pray.' And we pray over the phone. And if we're together in person, we'll usually say a prayer before we split up, unless the entire family is together in which case it's usually done over dinner."

Although Louise continues to place her life in the hands of her Maker, she readily acknowledges that many people find it difficult to do so.

"They pray about something and then they're ready to answer it for God instead of letting God take care of it. But my mom raised me differently. She said, 'If you pray about something and give it to God, don't take it back.' Sometimes you have to stop yourself and say, 'Wait a minute, why don't I give that to God to take care of?'

"But you have to understand that anyone who has a strong personality doesn't usually give their problems to anybody because they think they can handle things better than anybody else. The truth is, of course, that we have to remember that we don't always have all the answers. And that when we give a problem to God, He will fix it."

Although Louise is quick to admit that her own spiritual life is far from perfect, she adds that she has learned how to forgive herself. "One of the things we need to know is that we're going to make mistakes. And during such times you have to learn how to forgive yourself."

To emphasize her point, Louise tells the story of a close friend who once confessed to her that after twenty years he was still unhappy about something he had once done in life.

"I said, 'Do you love the Lord?' And he said, 'Well, yes I do.' And I said, 'Do you believe God forgave you for that?' And he said, 'Well, of course.' And I said, 'Well then, who are you to think you're more important than God that you can't forgive yourself?'

"And that's my message to other people. I've been through several divorces and no one could have been harder or judged me harder than I did. But you know what? The good news is that I finally realized that God forgave me. And if He can forgive me, who am I not to? We get to make mistakes and we get to go on again.

"And even if I could go back and relive my life and try to fix all those mistakes, I wouldn't. The mistakes make up who I am. I have learned from them. I've grown from them. I am the person I am today because of all the good and all the bad things that have happened to me . . ."

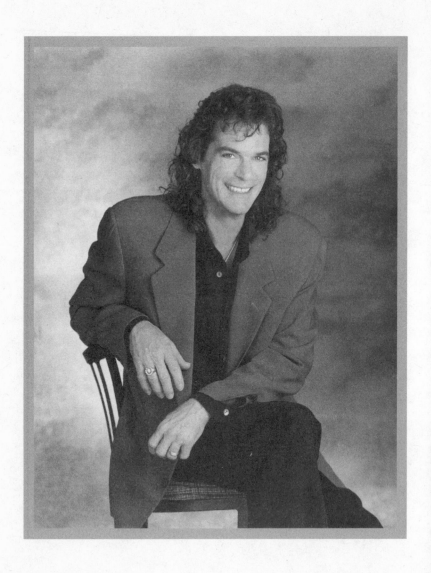

B.J. Thomas

Academy Award–winning singer and songwriter B.J. Thomas's personal life scraped rock bottom at just about the same time that he was nearing the peak of his career.

While the five-time Grammy Award winner was impressing critics and audiences with his remarkable vocal talent, the handsome Country/pop recording superstar was leading a secret life of drug and alcohol abuse that was destroying him.

It would take a frightening brush with evil for the fifty-five-year-old Texas-raised entertainer to mend his ways. Since that encounter, B.J., who is perhaps best known for such hits as "Raindrops

Keep Falling on My Head" and "(Hey won't You Play), Another Somebody's Done Somebody Wrong Song," has not done anybody wrong—particularly himself.

Nowadays, the still-popular entertainer is basking in the sunshine of a successful career, a loving family, and, most important of all, a devoted spiritual life that provides him with the kind of high which he cannot seem to get enough of . . .

As a youngster growing up in Houston, Texas, B.J. Thomas recollects being so attracted to religion that at age twelve he and his older brother, Jerry, would find ways to sneak into the local church building if it was closed.

"We'd go to church on Sunday mornings and Sunday nights and Wednesday nights. We'd go all the time. We really liked it. If the church was locked, we'd go through a window or something and go inside and we'd play Ping-Pong and we'd get the hymnals out and we'd sing from them and read some Scripture."

He attributes much of this religious attraction to his mother, whom he describes as "a very spiritual person. My dad, well, he was just the opposite. He was an alcoholic and he wasn't spiritual whatsoever.

"He was a great guy, but he never knew it, and probably, of all the kids, I'm more like him than any of the others. It was my mother who encouraged us kids to go to church when we were younger."

Not that B.J. needed much encouragement to do so. It was in church where he experienced what was often lacking at home—a harmonious environment.

"There was a real block against closeness in my family. My father's drinking caused a real separation. So as a young kid growing up my real inspiration came from the Church. That's where I also learned about prayer and togetherness."

During those times when his father would be hitting the bottle, B.J. remembers turning to the pastor of his church for solace. The minister liked both the Thomas kids, and would invite them to accompany him on his family visitations—an experience that was to leave a lasting impression on the youngster.

Reflecting back on those days, B.J. recollects that one of the best things about church was the music. He fell in love with Gospel music at a young age, and by fourteen was a regular in his church's Gospel choir.

"If there was a group of kids that were getting a quartet together or anything that had to do with Gospel music me and Jerry would be part of that. A lot of times the young people would get together on a certain night during the week, and I remember that for a time I was the song leader—that kind of thing."

As he grew older, his love of music embraced other forms. B.J. recalls falling under the spell of such Country greats as Hank Williams and Ernest Tubb. Another of his favorites was soul music great Jackie Wilson.

His family relocated to the small town of Rosenberg, Texas, and while still in high school, B.J. joined a rock 'n' roll band called the Triumphs.

"This was the summer between my freshman and sophomore years. It was this little band that some friends of my brother were starting. We played mostly in the Houston area."

His affiliation with that band would last into the mid-sixties, when B.J. took over as lead singer and changed its name to B.J. Thomas and the Triumphs.

After a series of local hits on a small label, the band signed with the larger Scepter Records Company and recorded a remake of a Hank Williams song, "I'm So Lonesome I Could Cry."

That song reached the top of the pop charts, and B.J.'s career finally began to take off. The then-twenty-two-year-old singer left the band to begin recording on his own.

By 1966, both *Cashbox* and *Billboard* magazines were describing B.J. as the "Most Promising Vocalist." That assessment would come true when he wrote and recorded the song "Raindrops Keep Falling on My Head" for the movie *Butch Cassidy and the Sundance Kid*. The song went on to win an Oscar in 1969 for "Best Song of the Year." B.J. was now firmly established as a star.

With a new recording contract from Paramount Records in hand, the rising young star was rapidly approaching the pinnacle of his career. What neither the record company nor his fans realized was the high price that the talented entertainer was paying for his fame.

"I'd been drinking ever since I was fairly young—ever since my twenties, when I got out of athletics and got into music. I just had no sense getting into that. And I had a whole drug thing too. I'd been taking pills since I was about fifteen or sixteen.

"I was just caught up in that kind of lifestyle—speed, downers—that kind of thing. I never thought about it. I never thought it was anything worse than smoking a cigarette or something. And when I got out on the road and I would get sick, I would get me some speed. And I did that from time to time until I came to rely on it."

As his growing popularity brought more pressure to bear upon him, B.J. began to increase his dependence upon drugs and alcohol. That dependency, he recalls, worsened in 1968 after an incident in a New York City hotel lobby left him disabled.

"To make a long story short, I had just arrived in New York City from Memphis, and I had an altercation with this African-American guy behind the hotel desk where I was staying who had some words with me when he found out I was from Memphis. This was right after the assassination of Dr. Martin Luther King Jr.

"He stabbed me in my left lung, and I went into the hospital for twenty to twenty-two days. When I got out, I was under doctors' orders not to sing or go on the road for six months. So when I got back to Memphis, I stuck it out for about a month and the money was running out.

"So I went to a doctor and I said, 'Give me four or five prescriptions for speed and three or four for downs.' I would use the speed for energy to sing because basically I just had one lung at that time. But that's when I really got hooked up into it. And I was really hung up in a major, major way until 1976, when I turned things around in my life."

By now, B.J.'s career was skyrocketing, and so was his drug habit. He remembers residing in a neighborhood on New York City's Upper West Side where drugs were readily available and he was one of the drug dealers' best customers.

"I'd go over to this area in New York called Needle Park to buy drugs. I was a successful entertainer and I had all kinds of money, but I lived like a bum—like a drug addict. I looked like I was living on the street.

"I had dirty hair, dirt under my fingernails—you know. And then I'd go on the road and I wouldn't even take a shower for the show. I'd just get up there, do seven or eight songs, get the hell off, and go do my drugs. I was just a classic drughead.

"And I never thought I would ever get free from that. Like every once in a while I'd think, 'Well, yeah, I need to.' But I was caught. It was like I was handcuffed and there was no way out."

His drug habit soon began to take a toll on his career, as word started to spread about the star's unpredictable behavior. B.J. soon found himself with fewer and fewer bookings.

"Soon, everything I had was basically gone," he somberly recalls. "I just had a number-one pop record and I couldn't even get a booking at the Elks Club. I wouldn't show up and when I did show up I'd sing four or five songs and I might cuss somebody out or insult the crowd—or even Jesus.

"I was just awful. I'd go on the 'Merv Griffin Show' and the 'Mike Douglas Show'—all those shows—just blitzed out of my mind. I was so high, they couldn't talk to me. I just basically lost everything and I didn't know how I was going to support my family. I thought I was going to have to find me a job or something," he quips.

B.J.'s life continued to spin out of control until one fateful day while en route from Hawaii to one of the smaller islands where he was scheduled to perform a concert. "I had been going too strong that week and in the last two days previous to this I had not gotten any sleep. So I was really trying to just keep going on the speed, and I finally went too far."

The entertainer suffered a severe drug overdose in mid-flight, regaining consciousness in a hospital room nearly forty-eight hours later. B.J. learned from doctors that he had only been moments away from death.

"They said my lips and my fingernails had turned black, and they couldn't get a pulse. I had gone to the bathroom all over myself—that's what you do when you die—you go to the bathroom all over yourself.

"They assumed on the plane that I had died. They called the emergency squad and they took me off the plane and they got me to the hospital. The thing that saved my life was that it was only a fourteen-minute flight. If it had been another twenty minutes I probably would've died."

Years later, B.J. still remembers the depression he felt as he lay alone in that hospital room. He also recalls how while in the midst of gloomy thoughts about his future, the door to his room opened and a nurse entered to fix his bed.

The sight of the nurse made him feel better, B.J. recalls. He was lonely for company and eager for someone to talk to. "I was thinking about my wife Gloria, who I was separated from at that time. And I said to the nurse, who was straightening my bed, 'You know, I don't know why I just didn't die. Do you?' "

Long moments passed while the nurse stared at her patient. "Yes, I do," she finally replied. "You didn't die because God has something for you to do." She then resumed her duties without uttering another word.

For B.J., those few words nearly brought him to the brink of tears. He remembers not feeling so spiritually touched since the days when he and his brother would visit families with their minister.

"It was a real matter-of-fact kinda thing the way she said it, you know. But for the first time, I guess, since I had been a boy, it dawned on me 'Yeah, hey, wait a minute. God's part of all this stuff. Maybe He does have a plan for me.' "

Upon returning home to New York City, there was a pleasant surprise awaiting him. "Gloria called me. We'd been separated for probably eight months. And she says to me, 'B.J., will you come home?' "

Two days later, B.J. was back in Memphis where a tearful reunion took place between the entertainer, his wife, and their five-year-old daughter, Paige.

There was even more surprising news in store for him. "Gloria told me that she had a spiritual awakening and that she was born again. She also told me that she had called my agency and asked them not to let me go to Hawaii because she had a premonition that I would die there, and that she and my daughter had prayed for me."

Although deeply touched by his wife's concern, B.J. remembers bridling when Gloria suggested that he meet two lay ministers who were instrumental in her own religious conversion. "I said 'Absolutely not. No way.' Two days later I ended up at this family's house where I met them."

Jim Reeves, a Texas cattleman, and his associate, Bobby Guess, were already waiting for B.J. when the performer arrived. "I looked at Gloria and at these guys who I knew were going to talk to me about spiritual things, and I was ready for a good discussion."

But unknown to the performer, more than just a discussion was about to take place—it would be an event that would transform his entire life.

"Jim and Bobby asked me to step into another room where Jim did most of the talking. He said to me, 'B.J., when I look at you in your eyes, you scare me. Can I pray a prayer of protection?' "

His first reaction to that was to say no, B.J. recollects, but he changed his mind. "I said, 'Sure, what do I care?' But what I was thinking is 'Boy, is this guy a jerk.' I was also thinking at the same time, 'Well, he's a nice guy for doing this' and 'Who is this cowboy?' "

Reeves next asked the entertainer if he was religious or spiritual. "I'm spiritual," B.J. recalls replying, drawing a nod of approval from the lay minister. "Good," Reeves exclaimed, "then you'll know what I'm talking about."

"He started praying for me. He was asking Jesus to protect me from Satan. He was offering up prayers saying something like, 'Lord, by the shed blood of Jesus Christ, I ask your protection over B.J.' "

What happened next is something that the recording star asserts he will never forget. "All of a sudden I hear this loud snap. It was like a shot or a tree limb breaking. It was this big crack coming from the left side of my chest.

"I just knew that when I looked down my rib was going to be sticking through my chest or something. I thought I had broken a bone or a rib."

Instead, what B.J. saw when he glanced down at his chest was not a broken bone emerging from his body, but something much more sinister.

"It was something that was almost like air or almost like wind. It came out of my chest and kind of curved around and went right by Jim's head and out the windowpane behind his head. There wasn't any form to it.

"It was unbelievable. I mean it was just plain unbelievable. It was like a special effects thing—like maybe they were doing the special effects for a *Casper* movie or something. Or *Ghostbusters*."

Frightened by what he was experiencing, B.J. recalls searching the eyes of the two ministers to see how they were reacting to this phenomenon. He quickly realized that no one else was witnessing this evil presence.

"I thought for sure they would at least have heard the cracking sound. But no one did. Meanwhile, I was having this illusion of this thing coming right out of my chest."

What began as a terrifying experience gradually developed into a much more comforting one, he recalls. "I now had these mellow and receptive feelings. I felt that something that had been blocking my heart had been removed by a simple prayer.

"I just knew that something had been standing between my heart and my soul and it was no longer there. I know it just happened and it's something that I've never been quite able to explain.

"I went home that night, threw away like over a pound of drugs —just threw it all away—and I gave up booze that evening as well. I gave it all up in one evening after that experience and I did not experience even one second of withdrawal. Not one minute. And I've been through withdrawal many times in my life."

Was it the devil that was exorcised that evening? B.J. simply shrugs in bewilderment. "I'm not necessarily a big believer in the devil, and I've never been particularly interested in whether or not there were principalities of demons or whatever those people talk about. I didn't concern myself with that because if I did, what good would it do me? I couldn't defeat any of them.

"Instead, I've always just trusted my guardian angels and whoever else wants me to go through this life that they would keep me from being destroyed by anything like that. But I do think that during the years of my drug addiction there were thought patterns due to the way I was living that can create certain buildups.

"Whatever it was, the simple prayer that this guy said had cleaned out that stuff. It was like something had gotten into my closet—I hesitate to say it was a demonic power or something. But what I saw was something I sure have never been able to explain, and now all the junky stuff in the closet had been cleaned out."

Feeling as if he had been given a new lease on life, B.J. began to ponder what he should do about his career. "I just didn't know what I was going to do—whether I was still going to be an entertainer or not. Jim was talking to me about going into the cattle business, and I bought a truck and I was thinking about doing that kind of thing."

A phone call would help him make up his mind. On the other end of the line was an executive from Myrrh Records, a religious label with a stable of top-of-the-line Gospel artists, making an enticing offer to the performer.

"I'd never heard of them. But when they asked me if I wanted to make a Gospel record, I said, 'I really would. I'd like to express how I'm feeling right now.' And, of course, we made the record 'Home Is Where I Belong.' "

That 1977 Gospel album would go on to earn B.J. his first Grammy Award for "Best Inspirational Performance." It would be the first of five Grammy Awards that he received for performing Gospel music before switching back to a secular format in the mid-eighties. That comeback resulted in more hit records for the talented singer and songwriter.

"Everything good started happening to me from that evening. My wife and I had some more kids and we did a Gospel tour where we went to China and eventually adopted a Korean girl. It was all quite incredible."

Today, when reflecting back upon his long and successful career, what B.J. is most proud of is his renewal of faith. "I'm even prouder of that than the Academy Award and all the Grammys," he proclaims. "It resulted in me singing spiritual music, and I think performing spiritual music may have been the whole point for me to even be a singer.

"And it all stems from that nurse saying one simple thing to me. And it probably also originated with the prayers for me from my wife and my daughter. I think prayer is a pretty powerful thing."

The popular entertainer, who still packs them in at his theater in Branson, Missouri, also credits his religious conversion for giving him a greater understanding of himself.

"One of the best things I got out of all this is knowing who I am. I used to think that I was this vocalist who if I did my thing in the correct manner I could change the world.

"What I understand now is that I am a man. I'm a man who loves his wife and who cherishes his children. That's who I am. And what a lighter load that is to carry. It's a load that's even a pleasure to carry."

While trying not to sound too much like a preacher, B.J. is nonetheless eager to share some of the lessons he has learned—the hard way —about the power of God to heal.

"If you don't block your faith off with addiction and a list of other things I can name, faith will win out sooner or later. Faith is the strongest part of things and your prayer is your tool to get to the spiritual essence of things.

"I'm not very traditional in my beliefs, but I do believe that everyone has faith and spirituality built into them—even if they have to take years of real trial with drugs and alcohol the way I did. There's a part of the Creator in everyone.

"Faith is an eternal spirit that's inside all of us. If you want it bad enough, you'll find it. It's the lucky ones who get it when they're young."

After B.J. left the house where he had his brush with evil, he recalls that one of his first actions was to purchase a Bible, which, to this day, he continues to read on a daily basis. He also developed a prayer life.

"I believe that real prayer works and changes things and tells us things that happen. It's not so much a language as a feeling—a deep, inner yearning. My girls pray on their own and my wife and I pray a lot together. We try to stay in a state of prayer and we pray for just about everything."

For anyone seeking to renew their own faith, the award-winning entertainer suggests that they pray in order to gain such a feeling. "Keep it positive and simple. Get up in the morning—you don't even have to do this every morning—and try to realize that the day is made for you and the Lord is there for you. Just start out with that.

"Say to yourself, 'I love myself. I love everybody and everybody loves me. I forgive everybody and everybody forgives me. And I forgive myself.' It's that simple. Sometimes faith can be so illusive because it is that simple. It all has to do with your thoughts and your spoken word.

"Just remember when you were young and how things happened when you asked your own father for something. You would say, 'Dad, can I have the keys to the car?' And he would say, 'Yeah, son. Be back by 10 P.M.' It was no big deal. Just ask and the words and the thought pattern will cause a whole series of events to take place . . ."

Charlie Daniels

With his bushy beard and trademark cowboy hat slung low over his eyes, Charlie Daniels, a Southern Country rocker who blends boogie and traditional Country fiddle-playing, has over his long career been better known as a good ol' boy than an altar boy.

But nowadays the sixty-one-year-old Wilmington, North Carolina, native, best known for his 1979 Country/pop hit "The Devil Went Down to Georgia," is finally lifting that wide-brimmed hat from over his eyes and revealing his more spiritual side. Charlie has even recorded a series of Gospel albums—one of which recently won a Dove Award for Country Album of the Year.

Charlie was a self-taught fiddler at the age of fifteen, who, according to one popular account, was so flashy a fiddle player, that he actually "defeated" the devil in a fiddling contest.

The six-foot-four giant of a man will only grin and give a broad wink when asked to verify that story. But the legendary musician, who has been heading up the Charlie Daniels Band since 1972, is more than eager to talk about a second encounter with Satan—one in which prayer was the instrument that defeated the devil . . .

Charlie Daniels says he is unlikely ever to forget the summer when he was on his way to perform with Willie Nelson at the first Farm Aid concert in Three Rivers, Michigan. Accompanying him at the time was his wife, Hazel, who suddenly fell ill.

"She was hurting and I said, 'I'm taking you to the hospital.' And she said, 'No, we're going home.' And I said, 'No, I'm not going to wait until we get home, I'm taking you to the hospital right now.' So we went to the local hospital and they found that she had something inside her fallopian tubes that didn't look good."

When doctors told a worried Charlie that his wife would require surgery, he and Hazel decided to have the operation performed closer to home—in Nashville. "So I put her on an ambulance plane and we flew straight back to the hospital in Nashville."

Charlie's voice cracks with emotion as he recalls that upsetting period in his life. "It was a hard time for me because I'm very close to my wife. I love her very dearly. In fact, I love her more than I love myself. And I didn't know what it was exactly that was wrong with her. And, of course, the first thing you think about is always cancer."

As he left the hospital that day, there was something else on Charlie's mind—a growing conviction that the devil was somehow responsible for Hazel's illness. Maybe it wasn't exactly logical thinking, but that was how he felt nonetheless.

That thought continued to occupy his mind as he returned home to freshen up. "I turned on the shower and I stood there. And if I've ever done spiritual warfare in my life it was at that moment.

"And I said, I just told the devil, 'You can't have her. You're not getting her.' I prayed and I prayed and when I walked out of that shower I just knew that she was going to be all right.

"And, sure enough, the next morning they operated on her and the doctor told me that her fallopian tubes were gangrenous, but that she was going to be just fine. And I also knew that through my faith, God had given me comfort and I beat the devil."

Charlie remembers rejoicing when doctors gave him the good news about his wife's condition. As tears streaked down his cheeks, he also recalls vowing to better serve his Maker—a pledge which he has kept since that day.

"My faith was not always steadfast. I had gotten away from it for many years, although I never quit believing. I got away for many years from the way I was supposed to be living.

"And that was not right because I was raised in a God-fearing family. There was a time when I was a kid that I didn't even know anybody who didn't believe in God.

"I mean, we used to hear tales of atheists, but I never knew one. We were a religious family right back through the generations. Most of my folks were Methodists, but we'd also go to the Baptist church. We were a family of believers.

"My grandmother was a very devout lady. I don't remember my grandfather very well on my dad's side because he died before I was three or four years old. My granddad on my mother's side, he went through his wild times when he was younger, but he was a very devout man. And right up through my aunts and uncles and cousins—I mean, we were all believers.

"Sure I got away from the way I was supposed to be living, and I slipped off the path a lot. But now I came back to trying to do like I should do. The potential for believing was always inside me. It was trying to make a commitment to stop doing the things that I shouldn't be doing that was hard."

The son of a North Carolina lumberjack, Charlie Daniels was a self-taught fiddler and guitar player at the age of fifteen. Music was always part of his life, and he recalls being influenced mostly by Country, bluegrass, and rock 'n' roll.

While in high school, Charlie displayed his flashy fiddle- and mandolin-playing style as a member of a local bluegrass band, the Misty Mountain Boys. When Charlie wasn't making music he was making money working in a creosote factory alongside his father and grandfather.

After graduating from high school, Charlie continued working at the factory, playing rock 'n' roll on weekends with the Rockets, a Jacksonville, North Carolina, band.

Those days with that band were wild ones, he recalls, a period of time when Charlie admits not trodding the spiritual path. "I had learned the Gospel message when I was young but I just didn't understand it. I didn't understand it at all.

"I wasn't sticking needles in my arms, but there was plenty of times when I was drunk and I've done all kinds of other wild things. I wasn't walking the path then."

Although someone might find fault with his spiritual life back then, Charlie's outspoken popularism never suffered. When a black worker with a family to support was laid off at the plant where he worked, Charlie chose to give up his own job so that the family would still have a breadwinner.

Now out of work, Charlie decided to spend more time playing the music he enjoyed so much. He and the Rockets took off for Washington, D.C., where the band eventually changed its name to the Jaguars after the title of their first Epic Records release.

Charlie continued performing with the Jaguars for about eight years. As the band began to experiment musically—utilizing jazz styling more and more—the classic Charlie Daniels Band sound started to solidify.

After recording a solo album for Capitol, Charlie formed his Charlie Daniels Band in 1972, and seven years later the band had its biggest hit—a hot fiddle number called "The Devil Went Down to Georgia."

The song topped the Country charts, and that year the Charlie Daniels Band received a Grammy for Best Country Performance by a Duo or Group. Numerous other awards followed, and by the late eighties the band had sold more than a million records.

By now, the singer/songwriter and master fiddler had also earned a reputation as a colorful guy, successfully creating an image for himself as a beloved, uncompromising outlaw in the Waylon-Willie-Hank Junior mold.

Despite that notorious public image, his personal life was something altogether different, he insists. "There was never a second in my life that I can ever remember that I did not believe that there was a God and that Jesus Christ was the Son of God.

"I had a lot of baggage, I had a lot of temptations, and I slipped off that old slippery log, but I was a believer. I always have been no matter what people thought of me."

Although Charlie candidly admits that there have been times in his life when his faith failed him, he tries not to be too hard on himself. "We've all done things which we're not really proud of, but the idea is to strive to do better the next time.

"Sure my faith has been challenged—it's still constantly challenged. It's just something that is going to happen. I slip off the path a lot—even today—but I do try to walk the path. I very much am a believer. I believe with all my heart."

One thing Charlie states that he has learned over the years, is to place his complete trust in God. "I still sometimes get so tied up in knots thinking that things are going to go wrong, or what's going to happen to me. And then all of a sudden I realize that it's something in the future that I can't do anything about.

"And I just finally have to say, 'Lord, I can't handle this. I just cannot handle this and I don't know what to do about it. I'm sick and tired of worrying about it.'

"But you *can* do something about it. You can turn your problems over to God and have faith that He will take care of them even though it's hard a lot of times to keep from being concerned."

Keeping faith, he acknowledges, is not always an easy thing to do. "It's believing in things that haven't yet happened. That's one of the hardest things to believe—that the things you pray for are going to happen. But the basis of faith to me is that you trust in Jesus Christ."

During uncertain moments when he feels his faith needs some shoring up, Charlie states that he turns to prayer to do so. "Sometimes I fall on my knees and sometimes I'll lie in bed. It depends on where I am and what I'm doing. A lot of times my praying is talking to God.

"Sometimes I'll say a fairly long prayer and sometimes it's a shorter prayer. I may say several prayers during the day. When we get up in the morning, my wife and I usually read the Bible. We try to start the day with prayer.

" 'The Lord's Prayer' is one of my favorite prayers, I think that it's put there as a guide for us. It contains in it everything we need. It starts off praising the Lord and it goes on to answer our daily needs—you know, 'lead us not into temptation' and 'forgive us our debts.' "

Nowadays, in addition to a busy concert schedule, the "King of Southern Country Rock" can also be found performing spiritual music. Although a relative newcomer to the Gospel field, one of his first efforts, *The Door,* won a 1995 Dove Award for Country Album of the Year.

"I had always intended to do a Gospel album," he declares. "It was a real opportunity for me to try and reach people who have kinda fallen into the cracks as far as organized religion goes. They think that to have God's love you have to be good enough and never commit a sin —that sort of thing.

"And, of course, we all know that's not true. If it was we'd all be lost because we all sin. I wanted to tell these people, 'Look, you may think that you're the worst person in the world, and that you may have done and still do things that you're not really proud of, yet there is salvation and an eternal home waiting for you."

Although deeply religious, Charlie is still haunted by his old reputation as a hard-drinking, carousing, good ol' boy. He is amused by that image, stating that nowadays he feels more like an altar boy than a good ol' boy.

"Let the chips fall where they will," he sniffs. "I'm chopping my own log. I guess a lot of people just don't think that I'm a sincere Christian. But there's always somebody who's got to criticize you. No matter what you do, there'll always be doubters.

"I still play secular music, and I've mentioned the name of Jesus Christ in places that no preacher would ever go into. I'm not saying that to take any credit, but it's a way to reach people even though I'll be criticized for being in those places in the first place. That's a self-righteous attitude. If you listen to everything everybody tells you, you can never do right.

"Sure I have some of the same temptations, the same problems that I've always had. But when I slip off that old slippery log I know there's forgiveness. That's the Gospel message to me—that we strive to be as good as we possibly can and that's what I'm trying to do."

Charlie likes to reach out to people who feel estranged from religion because he once felt that way himself. "I remember coming home one morning after a night of carousing. I turned on the television and there's this beautiful church service going on.

"And I didn't feel part of that—all those people dressed up and singing hymns of praise and enjoying their faith as they should be. I didn't feel a part of what the preacher was preaching about. I didn't feel like the preacher was talking to me.

"He's talking to everybody else, but he's not talking to me. Unless somebody sits down and talks to that person, to explain things to him and then have him read the Bible, he'll stay lost. I think somebody needs to be reaching out and teaching these people. They've got to know that even Adam and Eve took a fall.

"And through my music I just want to get that word across to these people that nobody seems to be talking to or that nobody is reaching. I want to reach people that have kind of fallen through the cracks when it comes to religion."

Although quite vocal on the subject of religious divisiveness—and a slew of other subjects as well, from patriotism to tithing to homosexuality, which he does not condone—Charlie is not interested in taking to the pulpit to preach his message.

Mainly, he wishes that all the squabbling over which religious denomination is the best, and arguments about the proper way to practice Christianity, would come to a halt.

"When are we going to stop wounding each other with all these self-righteous attitudes with everyone telling everyone else how to live their lives?

"My Bible says if you believe in your heart, confess with your mouth that Jesus Christ is Lord and that God raised Him from the dead, you shall be saved.

"Now if you believe in that, you're a Christian. If you wear your hair long or short or any of the other little things that people get involved in, that's none of my business. I'm so sick and tired of the denominations fighting among themselves.

"I'm sick and tired of these little theological bits causing division in the body of Christ. Can you imagine what it would be like if we were all united with each other?

"There's only one Gospel message for me—that we strive to be as good as we possibly can. That's also my message for people who have never known the Lord. By living in that simple manner they will be able to approach the Lord . . ."

Ferlin Husky

When Ferlin Husky's seventeen-year-old son Danny was killed in a 1970 automobile accident, the legendary Country music star's life took a tumble and he grew resentful toward God.

It would take nearly fourteen years for the seventy-year-old Missouri-born singer and songwriter to overcome that resentment. His feelings would change when Ferlin was unexpectedly touched by God while attending a Sunday morning church service with his children.

Since then, and despite two near-fatal heart attacks, the singer, songwriter, and comedian has remained in close touch with his Creator, sharing his faith with his audiences whenever he performs.

During such moments the veteran entertainer points to himself as an example that it is never too late to return to God's loving light.

"Even if you feel you've slipped and can never get up, just remember that none of us are perfect and that the Lord is always ready to take you back . . ."

Although many years have passed since his son's death, Ferlin's voice still quivers with emotion when he speaks about that painful time in his life.

He remembers the days just before Danny's death, when he and his son were at home in Hendersonville, Tennessee, discussing a fishing trip that the teenager wanted to go on.

"Danny was playin' drums in my band at the time and he kept asking me if he could drive down to Florida. He wasn't eighteen, yet, and I knew he could drive and all, but I was just afraid for him to go.

"I said, 'Son, I think it's best if you don't go.' Well, what happened is that I finally said okay. So he stopped in the Fort Campbell area near Hopkinsville, Kentucky.

"He had some friends there that he had gone to school with, and he was visiting them. He called me the night before to say where he was and to tell me that I shouldn't worry—that he was all right."

Those were the final words that Ferlin would ever hear spoken by his teenager. That evening Danny would die in a head-on automobile collision.

Ferlin recalls that he first learned of his son's death the following morning. He recollects that there was a knock on his door, and when he went to open it, standing outside with a grim expression etched on his face was a police officer.

"When I saw it was one of the deputies in the sheriff's department I threw up my arms and I started joking with him like, 'Hey, I'm not guilty, I didn't do it.' " But the unsmiling expression on the police officer's face quickly convinced the entertainer that this was no joking matter.

"He said, 'You got a son named Danny?' And then he told me what happened. Danny had died in a car crash. And from then on I don't remember a whole lot because I was sedated most of the time."

What the Country music star does remember of the days that followed is a procession of visitors arriving at his house to console him —including Johnny Cash.

"Johnny was and still is one of my best friends, and I love him like a blood brother," Ferlin declares. "So he comes in through the kitchen and into the den where I was and we embraced.

"We both shed some tears there. And he said, 'Well, I guess we'll never understand it, Ferlin. They take yours away and they give me one.' That was the day that his son John Carter Cash was born—it was on March 3. And then he said, 'Just keep the faith and we'll understand it. It's all for a reason.'"

But the grief-stricken entertainer recollects not being able to believe that God had a good reason for taking his son. Although he had been raised with a strict Baptist faith, Ferlin remembers feeling betrayed by his Maker.

"I sort of rebelled against God. I did everything but curse God Almighty. I was out of my head—hysterical—and I was saying, 'Why me, God?' I was saying, 'Why'd this have to happen to me?' I guess it was a time when I was feeling sorry for myself."

As the months passed by, Ferlin's feelings of resentment toward God did not lessen. He remembers trying to conceal those feelings from friends and family members who continued to console him.

"I never wanted to say anything that would cause somebody else to lose their faith. I'd just go ahead and listen to everybody talk but I didn't believe it. Even when they started talking about the hereafter, I didn't believe it. But I wouldn't say anything against ministers or preachers or anything."

Then what Ferlin believes was the first of two miracles in his life took place. It began with the joyful birth of his son Terry on Christmas Eve. The second miracle would take place sometime in the not-too-distant future—a renewal of his faith.

At the moment, after months of depression, Ferlin remembers feeling cheered by Terry's birth. It was an event, he recalls, "that made me feel like I was walking on cloud nine.

"I was grateful, but I still didn't go back to church. I still had this feeling in my heart like, 'God, why did you let Danny's death happen?'"

Ferlin remembers a Sunday in the fall of 1984, when he was preparing to attend services at the Holiday Heights Baptist Church in Hendersonville, Tennessee.

"My son, my daughters, and about eight or nine more kids were scheduled to walk down the aisle for altar call in this little church. It was a ceremony in which they were going to accept Jesus Christ.

"Well, I've heard of people—and I've seen people—who get touched by God or the Holy Ghost or whatever, but with the feelings I was carrying in my heart I never in a million years expected it to happen to me. But it did!

"All of a sudden I got so loose that I couldn't even stand up. I tried to walk and I just got to laughing and crying at the same time. I was touched by God. I never felt so good in my life before. My kids and some of their friends were walking down the aisle to accept Jesus and this just came out of me.

"I couldn't keep my mouth shut—I don't even know what I was saying. I was just blabbering and I wanted to laugh and I wanted to cry and I couldn't walk."

Ferlin remembers suddenly feeling released from all the bitterness that he had been harboring toward God. Now he felt only love for his Creator.

It was a feeling, he recollects, that he had not experienced with such intensity since his boyhood days growing up in southeast Missouri, when, full of spirit, he sang Gospel music in a church very much like this one.

"My folks were sharecroppers and we traveled around a bit. Whatever town we lived closest to, that was the church we went to. It was mostly Holy Roller churches that we went to. I guess I went to the Methodist church the longest, 'cause that's what I was raised around. Later in life I started going to a Baptist church—my grandfather was a Baptist minister.

"I grew up in a religious home where we practiced prayer. I believed in God all the time and I prayed all the time. I had prayed and I accepted Jesus Christ as my personal Savior. I had left Him after Danny's death, but He never left me.

"And this time when I left Him I had never really forgiven Him until this moment. Now after fourteen years I was finally able to say that God took Danny for a reason."

The morning after his religious conversion, Ferlin remembers feeling as if he were starting life anew. "I threw my cigarettes away. I said, 'That's it. If God's done this for me, I'm going to stop smoking.' And I also stopped drinking."

Ferlin, whose career was built on secular Country music and comedy, also began to sing more Gospel music—the kind of inspirational music he had grown up singing but was not usually encouraged to perform as a secular Country music artist.

"I couldn't sing Gospel songs because in these kinds of places where I worked—like nightclubs and dinner clubs—people would walk out if I did. They didn't want to hear about religion when they were drinking and having a good time."

Another change he made in his life was to avoid performing in clubs where alcohol was served. "I would take my family along to different shows and places where I could do Gospel songs and feel really blessed. I would play some fairs and things with the whole family joining in when I was doing Gospel singing."

Even when he was asked by concert promoters to stick to his popular hit songs, Ferlin recollects that he always managed to squeeze at least one Gospel number into his act.

He laughingly recalls how surprised his audiences often were to hear spiritual numbers from an entertainer who built his reputation on such songs as "Champagne Ladies and Blue Ribbon Babies," and "Truck Drivin' Son of a Gun." "People would see me and wonder if I was for real. But I was trying—and I continue to try—to set an example."

Although today he still remains primarily a secular act, Ferlin notes that when he performs at Branson, Missouri, he tries to work some spiritual material into his act.

"If I have an extra minute during one of my shows I always mention God Almighty and sing a Gospel song and give my testimony. And a lot of times I've had people come up after the show and ask me if I'd pray with them. It's a great feeling."

Ferlin speaks with great fervor about the importance of his spiritual life. "I pray to God not to let me slip and to keep me from temptations. I don't want to get up on a stage and profess to be something that I'm not.

"I don't want people saying, 'I don't believe him, he's a hypocrite.' But I'd say now that the majority of the people who come to hear me sing believe in me. And I've helped a lot of people find their own faith."

In 1977, after a long and successful career that spanned more than twenty years, Ferlin suffered a heart attack and required bypass surgery. Although the operation slowed him down a bit, he remembers it did not prevent him from eventually resuming his busy pace.

"I just believed and prayed that I was going to make it—and I did. Sure sometimes I got up and I would get mad or something, but I never lost faith that I would fully recover."

Ferlin suffered a second heart attack in 1990 after finishing a performance in Cody, Wyoming. The entertainer found himself back in the hospital, where the prognosis was not a good one. The entertainer learned that he would have to undergo triple bypass heart surgery.

The operation was a success, and Ferlin recollects feeling more grateful to God than ever before. "It actually strengthened my faith. I thanked God that He gave doctors the intelligence and skill to be able to treat my condition. It also forced me to lead a healthier lifestyle—like diet and stuff. These were all blessings from God."

Looking back at his career—one which has included numerous hit songs, several successful comedy albums, and featured roles in four movies, the Missouri farm boy believes his greatest achievement is being blessed by God.

"I've done all kinds of things in my life, and I know how to entertain, but what I thank Him for the most is what He has done for me spiritually.

"I've changed a lot. When I was this young kid I used to go up to the altar every time they had altar call. But I never had the feelings toward God that I have now that I'm older. It's by faith that I've received those feelings. I've grown into it."

As a survivor of two heart attacks, Ferlin counsels anyone suffering from a severe medical condition to "never lose your faith. Just look around and you'll see somebody in worse shape. And pray constantly. Open a Bible and turn to any page and read it. That's what I do.

"I thank God for my health. And if I'm down and can't get up, I'm still thanking Him for what He has done for me. And if you feel like you can't make it on your own, get the strength from somebody like your pastor."

Looking ahead, Ferlin states that he wants to continue sharing his faith with his audiences. "I've been blessed to receive a whole lot in my life. I want all those I can reach to receive through faith a lot in their lives as well.

"It's hard to tell anybody how to live, so I want to show them by being an example. I always tell people what He has done for me. I'd say the majority of people believe me. I've helped a lot of people turn to God. I want to continue doing that . . ."

Steve Gatlin

When the Gatlin Brothers decided after sixteen years of touring to quit the road and establish their own theater, Steve Gatlin remembers worrying about what effect such a move would have on the careers of the Grammy Award–winning trio.

The forty-six-year-old Texas-raised singer and songwriter recalls that it was "a scary thing to do. We were stepping out in a lot of faith."

That faith, however, was well rewarded. Today, the Gatlin Brothers continue to pack them in at their new performance home in Myrtle Beach, South Carolina.

This was not the first time that Steve, Larry, and Rudy relied on God to help them cope with a difficult situation in their lives.

When in the 1980s drug and alcohol abuse began to wreak havoc on their careers, the Gatlins turned to prayer to help rid themselves of their addictions. It was a three-year, up-and-down struggle that finally produced positive results.

As a result of such experiences, Steve firmly believes in the changing power of faith and prayer.

"Sometimes we're put through the fire," he reflects. "But I know that there are even better things in store for you when you do step out in faith . . ."

It was 1992 and the Gatlin Brothers Band was growing increasingly weary of life on the road.

After all these years of touring, Steve and his two brothers were tired of the endless hours spent traveling along monotonous highways, sleeping in hotels where the rooms all looked the same, and eating road food that never quite tasted like home cooking.

They were also older now—no longer the hot young band that had started playing together in the 1970s, eager and excited to be traveling from city to city to showcase their exceptional talents. Nowadays, Steve, Larry, and Rudy more often missed their families than their fans, and wanted to spend more time at home.

"The road was beating us up—it was a killer," Steve recalls. "You're away from your family, you're in a different hotel every night. Some artists like it—and it is exciting for a while—but not after you've done it for sixteen years."

It was decidedly a time for a change. The Gatlins, one of Country music's all-time premier close-harmony groups, wanted to write a new chapter in their history. But they also realized that this new chapter could not be written lightly.

"It was difficult when I first heard Larry mention that we should consider quitting the road," Steve recollects. "We had all these years of touring under our belt and people still wanted to hear us sing. We had performance dates booked and we were still making a nice living—those kind of things.

"It was like someone who has been doing something and they're successful at it, and it's going good for them, and all of a sudden they just decide they want to do it in a different way."

But the Gatlins now had a new goal in mind. They wanted to continue performing their special brand of music—but in a permanent concert hall—someplace where when the show ended, they could return home to their families instead of to a sterile hotel room.

There was yet another reason for wanting to make the change. Although still quite popular, Steve and his brothers were nonetheless witnessing a steady decline in the number of fans who were turning out for their road appearances.

"It was a tough part of our life because we felt like we were seeing the handwriting on the wall," Steve states. "We weren't drawing as many people as we used to, the hit records weren't happening, and we weren't on the radio anymore.

"We still felt like we were cutting good records and making good music, but it's just an aging process that happens to every entertainer and to every athlete.

"It was a decision that was coming to us sooner or later. Every act has to make this decision at some time. We were in our forties and we just thought we should take an active position in changing our careers rather than just sitting back and letting it happen. And to do that you have to step out in faith and think, 'Well, I hope this works.' "

Steve recollects the day when he and his brothers arrived in Branson, Missouri, to scout for a theater location and to buy some property to build new homes on.

"I remember walking up on a hill on property that I had bought. I took my wife aside and she and I just kind of prayed there. My brothers were there and two or three other people, but we just walked away from the group for a while.

"I remember specifically saying, 'God, if this is supposed to be, it will happen.' Well, it didn't. Two deals fell through and we eventually ended up in Myrtle Beach.

"So after three years of getting off the road and trying to go to Branson, it didn't work out and we ended up here in Myrtle Beach in a wonderful situation.

"There was a reason for all of that trial—and sometimes it felt like we were being put through the fire—but it all paid off and we're in a much better situation now than we ever were."

Steve enjoys recounting that story because in many ways it sums up his feelings about faith. "If you walk in the path you realize that everything that happens to you—whether it's good or bad—has a purpose in life. In all things—good and bad—you should give thanks.

"What happened to us is an example. Our hearts were set on Branson, but God had a different plan for us than performing there. It's just being able to see through the fog, knowing that the fog will clear. Sometimes that's very hard to do, but with faith it will.

"When we quit the road we felt like we were in the twilight of our career, so to speak. But we still wanted to sing and play. We had faith that it would all work out and it did. Things have been better for us than they ever were before."

Ever a realist, Steve acknowledges that it is not always easy to cultivate such firm faith. "Sometimes we get distraught about certain situations and we can't see the forest for the trees. But eventually you work your way out of that.

"You've got to have stamina and, in Christian terms, stamina simply means faith. You've got to have the faith to work through that situation because it will eventually remedy itself."

Faith and the power of prayer are two subjects that are quite familiar to the Odessa, Texas, native. "We come from a very spiritual family.

"There was lots of talk about religion and faith and prayer in our household when I was growing up. I don't think there's been a time in my life when I haven't felt not a Christian or thought about those things.

"I was raised on hellfire and brimstone in the Assembly of God Church. It's a Pentecostal church so I know what faith and prayer are all about. In fact, every once in a while I like to hear a preacher like that because he just kind of reminds me of my childhood."

As important as religion was in the Gatlins' lives, so was music—particularly Gospel and harmony music. Steve's father, an oil field worker, was often too busy with his job to travel the Gospel music circuit, so it was with his mother that Steve and his two brothers traveled. Steve was age four at the time, Rudy was two years old and Larry was six.

"We sang Gospel music all the time growing up. We traveled from church to church and from revival to revival all over the country.

That's kind of how we learned to sing. It was by growing up and singing in the church.

"Mostly we sang in the Pentecostal church, although sometimes we'd sing in some Baptist churches or at some Church of God camp meetings. My mother played piano and took us all over the country doing that.

"And when we weren't traveling, my granddad on our mother's side was an old Gospel quartet singer. He would love to sit down in the house and sing songs, and that's another way we learned to sing."

As Steve grew older and he and his brothers went on to attend college, that rich spiritual life was neglected. "There have been times in my life when I've been better and closer to God," he admits. "Things got a little funky during those years.

"It's the time you get away from home and you do what you want a little more. You stay out later and do all the things that go along with college. There's no one to make you get up at seven on a Sunday morning to go to church. So you kind of put God on the back burner.

"I don't think I was really lost, it all had to do with simple immaturity. I was twenty-four or twenty-five years old, I was married, and my brothers and I already had a hit record—so we got caught up in all of this.

"We were very fortunate. We didn't struggle too long. Before we knew it we had our second hit record and we were making good money—we had even won a Grammy."

Success did come easily to the talented trio with their distinct vocal stylings. By the mid-1970s the three brothers were performing together as a band, and were already drawing admiring audiences. But even before forming the group their careers were well on track.

Larry had been living in Nashville where he was establishing himself as a well-respected songwriter, while Steve and Rudy—then still in college at the time—upon graduation went on to form a band with their sister La Donna. The group, called Young Country, opened and sang backup for Country music superstar Tammy Wynette.

In the meantime, Larry was getting ready to release his debut album for Monument Records. He asked Steve and Rudy to join him, and they agreed to do so.

"There came a point when we decided that nobody else was going to make us stars," Steve recalls. "So we decided to do it ourselves.

We knew we had to go out and beat the bushes and that's what we did."

That album was a hit along with a second album that Larry released. In 1979 Larry and his brothers were performing on the Columbia Records label as Larry Gatlin & the Gatlin Brothers Band.

By the mid 1980s, the band's string of hits was not only earning them gold records and a stack of major music industry awards, but the Gatlins also began appearing on TV variety shows where they spread their appeal well beyond their Country music audiences.

Steve recalls that in the midst of all this success they began to fall prey to some of the perils of the indulgent world of Music City—particularly drugs and alcohol.

He prefers not to go into any detail about those wild days, noting that "It's been well documented about how we struggled with the craziness of the road in the late seventies and early eighties.

"It was a period when I thought it was never going to end—that we were going to continue forever making this kind of money. We bought an airplane and then another bus.

"It's very hard, sometimes, to step outside of all this and say, 'Where is this all leading?' And so because of that I think I did kind of what I did in college. I kind of put God on the back burner.

"Mike Tyson is a prime example of too much success at a very early age. A lot of these athletes that get a ton of money when they're straight out of college don't know how to handle it either. Nothing in life prepares you for this kind of success."

The Gatlins' day of reckoning came sometime in 1984, Steve remembers. It was then that he and his brothers began asking themselves where their lives were leading them.

Steve recalls that he and his brothers agreed that if they didn't quickly straighten themselves out, they might not live to enjoy all their hard-earned success.

"We got caught up in the machinery and we needed to sit back and take a look at it. We looked at what we had accomplished. We were very talented and we were having hit records and all this success. But we had gotten caught up in all this drug and alcohol stuff and now we needed to do something about it."

To deal with his cocaine addiction, Larry checked himself into a month-long rehabilitation program in California. Rudy and Steve also decided to break their pattern of alcohol and drug abuse.

"Larry especially realized that he was going to kill himself, because he couldn't keep going on this way. I don't know how much people know about Alcoholics Anonymous or Cocaine Anonymous, but their twelve-step program is based upon a higher power or some form of spirituality. And then every individual has to apply that to their own particular needs.

"We joined those programs and it gave us a chance to get back in touch with the God of our youth. It got us back in touch with Jesus Christ and with God and with the things that we'd kind of set on the side. You know, success is sometimes one of those things where you break your arm trying to pat yourself on your back.

"That happens to people who are not prepared for success. That's what happened to us. We were twenty-four, twenty-five, and we weren't ready. We weren't ready to handle it."

Although more than a decade has passed since the Gatlins turned their lives around, Steve becomes angry that he and his brothers still remain the subject of criticism for their one-time chemical dependence.

"Look, I made mistakes. We all did. I still make mistakes. I do things I shouldn't do and that I regret. We're not called upon to be perfect. We're called to be more Christ-like.

"The Bible is filled with great men of God, great prophets, who made mistakes. There's only one person in the Bible who didn't—and He was the Son of God.

"I don't know of any Christians who stay on a continuous spiritual high, because life deals you some pretty hard blows sometimes. It may not be as devastating as drugs and alcohol—it might just be a simple thing like suddenly losing a job. So maybe you're down for a while and you get high on something.

"Maybe for two or three months you don't read as much of the Bible as you should, or go to church as much. You might even find a drug that keeps you on a continuous high because you've been dealt a pretty hard blow. All I have to say is that you just have to fight your way through it."

For anyone struggling to overcome an addiction, Steve advises that they rely on a combination of prayer and professional treatment.

"You should discipline yourself to pray every day—or meditate—or just go for a walk and think about the Lord, because everyone has their own particular style of trying to reach God.

"Read the Word, and try to go to church on a regular basis. My brothers and I say a specific prayer every night—it's 'The Serenity Prayer.' We gather together with the band and right before we go on stage we pray.

"It's a prayer that means so much to our lives because it saved our career and turned us around twelve years ago. It's a simple prayer." He then goes on to recite it:

> *"God, give us grace to*
> *accept with serenity the things that cannot be changed,*
> *courage to change the things which should be changed,*
> *and the wisdom to distinguish the one from the other."*

"We have guys of different faiths in our band. One guy is Jewish, and I've got one guy who is a Mormon. It's not a prayer that will offend anyone's faith.

"All this prayer says is that if I can do something about a situation, let me do it. Let me try to fix it. If I can't, it's out of my hands. Don't let me try to mess it up and make it worse. Just let it go and accept life on life's terms.

"We all say this prayer and accept that there's a higher power— higher than we are. And whether you call that God"—which the brothers do—"or something else, it's a prayer that bonds us together and reminds us of a time in our lives when things weren't as good and we needed sobering up."

Besides prayer, Steve also believes it is important to attend church. "I'm not saying you have to go to church every Sunday morning or every Sunday night or whatever, but I just believe that you have to have some kind of worship structure in your life. Church gives you a sense of purpose."

Although the talented performer contends that he is not interested in preaching from a pulpit, Steve professes that he does try to share some of his spiritual feelings with his audiences. "In our show I sing— or we sing—a Gospel song from my Gospel album.

"I'm a very private person, but the show we're doing gives me a chance to share a little of my faith. It's a chance for me to step out in faith and do something for people who need to hear it.

"I guess it's because I do that every night that I just want to make sure it doesn't become rote. I don't want to just sit back and say, 'Well, I'm doing enough. That's enough.' It should never be enough."

Looking ahead to the future, Steve, who recently released his first solo spiritual album, *Love Can Carry,* which was nominated for a Dove Award, is hopeful that he and his brothers continue to attract new fans despite the current interest in Nashville's upcoming young talent.

"I'm not old, but I'm reaching the middle part of my life," he reflects wistfully. "I mean, I'm forty-six years old. Reality is setting in that the chances of us ever having a hit record again are slim. That's kind of disappointing because I think we sing and play better than we ever did.

"But it's just the time and what's going on in Nashville and what's going in the music business today. Our time in the sunshine is over, as it has been for many artists of our age and stature.

"I guess you're not supposed to worry about these kinds of things. I'm trying not to. My favorite chapter in the Bible is the sixth chapter of Matthew where he talks about the anxiety of what tomorrow may bring. He says just don't worry about it. That's hard to do because we still are all human and we all have those fears.

"It takes me back to 'The Serenity Prayer'—the line about 'God, give us grace to accept with serenity the things that cannot be changed.' Thinking about that line helps give me a way to step out in faith, and that gives me strength . . ."

Donna Fargo

As a young girl growing up in Mount Airy, North Carolina, the heart of mountain-music country, Country music superstar Donna Fargo was often frightened by the hellfire and brimstone sermons that she heard preached at the local Baptist church.

Which is why Donna, a mid-seventies' singing sensation best known for such smash hits as "The Happiest Girl in the Whole USA" and "Funny Face," shied away from organized religion as she grew older.

The award-winning songwriter came home to God after being

stricken by multiple sclerosis, a debilitating degenerative disease, while at the height of her successful career.

It was during that period of time that Donna progressed from a vague belief in God to absolute certitude that He would see her successfully through her ordeal.

Today, Donna continues to successfully manage her illness while continuing to perform and write music. She tells her audiences that anyone who is ill can achieve the same goal by using a combination of mind, body, and spirit.

"You can't separate mind, body, and spirit—it's all connected," she states. "But developing yourself spiritually is the most important thing to do if you're faced with a crisis. Have faith and invite God into the picture . . ."

Take a sensitive and impressionable young girl, bring her to a church where a Baptist minister is spewing forth about eternal damnation, and what do you get?

A frightened young girl.

That young girl was Country music legend Donna Fargo, the fourth child of a North Carolina tobacco farmer, who clearly remembers as a youngster her trepidation about attending Sunday morning services with her grandmother at the Mount Airy Baptist Church.

"There was always too much fear and not enough love," she recalls. "It was always the hellfire and damnation types of messages and nothing much past that to nurture one's soul. It was not the best thing for a child to hear."

Besides what she heard in church, Donna doesn't recall having much of a religious home life. Both her parents worked long hours, and any religious lessons that she did receive came from her grandmother.

"She was very high on spiritual things. Very religious, but tough. She was real independent and really helped me a lot with my thinking. But my parents didn't go to church much with me and we really didn't talk about it or anything.

"I don't think I had a lot of faith growing up. I was baptized when I was sixteen, and I went to church when I was in high school and college and all. And I think I had a hunger for religion in my heart, but I didn't know the importance of faith.

"You see, I think faith has to be developed, otherwise you'll never get past your five senses. In order to develop the kind of faith the Bible talks about, you really need to study and chew on the Word and inform yourself of spiritual issues.

"I didn't do that because in my background I had to deal with a lot of fear. It was like I was afraid all the time, and that's not healthy. What I needed to hear preached was the love of God. The preacher could have preached it, but I didn't get that.

"It was only after I became an adult that I realized that I needed to know more about that. We need to know how to love God and receive and trust that He loves us."

Instead of believing in God from the heart, Donna remembers adopting a more intellectual approach to religion. "I was getting along just fine with my humanistic faith, making decisions primarily based on my five senses.

"I was a product of that humanistic kind of belief system where you're limited by your five senses. I believed in God, but my mind was restricting me from feeling Him on the physical level."

If her attitude toward religion was medium cool, she does recall feeling zealous about teaching and music. "I had always wanted to be a teacher even when I was a little girl.

"And I also wanted to be a singer, although I sort of kept that dream to myself. I thought, 'Well, I may never be either one and I don't want people to laugh at me if I don't reach my goals.' "

It was a career as a teacher that Donna pursued first, earning her teaching degrees at High Point College in North Carolina and, later, at the University of Southern California.

She went on to become a high school English teacher, eventually rising to the rank of chairman of the English Department. With that accomplishment under her belt, Donna next turned to her second love —music.

"I had reached my ambition of being a teacher, but now I decided that it was time to work on the other goal of becoming a singer. So I prayed about it. I think I was in a constant state of prayer. I believed in God and I believed in prayer, but I didn't really develop a close relationship with God even though I talked to Him a lot.

"You know what I'm saying? I just didn't know enough. I didn't know enough to really study the Bible and to study how to develop one's faith and so on."

Having been raised in the Mount Airy region of North Carolina, home to countless old-time and bluegrass musicians, Donna had been surrounded by music ever since she was a youngster. Back then, however, although she did some singing, Donna had no ambitions for stardom.

Now, however, she began giving that some thought, writing music and performing in local clubs.

Although Donna considered continuing her education and, perhaps, someday becoming a high school principal or taking a position with the school board, it was her love for music that eventually won out.

"I taught myself to write by listening to the radio and analyzing songs and thinking about what interested people. And I really started liking the songs I was writing and I thought that maybe there was a chance for me here.

"At the same time—and here's another benefit to prayer—I stopped smoking. I was addicted to smoking and I kept thinking, 'How stupid, Donna. I had asked God to become a singer, and here I was, destroying my lungs with these cigarettes. It wasn't easy to quit. I must have quit seventy-eight zillion times, but finally I quit."

Donna's singing career would receive a boost when she met and fell in love with a young singer and music producer by the name of Stan Silver. Stan would not only become her biggest supporter and manager but her husband as well.

It was Stan who taught the young high school teacher how to play the guitar, and encouraged Donna to continue writing her own material. In addition, he helped to find her work in the Los Angeles area, so that she could gain more experience as a performer.

"He guided my musical career and he knew lots more about the business than I did," Donna recollects. "I really didn't know anything about it."

Donna soon had a hit single followed by another song which she wrote—"Who's Been Sleeping on My Side of the Bed?" Because of its controversial lyrics, that song gained her major notoriety but little radio play time. Many radio station managers believed the song was too provocative—especially for a girl singer—so they simply refused to play it.

Donna did not let that discourage her. She went on to write and record another hit song, "The Happiest Girl in the Whole USA." That 1972 Dot Records single skyrocketed to number one on the Country charts, and was followed by another smash hit, "Funny Face."

Now on the brink of stardom, Donna quit her teaching job and relocated to Nashville. More hits followed, and by 1978 the tobacco farmer's daughter not only had a million-dollar recording contract with Warner Brothers Records, but was also hosting her own coast-to-coast television show.

That same year her wave of success crashed disastrously against the shore when the superstar was diagnosed in a Nashville hospital as having multiple sclerosis, a crippling degenerative disease of the central nervous system for which there is no cure. Although Donna remembers feeling devastated, the diagnosis was not entirely unexpected.

"It was suggested that I might have MS two years before, but I was trying to believe that I didn't. That's why I wasn't shocked in 1978 when I got the diagnosis. For two years I had been hoping against hope that they'd find something simple and easy to heal. But it became more and more apparent that it wasn't going to be that way."

Although feeling depressed, Donna recalls harboring no resentment toward her Maker. "It soon sank in that I had an incurable disease and an uncertain future. Although everybody's future is unknown, it felt like the ultimate rejection. My body was rejecting me. I felt helpless and confused about what to do.

"I wasn't angry at God. It was like, 'Wow, I'm not prepared for this. What will happen to me?' The doctors didn't know much about MS in those years and it was no solace to me that they had no medicine that could help me. I thought, 'Wow, I'm really all alone in this.'"

In the midst of her distress, Donna recalls coming to the sudden realization that she need not face this crisis alone. There was always a friend upon whom she could rely upon, one whom she had ignored for far too long.

"I prayed in that hospital room. And God didn't hold my ignorance and confusion against me. He just answered what I needed to know with a Scripture—I didn't even know I knew that Scripture: 'You can't get to the Father except by Him.'

"It was then that my relationship with God and Jesus got meaningful and personal. I just knew He was definitely talking to me.

"So, my first real lesson in building my faith was born when I depended on God to help me and He did. I now started to think about God. I started to try to find God again.

"I got busy. Not only did I start learning all I could about my disease, but I also began to study about the spirit, mind, and body, and how others had helped themselves overcome all kinds of diseases.

"What I found was that developing the spiritual self is the most important thing anybody can do when they're faced with a crisis—or at any other time, for that matter.

"That's because in my opinion the spirit should direct the mind and the body rather than the mind and the body directing the spirit. If your spirit is in charge, it will guide the mind and the body to make better decisions.

"If your body and mind are just kind of running loose out there, kind of doing whatever you're reacting to, you might be ill-informed. You might be getting wrong information. Being a humanistic Christian, my body and my mind had been in charge all these years. It was now up to me to change that.

"So what I had to do was get my spirit in charge. I believe I always knew that the answers are inside us and that is our spirit trying to direct us. I began to try to apply this newfound knowledge to myself personally by renewing my mind with the Word of God."

Donna recollects that one of her most difficult battles was against depression. "I had to fight hard against depression because there's a lot of that with this disease. I suppose it's because the central nervous system is affected.

"It's also depressing because even though you look okay, you just don't feel well. It's not something you can talk about because nobody really understands.

"But by developing myself spiritually it helped me face the reality of my situation and taught me how to use my spiritual knowledge to get through it. And I tried to stay busy all the time to keep my mind off the way I felt. I also rebuked fear with the Word, because the Bible says not to fear."

Donna gives much credit to the Bible as a healing tool. "I should have known that from the start, but I overanalyzed things. But now I discovered it was the best thing I could have done to help myself when the doctors couldn't help me.

"I felt the Bible was the answer to my prayers and that if I could believe in Jesus I would really be saved. I had to confess this. I had to admit that my perception had been wrong about those people who, when I was a little girl, used to holler that they were saved. Then, I didn't think you'd know you were saved until you got to heaven. Now I knew better.

"I had tried to believe that Jesus was raised from the dead before, but I just hadn't gotten there. I had to progress from a vague belief in God to believing He is my very own father and I am His very own child. My Christianity had to finally get personal with me to be meaningful, and not just a fairy tale.

"Now I finally knew in my heart that I believed that Jesus was raised from the dead. I believed now that I was saved and that I could go on and I could handle this disease and whatever it did to me. I really knew this in my heart and spirit.

"There was no doubt anymore. I felt like I had reconnected with God and that He was really in charge, even though I also knew I possibly had a long road ahead and much, much more to learn."

Renewing her faith was not an easy task, she acknowledges. "I had to learn how to develop it because it had been kind of subconscious before. You begin to increase your faith when you start studying the Bible—particularly the New Testament—because the Bible says faith comes from hearing. And I studied it and I studied it.

"I had to unlearn all that hellfire and damnation stuff—the part about trying to be good enough for God to love me. It was hard for me. When it came to faith as a personal thing, I just never had related to God really that closely, although I had really known that I needed to.

"I had to learn how to trust God and to believe what the Word says about how to develop faith because it had all been knowledge based on my five senses before and now I had to put my spirit in charge."

Donna also read anything that emphasized positive thinking. "I was just a voracious reader. I tried to keep positive thoughts all the time and to have hope. Hope may not be as good as faith, but it's better than nothing.

"If I had to say, 'Would you rather be in a state of hope for twenty years or a state of hopelessness, I would take hope any day.' But hope is hoping, faith is believing. Faith's where we all need to get—a place where there's no doubt, just trust.

"I'd say the one person who probably helped me the most—his tapes and books—was Kenneth Hagin. He's a Tulsa, Oklahoma, minister. And I had good friends who would bring me all kinds of books and stuff.

"I studied the spirit, mind, and body and I studied about nutrition and I also tried to change my diet. But my ultimate goal was to increase my faith because the Bible says that without faith it's impossible to please God."

In 1979, Donna was able to begin performing again. She scored a comeback Top Ten hit with her song "Somebody Special." This was followed by a well-received Gospel album, and several other singles which also made it to the top of the charts.

Nowadays, besides having a busy songwriting schedule, Donna still tours nationally and internationally, performing a highly galvanized stage show. She is also at work on her autobiography, which she hopes someday to see turned into a screenplay.

"It's been a long process for me," she sighs. "Once I reconnected with God and felt that He was really in charge, then I felt I could go on. That helped me want to go on."

Donna is also dedicated to helping others who are struggling through illness, always counseling that they keep their faith and pray for God's help.

"Prayer doesn't have to be a really formal thing. It doesn't have to be just when you go to church or when you get down on your knees. You can just talk to God walking along. But I think it does need to be serious.

"I also advise that people who are ill study the Bible and read other good books that can help them, and really be in the business of doing positive things for themselves and other people."

In her own life, prayer also continues to play an important role. "I pray anywhere and everywhere. I always pray before every show I do and I say, 'Let your love flow through us to all these people. And get them home safe and sound and let them have a good time. And let me not fall on my face and make a fool out of myself.' That kind of thing.

"And I always pray for my husband's safety and well-being. And I pray for specific people that I think need God in their lives or need direction from God.

"I really think you can help people more by praying for them than you can by trying to stuff them with religion when they're not even hungry. And I do pray for people who are sick. I'm just in a state of prayer a lot of the time."

Although Donna regrets having been stricken by multiple sclerosis, she also believes that something positive came out of that experience —a renewal of her spiritual life.

"An incurable disease has an odd way of getting you on track," she asserts. "I think that tragedy and crisis sometimes can shake us in our booties and get us to realize that we've just been out there drifting along and kind of living life as it came to us. It forces one to get serious about what's important.

"I'm still learning a lot and have certainly gone in a different direction than I ever thought I would ever need or want to go. I'm very thankful for everything I think I'm learning, but my ultimate goal is to learn enough to get well and to help others get well. This goal drives me.

"I've had some exciting exchanges with the Lord since then, and although I'm far from a state of perfection or spiritual maturity, I stay very close to Him. Even if I never reach another goal, I know He'll never forsake me."

Donna scoffs at any suggestion that her illness is a punishment from God for the years she spent not being a devout Christian. "This disease is most likely a genetic thing—like the way accidents happen. I can't believe this is God's doing that I have MS, and I don't. But I do believe it will be His doing if I ever get rid of it."

Instead of dwelling on the possible causes for her disease, Donna states that she prefers to focus her thoughts on enjoying life—and encourages others who are ill to follow her example.

"Each day is a celebration for me. I've learned that it's important to be satisfied with life in the moment and appreciate life each moment that you are alive. Just stay on course with God and be open to wherever He may lead you.

"The diagnosis of MS got me on the right course, and now being on the right course I just remain open to where God leads me. So don't just sit around thinking negative thoughts. Translate those thoughts into positive thoughts and invite God into the picture . . ."

George Hamilton IV

For Country music legend George Hamilton IV, it would take a visit to Czechoslovakia and Russia in 1972 to revitalize his religious faith.

It was while on that concert tour behind the Iron Curtain that the popular entertainer witnessed members of his Moravian faith—a Christian sect dating back to the early sixteenth century—joyously practicing their religion in the face of severe Communist government persecution.

What the singer came to realize as a result of that experience is the matter-of-fact attitude he had toward his own faith.

Since then, the sixty-year-old "International Ambassador of

Country Music," whose career spans more than four decades, has been encouraging people to join him in practicing their faith more intensely.

Wherever the North Carolina native happens to be performing, George speaks out against the dangers of complacency in spiritual life. He contends that while any kind of faith is certainly worthwhile, ardent faith is even better . . .

A church could be found on almost every street corner in Winston-Salem's Moravian community where Country music singer George Hamilton IV was born and raised.

George remembers the community as being a tightly knit one where everyone knew each other. It was the type of neighborhood, he explains, where Sunday school was often considered more important than public school.

"My father was a Sunday school superintendent and we were a churchgoing family. My mother was the type that made sure we were there every time the church door opened."

Religion was so much the center of the community's social and family life that George recalls it was almost taken for granted.

"Looking back on it, I think I also sort of took it all for granted. I thought I was goin' to heaven in a three-piece blue suit and singing 'Amazing Grace.'

"It was like I'm okay and you're okay and we're all going to heaven arm in arm and hand in hand because we're nice folks. It was a little too easy and too ever-present."

Besides religion, another early influence in George's life was music. The tall, gangly teenager recollects developing a passion for Country music while watching Gene Autry and Tex Ritter movies at the local movie house.

George was twelve when he purchased his first guitar and, while still in high school, formed a pop-Country band.

In 1956, while attending the University of South Carolina, George met Country/rock songwriter John D. Loudermilk. The writer, who had heard one of George's demos, was impressed enough with the singer's talent to give him one of his compositions to record—"A Rose and a Baby Ruth."

That single launched George's career, racing up the charts like a frisky thoroughbred and going on to become a million-seller record.

As a result of that smash hit, George now suddenly found himself a teenybopper star, performing with such legendary hit acts as the Everly Brothers, Buddy Holly, and Gene Vincent.

His quick rise in popularity continued. George was booked as a regular guest on television programs such as the "Jimmy Dean Show" and the "Steve Allen Show," and by 1959 he was even hosting his own television program.

That same year George decided to move to Nashville, signing up with RCA records. There, he began to record mainstream Country music.

"I had for about three years been touring on the rock 'n' roll shows and rockabilly shows and all that. And my heart was in Country music. I wanted to be in Nashville. I wanted to be on the 'Grand Ole Opry.'

"I was being promoted as a teen balladeer and pop singer and all that, and really, at heart, I was a Country singer. That's what I really felt. That's where I felt I belonged. So I just kind of tired of pretending to be something that I wasn't."

It was a radical move for an already established pop singer at a time when rock 'n' roll—not Country music—was at its height. But George's instincts paid off and he soon had his first number-one Country hit with another John D. Loudermilk song, "Abilene."

George's reputation as a Country music star got a boost when, in the early sixties, he joined the "Grand Ole Opry" and remained a fixture there throughout the decade.

Despite his continuing success, the entertainer remembers always feeling that some important piece of his life was missing—one involving his spiritual side.

"It was kind of easy to put on the church suit and go off and sit in church and sing the hymns, but I wasn't putting my faith into action. I just wasn't growing as a Christian. I was feeling like an amateur Christian and a take-it-for-granted one as well."

George would discover the intense religious experience he was seeking in 1972, when the Country music star was invited to tour Eastern Europe with a Czechoslovakian Country music band.

"I wasn't going there as a Gospel singer or to do Gospel music, but to perform Country music with this band. It was during this visit that I attended a little Moravian church in Prague, and came face-to-face with people that seemed so full of love for the Lord and all."

When George, curious about the intensity of the worship service, questioned the Moravian minister about it, what he learned stunned him. The minister told him that what he was witnessing was a living example of faith under fire.

"When I told the minister that these young people seemed to have something that I didn't have, even though I was also a member of the Church, he said, 'Yes, but it's a little different here.'

"He explained that because these young people had accepted the Lord and joined his church and were publicly confessing Christians, they would never be able to attend the university, go to college, or have any higher education.

"That was a sort of subtle way of putting the pressure on by the government they had in the days of the Iron Curtain. And if these young people wanted to be a doctor or a lawyer or something, they could just forget it.

"The minister's wife wasn't even allowed to teach school in the city—she was forced to travel fifty miles out in the country to teach school—all because her great sin was being the wife of a Moravian minister, as far as the state was concerned.

"Yet despite all this persecution, these people were so much more joyful about their faith—so much more committed and on fire with their faith than I was.

"It was really a turning point for me. I began to realize that there's more to being a Christian than going to church a lot, obeying the Ten Commandments, and trying to be a good ol' boy.

"I'd never really been faced with the cross or sacrifice or surrender of self until I went to Eastern Europe. The things I saw—like in Poland I saw people being arrested for making a cross of flowers on the streets of Warsaw—made me realize I was just a Sunday morning Christian.

"My European experience caused me basically to reassess my own faith and start thinking about what do I really believe and do I believe it. It was kind of a jarring experience to realize that there are people in the world who actually get arrested for their faith."

Upon returning home from Eastern Europe, George remembers undergoing a period of soul searching about the meaning of faith, deciding that it had value only if it was intensely practiced. He recalls also coming to the conclusion that there was some merit in religious persecution.

"If Christianity is true, it can't be just a file drawer in our crowded lives. It must be the central truth from which all of our behavior, relationships, and philosophy flow. We all must be called upon to carry the cross.

"The finest Christians I've met in my life have been in places where it's not all that easy to be a churchgoer or to be a Christian. I'm not just thinking about Eastern Europe, but Africa and India—places that I've been where people are persecuted for their faith.

"What I found missing in my life, really, was commitment and sacrifice. I didn't hurt anybody or break the Ten Commandments. But that wasn't enough. I felt that I needed to reawaken—renew—my religious convictions."

Now determined to make some much needed changes in his own spiritual life, George recalls embarking on a worldwide mission to seek out Christian artists.

"I started going to Christian artists seminars in Europe, and I had other experiences where I met lots of singers and musicians who were Christians. These were strong believers who were willing to walk the talk and put their faith into action. We often spent long hours into the night discussing issues related to religion and faith."

His opportunity to put his faith into action came in 1984, when George recalls being invited to sing with the Billy Graham Crusade.

"Being part of that made me more and more aware of what being a Christian is all about. And I had some very powerful role models there. It was a reawakening—a growth period. I finally felt like I was moving people through my music.

"It was through that crusade that I kept coming face-to-face with people around the world who had so little materially, yet seemed to be so much more deeply committed and deeply rooted in their faith—like in India, Tanzania, and even Jamaica. That reminded me of my Eastern European experience. It was an ongoing reawakening, a growth period."

Although George is, today, no longer a superstar on the Country music scene, the legendary entertainer, who has done more international tours than any Country music artist in history, continues to perform regularly. These days, however, he likes to refer to himself as a "musicianary."

"I'm not a professional Gospel singer. I still earn my living in Country music mostly from concerts and tours. But I also do these things in churches on a very low-key, sort of love-offering basis with no fees or honorariums or anything. It gives me a chance to talk about some of the things I've seen and learned about faith."

George, who has recorded more than five dozen albums featuring his diverse styles of pop, Country, folk, and religious music, also remains actively involved with international church-based tours.

On such tours, like one he recently undertook throughout North America, the veteran entertainer often combines Gospel music with the spoken word. "It was called a *Moravian Country Christmas* and we were performing in all these churches.

"I'd be telling the Christmas story with poems and readings from Scripture and folk hymns and carols. And there was a little bit of Moravian history woven in as well."

Although his own spiritual renewal was sparked by what he witnessed in Eastern Europe, George does not believe that it requires such a dramatic incident to bolster one's faith. Instead, he favors self-contemplation as the best method of getting in touch with one's spiritual core.

"We've got it pretty easy here in America, especially in the Bible Belt. A lot of people do a lot of religious things and go through a lot of religious motions, but it doesn't always mean a lot.

"I think that when you come from the kind of background I did, where all your life you've known church life, you begin to coast and take it for granted. In my own case, I never have been a dope addict or a drunk or whatever and then had some sort of life-changing, thunder and lightning experience overnight.

"My renewal came in the knowledge that I was a take-it-for-granted Christian, so I guess you can say my present walk is more of a gradual maturing exercise. What you need to do is think about whether or not you're just going through religious motions."

George also has some simple words of advice for anyone struggling to renew their own faith: read the Bible. "That's the best place to find your answers. I also think it's a good idea to get involved in a church or a prayer group or a Bible study where you can be nourished and encouraged by fellow believers.

"It's always helpful to have people around you who can kind of nourish and support you. I think a combination of this and reading the Scriptures—getting into the Word—are the best ways to get back on track and get grounded."

When asked to describe his own spirituality, George describes himself as a "work in progress. I've never felt like much of a religious success or whatever. I guess we all feel like that. I'm somebody trying to do what I do better.

"I just know that since my own spiritual awakening and reawakening, and since coming to—hopefully—a more spiritual maturity, my life has been much more meaningful. Much happier.

"These days I find myself more satisfied and more fulfilled and uplifted singing in a little church in some remote village in Scotland, just with a guitar and no band and no sound system whatsoever, than I sometimes do on a big stage, or a big arena, or on a television program."

"I'm also not one of those who believes in the so-called Prosperity Doctrine. I don't necessarily think that if I love the Lord and I'm a nice, good, Christian fellow, that I'm gonna have a big Cadillac and a big house. I don't think that they always go hand in hand.

"That was one of the main things about the Eastern European experience—to find out that there were people over there who seemed to have so much less financially and materially, but, yet, were much, much richer than I in other ways.

"I guess what I'm trying to say is that I feel like I've been richly blessed, but not necessarily financially. But that doesn't seem as important as it used to be. It's just priorities, really.

"As you become more like He would have us be I think we all become more grateful and more satisfied with our station in life and we appreciate simple things much more.

"I try not to ask God for selfish things; I try to ask for improvement and try to ask for the Lord's continued blessing and His help in what I'm doing. You know, there's lots of times you almost can't help but pray for financial help. But I try to avoid that.

"Some Christians that I've met have kind of, sometimes, judged their fellow Christians' merit based on how many gifts they do or don't have. I'm not much for that. I feel like the Lord spreads His gifts around where He pleases and where He feels they'll do the most good."

What George states he considers much more important than financial success is that he and his family remain healthy, and that God gives him more years to continue performing the Country music he so much loves.

"I want to use my music in the right context—to serve Him. Rather than sort of a selfish drive to attain goals and amass financial blessings, I want to become closer and closer to the Lord and walk closer to Him.

"I guess that's what I'm really working on these days. I'm trying to be more what I think He would have me be and less starring in my own movie, hopefully . . ."

Penny DeHaven

Beneath Penny DeHaven's public persona as a glamorous and successful Country music star has always existed a dark tapestry of abusive childhood memories, a suicide attempt at age twenty-one, and a diagnosis of cancer in 1992.

Despite such a traumatic background, the dynamic hazel-eyed beauty, who began her music career as a two-year-old in Winchester, Virginia, the birthplace of another famous Country singer—Patsy Cline—has flourished thanks to her faith in God. She praises God for helping her to pick up the shattered pieces of her life.

As someone who has passed through the fire and survived, Penny has much to say to others who are also hurting about God's life-changing power.

She does so on stages where she performs throughout the world, sharing with her audiences her personal message of faith, hope, and healing . . .

Having grown up in the shadow of a hard-drinking, abusive, truck-driving father, who would often beat his wife and show affection toward his children by tossing pocket change at them when he returned home from the road, Penny DeHaven's recollections about family life are not the fondest.

Her more affectionate memories are reserved for her mother, Opal, who sometimes taught Sunday school. "She always gave me so much love and had the most wonderful way of making me feel that all my dreams of being a singer would come true. I think they were really her dreams too."

It was Opal who also encouraged Penny and her older sister and brother to attend church each Sunday, which they often did. But short of the time spent in church, Penny recalls that there wasn't much religious instruction at home.

"I know this is awful to say, but I don't remember when I was a little kid much about religion. I think that's because there was a lot of drinking and fighting and stuff going on in the family at the time so church was never practiced at home. We hardly ever did anything in the home that was God-like at all.

"There was a lot of physical abuse of my mother and emotional abuse of the children. I remember Daddy coming home and fighting and cussing and yelling and hitting my mother. And us kids were hiding and listening to all this mess. And one time, Daddy was beating on Mama and I jumped on him and he turned around and started to hit me —but he never did.

"I remember seeing him running around the house with a sledgehammer in his hand cutting down doors and going after my mother. And he had a gun cocked and ready to fire on me one time, and my brother managed to get it away from him. But he was an alcoholic and I don't think he remembered anything he had done."

Although religion was never a family priority, Penny remembers always having strong feelings toward the church. In fact, it was at the local Congregational Christian church in Winchester, Virginia, that the two-and-a-half-year-old gave her first public performance.

"I was supposed to sing 'Jesus Loves Me' with a bunch of kids, but they all got scared and ran away. I just stood there by myself singing and that was kind of the start of my musical career."

Later, while in elementary school, Penny joined a Gospel quartet, attracted more by the music than the religious content of the songs. "I never did know the Lord Jesus, I just knew about Him," she reflects wistfully.

Penny recalls that while in the fourth grade, her family relocated from Winchester, Virginia, to Berkeley Springs, West Virginia, a sand-mining town where there was more opportunity for her truck-driving father.

There, the pretty young girl with a beautiful voice began to sing on local radio shows. Before graduating from high school, she became a regular on the popular WWVA "Jamboree USA" radio show in Wheeling, West Virginia, where she went by the stage name of Penny Starr.

Singing was something Penny recalls always wanting to do professionally. Her career got a boost when she won a local talent contest and was invited to go on a tour of Iceland, Puerto Rico, Bermuda, and Vietnam.

Hardly out of her teens, Penny felt ready for the big time. The teenager arrived in Nashville with a suitcase full of lovingly made stage dresses and a heart full of dreams. She was a young star in the making, having already made a name for herself on the WWVA "Jamboree."

By 1969, the young singer signed a contract with Imperial Records as Penny DeHaven. In a nine-month period of time, Penny had three hit records. When Penny switched to the United Artists label a year later, more success followed.

Meanwhile, the glamour and excitement of Nashville's Music Row with all its lures and temptations beckoned. As she pursued her dreams of stardom, Penny also pursued a fast-paced lifestyle—one which included a love affair that ended in a suicide attempt.

"I had just turned twenty-one and I started dating this man who I didn't know was married. I was in love with him, and his wife came in when we were celebrating my birthday and confronted us. Well, I found out all this stuff and I just took off."

Penny does not recall much of what happened next. What she does recollect is purchasing a batch of sleeping pills. "I bought sixty of them and came back to the apartment and took them all. I don't remember much after that except being half-carried down the steps. I do remember saying, 'God, I don't want to die.' And that's all I remember."

Doctors later informed the young singer that they had not expected her to survive her drug overdose. She was fortunate, they added, that the ambulance driver had rushed her to one of only two hospitals in the state equipped to perform a rarely employed procedure for such severe drug overdose cases.

She was informed that the complicated procedure had required that her entire blood supply be removed, filtered, and cleansed of toxins before being returned to her body.

Today, Penny is certain that God's hand was involved in saving her life. At the time, however, she remembers not giving much thought to such things as divine intervention.

"It was a miracle, but even when I came out of the hospital I didn't recognize it as such. If your eyes are blinded, the scales are still on them and you don't recognize miracles. And I didn't. I kept on doing the same things I was doing. That experience didn't straighten me out at all.

"I was still blinded because I hadn't asked Jesus Christ into my heart yet, and I was on a road straight to hell.

"I continued to drink and run around and lead a wild life. I never thought about the consequences. I just wanted to go out and have a good time.

"Here I had been saved by the intervention of the Lord, who knew there were better things ahead for me, but back then I didn't realize it. He knew that I had a purpose in my life and that someday I would be out there witnessing for the Lord, but only He knew it back then."

Despite her natural beauty and undeniable talent, the top-dollar concerts and the blitz of media attention all seemed to elude her. Although disappointed that the doors to success never quite swung fully open, Penny remembers not giving up on her dreams.

"Trust and optimism are things that have always come natural for me. Time after time in show business, or in life, I've been disappointed. But I'm so grateful to God that I've never become bitter about the music business, or with any of the people who've hurt me."

The talented entertainer came close to a smash record in 1970, when she recorded a duet with Country music star Del Reeves. The songstress hoped that by teaming up with this legendary recording artist, the recognition she sought to gain would be hers.

Again she was disappointed when the song, "Land Mark Tavern," made it to the Top Twenty, but never hit number one. Penny went on to perform other songs that also hit the charts, and even found herself performing at the "Grand Ole Opry," which she describes as among the most exciting experiences of her life.

But it was on one evening in 1978 that Penny experienced something which she contends has been much more valuable to her than superstardom or a gold or platinum record—her personal face-to-face encounter with Jesus Christ.

"I was visiting the home of a prominent show-business couple," she recollects. "They were very flamboyant people—wild even by music business standards—so I was surprised to see a large, well-worn Bible on the coffee table in their living room. And it looked so well used."

Penny recalls experiencing a rush of joy as she held the Bible in her hands. Somehow, just by holding the sacred book, she remembers feeling a closer connection to God.

"Then this couple led me in a prayer of salvation, and almost immediately a song came to mind that I had evidently sung when I was a kid in Sunday school." Penny goes on to recite a verse from that song:

> "Have thine own way, Lord
> Have thine own way
> Thou art the Potter,
> I am the clay . . ."

Although that evening would mark the beginning of her religious conversion, Penny recollects that it would take a while longer for her to firmly trod the spiritual path.

"I was praying for Jesus to come into my heart, but I went out that night and drank some and messed around a little bit. But as the days went on I couldn't do that anymore."

Her voice fills with pride as Penny recalls how with each passing day, her commitment to God grew stronger. "I stopped working clubs and those drinking situations. My necklines went higher and my hemlines lower when I was performing.

"I was a baby Christian—in the very beginning of things—but I was feeling better about myself. There was a different kind of light that was starting to glimmer in my eyes.

"I had become saved. I had confessed my sins. I now believed in my Savior with all my heart. Sometimes I failed, because we're not all perfect, but I still could not live the kind of lifestyle I used to.

"Now I was attracted to a different crowd of friends. I was drawn to the light. I was reading the Bible and talking about the Lord. Seeing the changes in my life, my mama, sister, and brother-in-law made a personal decision to accept the Lord."

In 1992, what easily might have proven to be a final chapter in Penny's life became, instead, an inspirational new preface to it. That's the year when Penny was diagnosed with cancer.

"It was very aggressive—already in the lymph nodes when diagnosed—and they gave me the strongest chemotherapy that they can give you. But it came back five months later."

The swift reoccurrence of the cancer worried Penny's doctors. "They said, 'We can go with the strong chemotherapy again or we can go with a new experimental process called a stem cell rescue.' They told me, 'If we go with the new process, it won't be easy.'"

She was further warned that the procedure was so new, doctors were not certain of all the side effects. "There were so many things that could have happened to me. I could have lost my voice, or my heart could have failed, or my kidneys shut down. I could have even died! But none of those things happened."

Along with her natural optimism, Penny remembers relying on her faith that God would get her through the procedure. As the treatment began, she recalls being in so much pain that there were moments when she regretted having agreed to undergo it.

"It was rough going. It really hurt bad. I was throwing up blood and it was just horrible. There was even a point when I called a friend and said, 'I think I'm going on to be with the Lord.' I thought I was dying."

Penny remembers that moment when she felt close to death as not being entirely unpleasant. "It was like this euphoria came over me. I wasn't alive and I wasn't dead. I just had this feeling that the Lord had me in the palm of His hand. Oh, what a glorious, glorious feeling that was.

"The Holy Spirit had to have been in that room. I just wanted to go on and be with the Lord. If I had a choice, I'd have gone on. I really would have. That's how glorious it was. It was like a near-death experience except that I hadn't died.

"I didn't see any tunnel but I knew it was the Lord there comforting me. I just want to cry when I think about it. It's the most peaceful moment I've ever had in my entire life."

When the procedure, which lasted for several weeks, was finally completed, Penny believed that prayer was responsible for helping to keep her alive. "My doctor was praying for me and the whole church I was attending at the time was praying for me and people all across the country were praying for me. I had so many prayers going for me.

"It was through my faith in the Lord that He healed me. I know several women who have had the same bone marrow transplant and didn't make it.

"He healed me and here I am today with a clean bill of health and I'm getting stronger and stronger. People who see me onstage say, 'Where do you get your energy?' They don't even know that I've been sick."

While some people diagnosed with life-threatening diseases might understandably express bitterness toward their Maker, Penny asserts that she did not feel that way.

"God is not the author of the bad things that happen to you. I didn't blame Him. In fact, I thanked the Lord Jesus for giving me an optimistic attitude to face this. I also knew He wouldn't leave me or forsake me, but would help me find a way out."

Nowadays, the talented performer continues to draw large audiences whenever she performs. Over the years, she has also been featured in several motion pictures, including the popular movie *Bronco Billy,* with Clint Eastwood, and *Honkytonk Man,* also starring Eastwood.

When she is onstage, Penny reminds members of her audience who are ill to rely on faith and prayer. "I always talk about the Lord and tell people to get the Lord as their Savior. If you get to know Him and you're ill, He's not going to allow you to go on and be with Him if He still has a purpose for you on earth.

"I try to comfort people the same way He comforted me. I tell them about what the Lord did for me and I tell them that I'm a miracle standing here.

"I'm really a miracle, so that's got to give them some encouragement. I tell them that no matter what their doctors might say, as long as you're a child of God and believe, reality does not mean finality . . ."

Doug Stone

oug Stone was close to realizing his dream of becoming a Country music star when tragedy suddenly befell him. The forty-one-year-old Georgia native, who has sold more than 3 million albums since his 1990 debut album, suffered a heart attack in 1992 while onstage and required emergency quadruple bypass surgery.

Instead of becoming angry toward his Maker for such an untimely affliction, Doug, in his typical low-key manner, blamed his heart attack on a lifestyle of "too much grits, grease, and gravy."

It is the same relaxed attitude which has characterized his approach to other trials in his life—including an impoverished childhood, a long period of debt, and two divorces.

"None of those things ever affected my faith," the superstar declares. "Anything I ever got I deserved, whether it be rewards or a kick in the butt . . ."

Doug Stone chuckles at the notion of himself as a "great Christian," although the Country music superstar admits that he has always been drawn to religion.

"I wish I could say, 'Yes, I'm a Billy Graham.' But there's not that many people walking the face of the earth that have that kind of faith," he asserts.

"I've never lost my faith. I know without a shadow of a doubt that there is a God. There's no doubt in my mind about that. It's just very hard to keep a close feeling with Him living in this physical body."

Raised in rural Georgia, Doug remembers being attracted to religion as far back as the age of twelve, when one Sunday morning he was suddenly seized by the spirit of God.

"I was in this small Baptist church in Marietta, Georgia, and I was sitting in the pew with Mama at the time. This preacher was preaching and I was listening, hanging on every word. And there was a tug on me.

"I couldn't help it. I actually ran away from my mama. Mama went, 'Where are you going?' And I ran down to the altar and that's the day I got saved. I remember everything about it."

Doug recalls that shortly after his own religious experience, his father, Jack, a longtime nonbeliever, also underwent a religious conversion.

"He was a hardworking and sometimes a hard-drinking man, but he got saved in a very mighty way. It was amazing to see what happened to him when he was touched. It changed him totally."

Doug recalls, however, that there was also a downside to his father's religious conversion, one which resulted in a divorce when Doug was only twelve. "He wasn't the same person. It was like my parents didn't know each other anymore. It changed him totally.

"It's almost like God separated the two of them because they were so different once he got saved. They couldn't even live together. So they just split up and my brothers and I went with Daddy.

"We went to church all the time. We started following a preacher who really seemed to be full of the spirit, and we were doing revivals and stuff. It was really interesting and we had a great time. The bad thing about it is that I've been unable to keep that same feeling continuously.

"I wish I could have that kind of faith again. I never found a way to do it. I had it in me then, and I had it again when I was twenty-one. But I ain't had it since."

Doug recalls that moment of religious intensity with a mixture of awe and regret. "Myself and Daddy were having church one night and there's one thing I wish I had never done, but I did it anyway. I had a gig to play that night.

"I was really having a good time with my daddy and the spirit, but I had to leave and go perform. My daddy didn't want me to leave.

"Well, I was driving down the road and I'm going, 'God, if you don't really want me to go, just let me know.' Well, it wasn't raining at the time. There wasn't a drop of rain falling anywhere.

"And then, all of a sudden, it was raining and within five seconds it rained so hard I had to come to a complete stop. As soon as I came to a complete stop the rain went away."

To this very day Doug remembers the sense of awe he felt as he sat in his car in the middle of the road—a feeling which he has been unable to recapture since.

"I shouldn't have went. But I'd contracted to do a job. So it's like, what do you do? Looking back, I think I should have just turned around and went back home."

Doug recalls that besides teaching him all about religion, there were other things he learned from his father as well—particularly that happiness was more important than money.

One piece of his father's advice which the Columbia Records artist is glad that he did ignore was not to become a singer like his mother, Gail, who also dreamed of becoming a Country music star.

While Doug's father taught him practical skills such as diesel mechanics, it was Gail who taught her young son how to play the guitar and encouraged his musical career. She would later act as Doug's manager as well.

"It's really strange, but all my life I felt like I was going to be a performer. I just didn't know when it would happen. I just knew that I was going to get my turn at bat and I was going to run around the bases."

His teenage years were restless ones, Doug recalls. He recollects being into bikes and motorcycles and running around with friends who, like himself, were a bit wild and liked to play music.

Music continued to beckon him, and Doug quit high school at age sixteen to perform in a band called Impact.

"I was sixteen when I had my band, but really my first band was me and Mama. Mama was a great singer, but she never made it—she came in the wrong era. She's still the inspiration behind me, and my greatest critic."

Not only did Doug have his own band at that age, but his own trailer as well—inside of which he built a recording studio. "I had my own trailer, my own property, my own car, my own problems, and my own job. And it's been that way ever since.

"If I made a mistake I'd stand on my own two feet and take the blow for it. That's how I am today. That's the way my daddy was. He said 'You always stand on your own two feet and take the blow for what you do. Don't blame other people for your failure. Blame yourself.' "

By age twenty-three, Doug had already been married five years and was the father of two young children. During the day he worked various jobs, but nights and weekends would find Doug performing music in local clubs or in his homemade recording studio.

His unsettled lifestyle of long hours away from home eventually took a toll on his first marriage—as it was also to do with his second marriage—and the young couple were divorced.

Doug recalls that his infatuation with music also got him into debt. "I hated mechanic work. I figured I was selling my life by the hour. When it came to music, I'd give the money away just to be able to play."

When Doug found himself unable to pay his bills, his creditors finally seized his trailer. Hounded by a variety of lawsuits, the young entertainer moved into a small well house that he, his father, and his brothers built. They later enlarged it into a house.

Although he continued to be plagued by years of debt and financial struggle, Doug remembers never losing his faith that someday his situation would improve.

"I wasn't too worried about things," he chuckles. "Living in that little house I remembered my daddy saying that 'the more stuff you got, the more stuff you've got to worry about.'

"I felt like I had gotten what I deserved and that I was proceeding in life the way God wanted me to go. The way I felt about it I never blamed God."

Meanwhile, Doug continued to perform, playing clubs and honky-tonks in the Newnan and Marietta areas. Although he remembers often wondering whether he would ever amount to more than a local performer, one person who didn't share Doug's doubts was his mother, a locally known singer and guitarist in her own right.

Not only did Gail provide her son with constant encouragement, she often booked him work as well. In fact, when Doug was only seven, Gail convinced Country music superstar Loretta Lynn to let Doug open a concert for her.

Doug grins that he might never have gained the confidence to push himself harder had he not fallen asleep one night while listening to his own tapes.

"I was working this second-shift job, and the way I relaxed when I got back to my trailer was to put on my headphones and listen to music. I had recorded some stuff and I fell asleep and when I woke up—for five or six seconds—I didn't know who was singing on that tape.

"It freaked me out when I figured it out," he chuckles. "I said, 'That's me singing?' Then I decided, 'Hey, maybe there is something here.' It really hit me then. I got cold chills all over me. It was like waking up with someone else's ears, and that's the first time I really knew I could sing."

Doug's first big break came in 1987 while he was performing at the VFW hall in Newnan, Georgia. After the show he was approached by Country music agent Phyllis Bennett.

"She came into the VFW hall one night to hear me and my band play, and decided that I was the guy. I had just turned thirty-one and I started to think, 'If I don't do something soon I'm going to be too old to do this.' "

When Bennett offered to become his manager, Doug gratefully accepted. His new manager quickly arranged for Doug's demo tape to be heard by Epic Records' director of Country music, who invited the young singer to a live audition. Doug left that audition with a record contract in hand.

Instead of being overjoyed, Doug recalls that his first reaction was to return home and pray. "I prayed during those moments. I said 'God, if this career is going to send me to hell then I don't want it.' I think that was my main prayer. I'd rather be poor and struggling and go to heaven than to be rich and go to hell."

It might seem like an odd prayer coming from someone whose career was about to take off, but Doug believed he had a good reason for his concern.

"It was just one of those times in my life when I couldn't stay as close to God as I wanted to be. I was playing music in bars and honky-tonks and doing some wild stuff. There was even a time when I holed up in my house for a while.

"I didn't want to go outside because I knew my personality. I was kind of wild. If I stayed at home nobody would bother me and I wouldn't get in trouble—no drinking, none of that stuff. So I stayed inside.

"I just think that we're living in the last days and the devil is walking around now and tempting us. It makes it rough out there for those people who have never felt the spirit. They're going to have a hard time.

"I was worried because I wasn't feeling the Presence the way I used to. I was constantly getting on my knees and saying, 'God, forgive me. I'm sorry. Put me back on track.'

"Even today I'm constantly on my knees. I pray at least once a day. It's just one of those things where I'm constantly wanting to get forgiveness for anything that I did years ago—or even that day."

By the spring of 1992, Doug's career finally seemed to be on track. The up-and-coming performer had just released several singles which were quickly climbing to the top of the charts, while his *From the Heart* album was well on its way to going gold.

In addition, the Grammy Award–nominated performer was drawing larger and more admiring crowds, gaining even more exposure as the opening act for superstar Kenny Rogers.

The handsome entertainer with the expressive, heart-rending delivery had certainly come a long way from those days when he was playing VFW halls.

With those years of scrambling behind him, he and his second wife, Carie, were even able to afford to move from their modest home in Georgia to Nashville, where they settled into a four-bedroom log house on fifty-one acres of land.

He was on a roll, so what could stop him?

During a concert in Princeville, Oregon, Doug experienced pain in his chest and down his arm that was so intense, he could hardly grip the microphone.

The thirty-five-year-old Country music star was flown back to Nashville where doctors decided that Doug needed to undergo immediate quadruple bypass surgery. Ironically, one of his songs reaching the top of the charts at that time was called "Come in Out of the Pain."

Characteristically, even as he was being prepped for surgery at Nashville's Park View Medical Center, Doug reacted to his situation with unflappable calm.

"I wasn't too worried about it," he laughingly recalls. "I felt that either I would come back to the room or go on. Either way was fine. I don't even remember reflecting on my life. I was just relaxed.

"If I was going to die it was going to be the easiest part of living, once I got to that point. I think death is going to be a transition from here to a better place, anyway.

"I think when you start to die you're going to be scared, but I think as you die it's going to get easier—if that makes any sense. I'm intrigued with near-death experiences—you know, where people go and then come back."

Doug nearly got the chance to learn about such experiences firsthand. "I almost died in my room the night before they operated on me. I had some kind of reaction and I almost died right there lying in my bed before they even got me to the surgical table. But they were able to get me back."

The operation was not only successful but just five weeks after leaving the hospital Doug was back onstage performing before an enthusiastic crowd of close to twenty-five thousand people at the annual Nashville Fan Fair. By the following summer he had returned to a full touring schedule.

Today, although Doug's tender crooner's style has not changed, much of his lifestyle has. Gone are his three-pack-a-day cigarette habit and the fried food binges he so loved.

There have been spiritual changes as well. "What happened to me brought to the forefront the thought that I was going to be in a pine box one day. So since then I've been trying to live my life differently.

"I live everyday like it was my last because it could be. It could have been even before the surgery. I just didn't know it. I've developed a greater appreciation of life and God. I'm living each day to its fullest."

Doug is eager to share his philosophy of life with anyone who cares to listen. "If you're looking for tomorrow that's fine. Have plans and have goals. But live every day. I put it this way. When I die they're not going to collect a whole bunch of money off of me because I've already spent it."

Doug concedes that his medical ordeal put him closer in touch with God, but he does not believe that a renewal of faith is dependent on such a crisis.

"I was just twelve years old when I embraced God. "Nothing bad had happened to me at that age. No sin or anything else. I don't think it takes surgery or an accident to bring God to the forefront in your life.

"All you need to do is seek Him out and you'll find Him. Faith is a one-on-one thing with God. It's between you and Him. If you want to find Him badly enough, you will. And if you're going to do that, you better start today because you're always one heartbeat away from hell if you don't."

In the Gospel-tinged title track of his 1994 best-selling album, *Faith in Me, Faith in You,* Doug emphasizes the importance of maintaining a close connection to God.

"That's true even if you're a sinner. I tell my kids that God always knows what you are doing, and if you've done something wrong all you need to do is get on your knees and ask for forgiveness. He's a forgiving God. And if you're ill, or you want to get through something bad enough, seek help from Him, you'll get through it."

Doug also becomes impatient with anyone who tells him that they lack faith, stating that he simply cannot understand how anyone can doubt God and His life-changing powers.

"My daddy used to have people come up to him and say, 'I don't believe there's a God.' And, of course, we were a family of mechanics.

"So my daddy would say, 'Well, let me stick this hot torch to your butt and see how long you can stand there before saying, 'Oh, God!' He said, 'You take the biggest atheist on earth, if they're dying, they're going, 'Oh, God!' I think we're all going to need Him sooner or later."

Prayer plays an important role in his life, Doug confides. "I pray that the Lord watches over the world, watches over my family, watches over me, and just forgives me for the sins I commit every day."

One thing which Doug states he will not pray for is material success. "I don't think I should do that. I don't think material things are something you should pray for. It doesn't make any sense to me.

"What you are really looking forward to is going to heaven—that's what you should be praying for. That's what our ultimate goal should be . . ."

Rick Trevino

Immediately after experiencing his own spiritual renewal at age fifteen, Country music superstar Rick Trevino offered up a special prayer that his father, who was a heavy drinker, would also see the light and cease his dependence on alcohol.

Although it took nearly a decade for his prayers to be answered, when that moment finally arrived, the twenty-six-year-old Texas native greeted it with joy.

Rick, a third-generation Mexican-American, and one of Country music's top young superstars, accepts the fact that "God moves in mysterious ways."

He emphasizes that what is most important is not the amount of time it takes for a miracle to occur, but that with faith and prayer it does happen.

"The future might seem kind of bleak—especially if you have some kind of addiction," he offers. "But always have faith in what lies ahead. Believe that you'll come out of it and you will . . ."

As one of the rising stars on the Country music scene, Rick Trevino confides that he works hard at avoiding the temptations that come his way in the music business.

And so far in his meteoric climb to the top of the charts, the bilingual performer with the well-modulated baritone voice and handsome good looks has done a good job at doing so—particularly the pitfalls of drug and alcohol abuse.

"I just want to be some kind of example that young people can count on," Rick declares with his slight down-home twang. "I had role models as a kid and I want to be a role model to these younger people. I never want to be in a bar offstage messed up or drunk or something. Or messed up while I'm singing.

"I just always want to be focused and carry myself in a classy manner so that the young kids can say, 'Hey, I wanna be like that guy.' I don't drink on the road. Occasionally, on special occasions, I might have a glass of wine or something. But for the most part I don't drink beer or anything else."

The multifaceted performer with his trademark black cowboy hat goes on to reveal that much of his aversion to alcohol stems from having been raised in a family where his father was a heavy drinker.

"I saw what alcohol can do to a family. I know because I was born and grew up in an alcoholic family. Even today my father will tell you that he is an alcoholic, although he doesn't drink anymore," Rick observes.

"And that really made me want to be different—not being into that lifestyle. I don't want to bring that into my life because I've been exposed to the negative side of alcohol.

"I just try to put on the best possible show, sign autographs, say 'hi' to everybody, and then, when I'm done, I try to call it an evening. I try to stay away from that alcohol and drug environment because you're in it every day."

Rick avows that the way he enjoys getting "high" is by pleasing his audiences. "I have fun every day just performing. I feel like every day is a blessing. I have so much fun in my everyday life, that I don't need to drink at all.

"Sure I've had my share of partying. I'm not the perfect person. But it's because of God and my relationship with Jesus that I can cope with everything without getting involved with drugs or alcohol."

With his youthful good looks, dazzling smile, and charming boyish manner, the singer and songwriter submits that another temptation he must contend with is his constant pursuit by female fans.

"There are a lot of ladies out there," he laughs, "but I've got a real strong relationship with my wife Karla whom I've known for six years. I want to keep that. So it's tough to be out on the road with those temptations and really try to walk the Christian walk."

Rick enthuses no end about Karla, his former college sweetheart and a student at the University of Texas. "She is one of those rare ladies that can deal with a long-distance relationship. It's hard for both of us, but it's so nice to have someone on this earth to share my career with.

"She's been my best friend through everything and she's always somebody that I want to come home to, talk to about what I've been doing. She keeps me accountable," acknowledges the young Country music singer.

Rick, the oldest of three siblings, reminisces about his days growing up on the outskirts of a Mexican neighborhood in Houston, Texas, and his spiritual upbringing.

"I was maybe five when my dad got transferred to Austin to work at IBM, and my folks and my brother moved there from Houston where I was born.

"We lived in a pretty pleasant neighborhood in Houston, although it was on the edge of a tough Hispanic neighborhood. But it wasn't as tough as the neighborhood where my mom and dad grew up.

"I guess my earliest memory of having a relationship with God is mostly around my mother taking me to church. My brother and I would go to a Catholic church in Austin called St. Thomas More. We went there many years, but it was an on-and-off kind of thing.

"We would go maybe two months where we wouldn't miss any Sundays, and then we wouldn't go for two or three months. And then we'd be back at Christmastime. We'd kind of go in streaks.

"I also remember how my mother used to pray with me. I remember very early on, even when we were living in Houston, that my mom would kneel down and pray with me. She had a real impact on me when it came to religion."

At St. Thomas More, Rick remembers taking part in all the rituals of the Catholic Church—from First Communion to baptism—yet sensing that something was spiritually missing.

"I've always wanted religion in my life. One of the priests even asked me if I'd like to go into the ministry, stuff like that. I've always been open to the Gospel and intrigued by the Bible—especially the history of Jesus Christ. I guess God was blessing me with an open heart.

"But by the time I was fifteen, I just started to feel like I wasn't being nourished by God. I started losing a little bit of my connection with Him. My relationship seemed to be more with the Church than with God.

"Then a friend invited me to go to a Bible church with her. It was a nondenominational church that was called the Hill Country Bible Church. I was fifteen and I really started to enjoy going there. I'd go there a lot by myself.

"And it was then when I finally accepted Christ as my Lord and Savior. This was kind of an eye-opener for me because it was different. It was the first time I felt an actual relationship with Christ."

Although most of his childhood memories are pleasant ones, some of them are marred by images of his father's indulgence in alcohol.

"My father drank a lot. They both had a tough life. So maybe that's why they were both very reluctant to devote their entire lives to Christian faith.

"After I had accepted Christ I think my parents started seeing the kind of spark that was in my eyes all of a sudden. I tried to explain to my folks what I was doing, and how I would like them to change. But I couldn't do much because they weren't willing to change."

But there is more to Rick's memories of his parents than their struggles with alcohol. Although Rick Trevino was the one who was musically talented, both he and Linda encouraged their son's interest in music. Young Rick was playing classical piano when he was five, and performing professionally at the age of fourteen.

He recollects that his mother spent most of her time at home caring for her three children, Rick, Adam, and Crystal, while his father was either at work or singing and playing guitar in the Houston clubs with a Tejano group called Neto Perez and the Originals.

"What I remember most is my dad performing and my mom kneeling down in prayer, cooking, always keeping us well dressed and saying, 'Okay, you gotta go to school tomorrow and remember to say your prayers.'

"My folks were very proud of me and supportive. The biggest influences at that time in my life were God and my parents. They continue to be supportive and protective of me."

Besides being musically gifted, Rick also was a talented athlete, and was once touted as one of the finest high school baseball players in Texas.

He decided to turn down a baseball scholarship offer from Memphis State University to concentrate on music, and began playing in bands again in the Austin area.

"I'm happy I closed the door on baseball. I'll never forget the time I played baseball, but I knew music was there for me and I wanted a Country music career."

While attending Texas A&M University, Rick kept his hand in the music scene, returning to Austin on weekends to play in clubs like the Broken Spoke or Dance Across Texas.

It was around that time when Rick decided to send some of his demo tapes to record companies in Nashville. "I was actually signed by Steve Buckingham of Sony Records. He was impressed by one song that I did, and he came down to Austin and signed me when I was nineteen."

His first self-titled album immediately went to the top of the charts, while Rick's single, "Just Enough Rope," also made a fast climb up the *Billboard* charts.

That record also made some Country music history by being simultaneously released in Spanish. Since then, Rick has blazed a swift and powerful path to Country music stardom.

Besides his appreciation of music, Rick recalls how his parents instilled in him his lasting moral values. "Even though they weren't consistent churchgoers, they gave me very positive values. It was old-fashioned-type values like knowing right from wrong that really rubbed off on me.

"One of the main things they taught me was the value of hard work. My father told me, 'If you stop working at your craft, whatever it is, and stop practicing and reach the point where you think you're better than everybody else, you should sit down and think about what you're doing. You never, ever, stop working—you never, ever, stop learning in anything you do.'

"Another thing that sticks out in my mind is that to this day I still get people saying, 'Don't call me sir.' I was always taught to say 'yes, sir,' and 'no, sir,' 'no, ma'am' and 'yes, ma'am.' They taught me that. I am an adult now and I'll still say that. I'm just not getting over that habit."

Rick remembers how at age fifteen, after his religious conversion, he began praying that his father would stop abusing alcohol. "I continued to pray and it took maybe ten years but it did happen. I remember that my dad had a breakdown or something due to alcohol and my mom said, 'Hey, that's it, I'm leaving.'

"And my dad called a friend of mine—her name's Jean Bringell—and she's kind of my spiritual leader. And he went to her house and said, 'Look, I need help.' And he got on his knees and accepted Christ. That's how his life changed.

"It's not that he hasn't stumbled in the last three years, but he sure is a different person. He gets up in the morning and prays and is completely different from how he was five years ago.

"And my mother also accepted Jesus. And here it is—you know, thirty or forty years later—and my mom and dad have finally rediscovered the true love that was lost for many years.

"I prayed a lot for that and it took some time, but I think that God just moves in mysterious ways. Now they're more in love than ever and Daddy has his alcoholism under control."

Merging the best of his Hispanic heritage with the legacy of traditional Country music, Rick has clearly become Country music's biggest star of Hispanic descent since Johnny Rodriguez and Freddy Fender. He is also one of the youngest Country artists to get a record deal since Tanya Tucker.

Reflecting upon his success at such a young age, Rick proclaims: "It's been a pleasant climb and has really gone well. I feel blessed by my life and my career and I thank God every day for these blessings.

"There are so many blessings that He has bestowed upon me, like my music, my family, my friends, my home, and the people I'm surrounded by.

"I pray every morning, thanking God for the day and for what I'm doing. I pray and I always ask for wisdom because I'm young and in this business the main thing is to have wisdom. You have to have the kind of wisdom to make smart career decisions.

"I never really pray for material success. I've never really said, 'Hey, I want a number-one record,' or 'Lord, help me. Let me have a gold album.' I've always just been thankful for my abilities and have always asked Him to keep me safe."

While Rick's career is currently at full throttle, he admits being concerned about how his faith will weather any possible future downturns. "Faith is very important to me. It's important that I have it in both the good times and the bad times.

"I honestly feel like God is one of these days really going to challenge me in my life. I feel like everyone has to go through such a time. And I always pray that I will not turn my face from God. I just pray that I'll have the same kind of faith that I have now.

"I know that my mother and father have had their time and they've met the devil. I know that one of these days I'm going to have my time whether it's twenty, thirty, or forty years from now."

While Rick admits that he is a trifle young to be dispensing any spiritual advice, he feels strongly enough about his faith to do so. The superstar encourages anyone who is feeling troubled not to forgo their faith.

"Quite honestly, I wouldn't blame someone for losing their faith if something devastating in life has happened—like losing a loved one. That's when it could be real easy to lose faith.

"But all I can tell you is to try to surround yourself with people who pray for you. Ask people to pray for you and pray yourself.

"Somewhere along the line He will knock at your door and you'll come out of it. That's kind of my whole advice to anyone who is down in the dumps."

Looking ahead, the Country music hit maker, who recently released his third album for Columbia Records, and was voted in 1995 Best New Country Artist by the Hispanic Music Awards Association, states that his goals are simple ones.

"I want to continue to write music and become a strong songwriter and better musician. I practice every day and try to find time to write every day to do that. That's hard to do, but it's something you have to force yourself to do.

* "I'd also really like to record some kind of Country Gospel album. I think God would want me to do that in the future and I think that would be very nice.

"And on the personal level I want to be the same person that I have been and to take care of the people who take care of me. I also want to do whatever God calls on me to do . . ."

John Berry

John Berry will never forget the highs and lows of 1994. Within a twelve-week period, the Country music superstar enjoyed his first number-one hit, "Your Love Amazes Me," the birth of a second child by his wife Robin, and emergency brain surgery to remove a life-threatening cyst.

It was a wild and crazy ride for the thirty-eight-year-old Aiken, South Carolina, native, who found himself on the operating table just when his fourteen-year struggle to gain recognition in the music business was within his grasp.

The Grammy-nominated singer and songwriter still cannot recall very much about that harrowing experience, except for a dim memory of praying that he would survive the operation and not have all his years of hard work come to such a terrible end.

John quickly recovered from the five-hour operation and was back performing onstage within a month—a miracle that he has never stopped being grateful for.

Among the credits on one of his recent albums, *Standing on the Edge,* can be found this thank-you note: "And to my Lord, God, for giving me another day . . ."

Although John Berry is still dealing with some temporary memory loss as a result of his 1994 brain surgery, the one thing he certainly hasn't lost is his keen sense of humor.

Before performing a song onstage, the Liberty Records artist still checks with his bass player to make sure that he's counted the correct number of frets on his guitar to put him in the right key with the rest of the band.

It's a ritual that always draws a laugh from John and members of his band. But behind this bit of humor are dark memories of one of the most harrowing moments in his life.

John recollects that it was shortly after Christmas 1993, when he began feeling "slightly out of it." He and his wife Robin, who is also his backup vocalist, were living with their two children on their hundred-acre farm eighteen miles outside of Athens, Georgia, at the time.

"I had some signs that something was wrong with me. I had quit eating—which is a pretty good sign with me that there's something really wrong—and I had lost fifty pounds. And I was feeling all the time like I was having a constant fever.

"And all the things that were important in my life—my family, my wife, my children, our farm where we live—all these things had become unimportant. And my career. Nothing seemed to matter to me."

Preoccupied with plans for a new concert tour and at work recording a new album in his Nashville studio, John didn't let on to anyone how he was feeling. But after six years of marriage, Robin, who reluctantly left the tour that February for the final months of her pregnancy, sensed that something was wrong with her husband.

"John was tired all the time and emotionally drained," she recollects. "He just seemed to be withdrawing, getting further and further away from himself."

The headaches were the worst, often keeping him from sleeping. John remembers continuing to ignore the warning signs, even though he confesses to having a phobia about aneurysms, a condition sometimes caused by weakness in a blood vessel wall.

That phobia was well founded. His father, at age thirty-one, had survived a cerebral aneurysm, while that same condition took his mother's life at fifty-two. John was twenty-one years old at the time of his mother's death.

"I knew there was something going wrong with me. And with my family history—both my parents had aneurysms—I was worried. But I just tried to forget about it and kept going."

Meanwhile, John's uncharacteristic behavior continued. "I remember one day I was on the road when Robin was delivering our second child. And she called me up to let me know she was going into labor.

"And I can remember telling her, 'That's great. Call me and let me know how it goes.' That was pretty bad. But there was so much pressure in my head, that everything was overcast to me—even the birth of our child." Somehow John was cognizant enough to get himself to the hospital.

When Robin finally went into labor, John arrived at St. Mary's Hospital in Athens, Georgia, to be by her side. "I was slumped on the floor outside of the room where my wife was delivering our baby and I had this continuous headache.

"A nurse came over to me and said, 'Are you okay?' And I told her I really wasn't. I was feeling weak and I could barely respond. And then I told her my family history. They took me to the emergency room to check me out."

The very next morning John found himself at the Emory University Hospital undergoing a battery of tests that confirmed his doctors' worst fears. John had a colloid cyst on his brain. The cyst, in itself, was not life threatening, but could be fatal if it caused a block in the flow of spinal fluid.

Meanwhile, Robin had delivered John's new son—a five-pound,

thirteen-ounce baby named Sean Thomas. But even before she could enjoy the birth of her new child, Robin despaired that at this blessed moment in their lives she might lose her husband.

For John, however, there was some good news. Doctors told him that by making two small openings in his skull, the cyst could be drained.

John recalls reacting with mixed feelings. On the one hand, he was relieved that doctors had finally discovered the source of his constant headaches. On the other, he feared that his condition was worse than doctors suspected.

"I was afraid that they'd find more than they were bargaining for. I was afraid that they would get in there in the midst of surgery and move something out of the way and there would be something worse that they would find. And they'd be like, 'Oh, wow, we didn't know this was going to be here.' That thought scared me to death."

Robin, meanwhile, remembers being relieved to learn that there was an actual physical cause for her husband's behavior, and not "a mental or emotional problem, or a problem in our marriage." She had even begun reading books about depression and prayed each morning that her husband was not suffering from mental illness.

Two weeks later, the entertainer found himself being prepared for surgery. A quietly religious person, John believes he prayed for God's help during that frightening time in his life—although he still cannot remember. To this very day, there are still many holes in his memory about what happened just before, during, and after his surgery.

"I know that I spent almost a month in that hospital, but I don't remember a lot about that period. One of the things I can't remember is whether I was praying or if there were any prayer sessions going on for me. I know that sounds weird, but I just can't recall."

Instead, John offers up some pretty good evidence why he believes he did call upon God to get him through the surgery. In doing so, he begins to reminisce about his boyhood days growing up in Aiken, South Carolina.

"Aiken was a small town with this picturesque downtown main street," John recollects. "We grew up in a little subdivision there with lots of family around—a lot of my dad's brothers and sisters lived in the same subdivision. There were cousins all around, aunts and uncles, so it was a real neat atmosphere to be in."

John was the youngest of three siblings—he had a brother and a sister. His father, Vernon, sold insurance while his mother, Geneva, mostly remained at home to raise the children. When John was eight, his father lost his job, so the family relocated to Atlanta, Georgia, where there was plenty of construction work available.

"Both my parents were very strong Christian people. And I remember as a kid, every night we would have dinner at 5:15 P.M. Everybody in the family would be there. Mom and Dad, my brother and my sister, we'd all sit down together to eat.

"Every night after dinner we would clear the table and my dad would get his Bible out. And we'd all sit around the table and we would read a chapter in Proverbs. And he would read some other Scriptures. And we would have family prayer time. It would last about half an hour and we would do that every day."

In addition to home Bible study, church attendance was an important part of his family life. The talented performer recalls that each Sunday he and his family would attend a nondenominational church. After the service, his family would return home for a religious discussion.

"That's how we lived. It amazes me when I think back on what a materially poor family we were, how financially poor we were, but what a spiritually rich family we were."

Religion remained an important focus of family life, and John became increasingly interested in religion through his teenage years, getting involved in Christian youth group meetings.

There was only one thing that John enjoyed as much as his religious activities, and that was music. Throughout his high school years, he was singing and playing guitar.

"I used to play in a lot of college coffee houses. I ended up getting into that quite a bit. That went on for a number of years and then, in 1984 or something like that, I finally did put a band together."

John, who was twenty-four at the time, recalls that his band was heavily influenced by Philadelphia bands like the Chi-Lites and the Stylistics. Music had become so much part of his life, that John began to dream of a career as a recording artist.

"I prayed about that all the time. It was very important to me to hopefully gather some guidance and knowledge about what I was supposed to be doing with my talent. I would pray about what direction I should be going in.

"I remember one night I went for a walk around the block and just really prayed about getting a chance to sing. It didn't matter what form or whatever. I just loved to do that. I loved it and I was really praying for that opportunity to come.

"I never lost faith that this would happen. I was never discouraged. I always knew that being a performer was what I was supposed to do. I just never had any doubt about that.

"I just knew that God would provide me with a break—whatever form that break might be. And I didn't focus on all the trappings of a successful career.

"I was never sitting around going, 'Okay, do I really want to have a career so I can have four Cadillacs and a mansion and a swimming pool?' That's not what it was about. It was about getting to perform for a lot of people. The trappings were not important."

That break did not happen overnight. But a phone call eventually brought an answer to his prayers. A promoter who had seen John's band perform offered the young musician and his bass player a job in one of the larger clubs in Athens, Georgia.

John remembers wasting no time in packing his things and heading out to Athens, which was then known for its thriving music scene. "It was like my prayers had finally been answered. My faith had been rewarded. It didn't happen fast, but there's not been anything that's happened fast in my life.

"It's all taken a long time, but my career has slowly developed. And I believe it was because of those prayers that I got that call and received direction in my life."

With his distinctive and emotionally charged voice, John quickly gained a reputation as one of the fine new voices in the Country music nightclub circuit. His bookings increased and soon he was playing some of the largest clubs in town.

"I found what I was supposed to be doing at least for that period of time. I went from practically starving in Atlanta to making quite a living playing in Athens. There was lots of music in Athens, and my style of performing was different from most of the bands."

Three years after moving to Athens, John fell in love and married his wife, Robin. He remembers those days as some of the happiest in his life.

"I was singing for a living and I was doing all right. The music allowed me to build my own house and raise a family. I was able to do what I wanted to do and I never had to take a day job at Kmart," he quips.

Still, he was growing increasingly restless. The years were passing by and John felt that he was not putting his God-given talents to full use. So he and his wife devised a plan. The couple agreed to go to Nashville every forty-five days where John would perform at show-cases, hoping to be discovered by some major record company.

"It was a test of faith in my own abilities. If I was any good I would find interest—serious interest. If not, then I would figure out what to do from there. Robin and I prayed a lot about it because at that time it was brand-new ground for us. We were going to Nashville and we were meeting a lot of people we didn't know, had never met, and had never heard of.

"We weren't sure what was in it for them and we didn't have anybody that we'd worked with for any long period of time that we could talk to about them. We didn't have anyone to tell us what we were doing and that who we were dealing with were the right people and the right way to go. So we asked for guidance."

John believes his faith was again rewarded when, in the spring of 1992, he played a showcase to which he had invited all the usual music executives and members of the press.

To the entertainer's disappointment, only one person showed up —Herky Williams, then an executive with Liberty Records. That disappointment turned to elation when the record company executive invited John to dinner after his performance.

An audition was arranged, and when John left Liberty Records that day he had a two-album contract in hand.

Twelve months later, the new recording artist was not only winning the praise of music critics but had already scored his first number-one hit, a song he wrote called, "Your Love Amazes Me."

As fate would have it, on the very day that John was wheeled into surgery—May 10, 1994—that song hit the top of the Country music charts.

For fourteen long years John had struggled to establish himself as a Country music artist. And now, just when his talents were beginning to be recognized, the singer and songwriter lay in critical condition in an Atlanta hospital where he was being prepped for a five-hour brain operation.

"All I can remember is that I came out of the surgery and I was feeling better. The pressure was gone. I can't remember much else except I was told that my fans were outside the hospital. There were flowers and telegrams streaming in."

On June 6, less than a month after his surgery, John appeared at a Nashville Fan Fair with Robin, his two children, and his mother-in-law in tow. All he can remember thinking about as he stood on that stage and gazed out at the wildly cheering audience, is that a miracle had somehow taken place in his life.

"It was quite an emotional experience, and to be quite honest it was nice to be emotional about something again. Part of what the cyst did was to block my emotions."

Today John considers himself a different person. "I've changed my attitude and the way I look at things. I now know what's important to me. I don't have any doubts that God and my family are what are most important to me. And I'm not in so much of a hurry anymore. I try to spend as much time as I can with my family."

Prayer also plays more of a role in his life than ever before, John offers. "It's part of my family's daily life maintenance plan," he chuckles. "Life isn't easy—there's lots going on—and prayer helps guide us in how to raise three children. It helps us on how to take care of our family and how to make the right decisions career-wise."

John states that he does most of his praying during the afternoon hours, although he often prays at night, as well. "Sometimes it's late at night, sitting on the couch, or in my car rolling down the highway that I'll pray. It's whenever I find the time to be able to have a few minutes."

The Country music superstar, who has sold more than one million albums, proclaims that he is not only grateful for his commercial success, but indebted to God for being alive. It is during the Christmas season, he adds, that he feels most thankful of all.

"We have all our family over and we go on a hayride. Then we have a big bonfire and we all sit around and my brother-in-law, Mark, reads "The Christmas Story." Then we all go around the circle of the whole family and close friends. We just talk about things that we're grateful for."

One Christmas gathering that was particularly special to him was the one which took place after his surgery. "When it came to my turn I just didn't know where to begin. I finally started with just being thankful for being here—just really thankful and glad to be able to spend another Christmas with my family. Just thankful to have made it through all these things."

As a result of his own harrowing experience, John urges anyone who may be facing surgery to "have faith in God and believe in God without a doubt. And if you don't have faith search for it from within.

"If you can't find it there, then go get some guidance—maybe a pastor of a church or even a good friend. Faith is a very wise thing to have in your life, especially if you're not feeling well—take it from me, I know . . ."

Marty Raybon
(Shenandoah)

Although surrounded by all the trappings and rewards of Country music stardom, singer and songwriter Marty Raybon sensed that he was headed in the wrong direction.

The thirty-seven-year-old lead vocalist for Shenandoah, one of Country music's most successful groups, was raised in a Christian home and had pledged himself to God when he was only six years old.

But when the superstar looked at himself in a mirror, all the Alabama-born entertainer could see gazing back was the face of a "hellbound pagan"—one who had forsaken his spiritual roots.

Early one morning, while recovering from a hangover and feeling "burnt to a frazzle, and at my rope's end," Marty decided that he had enough. He began to pray and it was then that he experienced a miracle in his life.

Over the years, Marty has endured his share of heartbreak and trial—including a bitter lawsuit involving the use of Shenandoah's name and his mother's diagnosis of cancer.

The award-winning performer credits his newfound faith with helping him get through those difficult times, testifying that "in the midst of these things I knew that through the power of faith and prayer that God would take care of me . . ."

Marty Raybon's roots run deep in the fertile soil of music, family, and faith.

Growing up with two brothers and two sisters in Sanford, Florida, his early years were saturated with hard work as a bricklayer, church activities, and tight, bluegrass harmonies which he sang in a family ensemble, the American Bluegrass Express.

At age six, his parents were divorced. It was an event which Marty recalls left him feeling more confused than hurt. "Let me say in all honesty that I never came off with a feeling that I had lost something very valuable in my life," he proclaims in a warm Southern drawl.

"I never felt hurt or insecure about that. It was a conflict that my mother and dad had. It did not have anything to do with us kids. In fact, my mother and dad loved each other so much that they remarried sixteen years later.

"And they continued to shower love on us continuously—even after they were separated. The three months out of the school year that we were off, we went and spent it with my dad.

"And the nine other months we spent with Mother. And we'd see our dad on the weekends, too. So I didn't feel like I had to walk around in life with a chip on my shoulder because things between them didn't work out."

Besides continuing to bestow love upon their children after their divorce, Marty's parents continued to provide them with religious instruction as well. Marty, however, remembers not paying too much attention to those lessons.

"I just kind of scuffled through it more or less. I was just a six-year-old kid and I thought I knew lots about religion, but I didn't know the first thing about a relationship with God.

"We were raised Southern Baptist and Mama took us to church and when I would go see Daddy it was the same. It's just that I was not moved to get into anything very deep about religion."

Despite that attitude, Marty does recall a day at Sunday school when he became so overwhelmed by the story of Jesus' sacrifice on the cross, that he walked down the aisle that very same day to receive Christ.

"I was a six-year-old kid at the time and I felt the spirit of God. I was destined to appreciate and hold on to God more than anything else. That day God had already set me forward on the path to belief and faith, although I lost my way for a while."

Marty's musical talent became apparent at an early age, when he and his family came to realize that he had been blessed with an incredible gift—his voice.

One of his first public performances took place in a third-grade talent show when Marty sang "The Battle of New Orleans." He won that show and went on to sing in other talent contests and school assemblies as well, always beating the competition.

Marty continued to perform music throughout his teenage years, singing and playing guitar with his father and two brothers in the family bluegrass ensemble. The talented group went on to win Florida's state-wide bluegrass competition for five consecutive years.

Even then Marty recalls having his sights set on larger opportunities than playing bluegrass music with the family band. He eventually left the group and departed for Nashville for what he likes to describe as his "starvation years."

"Those were the years when I was knocking on doors and not getting any answers. There was even one Christmas when I was so broke that all the lights in my house had been turned off and the heat was turned off. I was cold and alone and all I had to eat was a can of corn."

It was more ambition than faith which drove the performer in those days, Marty recollects. "It was a time when I wanted to be what I wanted to be rather than what He wanted me to be. It was the difference between being God-centered and self-centered. Back then I was self-centered."

Despite his lack of success, Marty remained determined not to fail at becoming a Country music artist. Upon hearing talk that things were happening musically in Muscle Shoals, Alabama, Marty packed his bags and headed south. There he hooked up with several other struggling musicians, and they formed a band that would soon become known as Shenandoah.

With its smooth harmonies, positive lyrics, and sparkling production, Shenandoah would go on to become one of the most successful and consistent bands in the competitive and ever-changing world of Country music.

Just two short years after its formation Shenandoah not only had a record deal, but Marty and his band had their first hit song as well.

Success followed swiftly. In 1989, the band won The Nashville Network's Viewers Choice Award for favorite newcomer. That same year, Shenandoah's second album, *The Road Not Taken,* had three singles go to number one on the Country music charts.

Although Marty recollects thoroughly enjoying Shenandoah's success and his newfound fame as one of Country music's top singers, he remembers the price he paid for that success.

"I was drinking, carousing, lying—you name it and I was guilty of it. I was a hell-bound pagan before I fell in love with Jesus.

"The wild stuff just happened and I guess it started when I was about fifteen. I was playing in a bluegrass band and stuff like that and before you know it, this fella's drinking and, you know, I'm going to drink too. Everyone wants to be 'one of us' and the thing about it is that God just wants us to be one of Him.'"

Those early successful years were wild days for the rising young star, and through most of it Marty remembers always having a feeling that he was heading in the wrong direction.

"I didn't want to have nothing to do with the Holy Ghost. I didn't want to have nothing to do with no ghost. I mean, that kinda stuff scared me when I was little.

"But I also knew that I had grown up in a Christian home and I had made a commitment to God when I was six. I was running away from the Lord. The whole world had gotten ahold of me instead of God and I knew it. And I continued doing that even after I had gotten married.

"And, brother, I'm not even going to get into what drinking and staying gone all the time playing music can do to a family. I had little ol' bitty young'uns at the time.

"And although I was good to my young'uns and to my wife, when you're drunk you don't have to beat a woman to hurt her, you can abuse a woman with your tongue. Sometimes it's the things you don't say when you're drinking that can hurt someone. The Bible says that life and death are in the tongue."

Marty asserts that even during his most drunken moments he always felt "the Lord pulling on me. The harder I ran from Him, the more He kept pulling on my life.

"It got to a point where I started remembering what my daddy had told me. He had said one day, 'Son, you keep rejecting, you're going to get to a point where you're not going to get it.'

"I just kept feeling more and more in my spirit that things with me weren't right. I just started to feel like my daddy said, that I was going to die without Him—I really did and it worried me."

It was on one March morning in 1991 that Marty recalls awakening in the basement of his house with a severe hangover. "I was drunk as a skunk at eleven-thirty in the morning. I was burnt to a frazzle, at my rope's end. This was in my home in Alabama. And, brother, I'm going to tell you. I was feeling like a hell-bound pagan."

When he glanced at his reflection in the mirror, the face gazing back at him filled him with loathing. Marty recalls thinking during those moments that if he didn't soon mend his ways, he might wreck his marriage as well as his health and career.

"I told the Lord I wanted a chance to raise my young'uns in the way of the Lord. I told Him that I couldn't go one more minute, one more hour like this. I was scared that I was going to die and that I was going to die without God.

"That morning in my basement, I came to Him with a heart as humble as a child. I said, 'Lord, I'm as stripped down as I can be. I'm as low as I can get. Father, more than anything else in the world, I know that unless I change I'm gonna die without you. What I need Lord is you.'"

There is still a trace of awe in Marty's voice when he relates what happened next. "I started praying and then I felt the spirit of the Lord come over me. I knew the goodness of God.

"It was a miracle. I came to the knowledge, the understanding, the belief, the faith, the trust, and the hope in the Lord. That morning I was at the River Jordan and I felt in my spirit what I am today."

Marty recollects falling down upon his knees and continuing to pray. He repeats the prayer that he offered up to his Maker that morning:

> *"Lord, you can give up on me*
> *and that's fine, Lord, because*
> *of the way I've lived. And I*
> *have done some ugly things. And,*
> *Lord, I'm ashamed of myself. And*
> *I come to you, Lord God, broken*
> *because of the way that I've done*
> *the things that I've done. But,*
> *Lord, I pray and ask that you give*
> *me the strength and the health to*
> *raise my young'uns in the way of*
> *the Lord."*

"That's where I was. I wanted to be a better husband and a better father. I wanted to be a better witness to the Lord. And I asked Him to take away my old nasty drinking habit and to get rid of my yearning for cigarettes.

"He made me into a new creature that morning. I've not touched a drop of alcohol since that day and I have not longed for one. And I've not smoked a cigarette since that day. I was totally cleansed that day.

"My daddy used to say, 'Son, there'll come a time in your life when the things you once loved you'll hate. And the things that you once hated you'll love.' And when I became a new creature in Christ, the old things in life passed away.

"I didn't want to have anything to do with the old ugly ways. I didn't want to have anything to do with drinking or smoking like I did. I no longer wanted to have anything to do with anything that was not pleasing to God."

Although deeply religious, Marty emphasizes that his spiritual walk is far from being a perfect one. "There are still some bad habits I need to get rid of, and the Lord is working with me on that. He needs to mold me.

"I want to be a better daddy. I want to be a more loving husband. And more than anything else in the world, I want to be a bona-fide child of God."

In those moments after his religious conversion, Marty recalls eagerly climbing the basement stairs to the bedroom where his wife, Melonie, lay sleeping.

"I awoke my wife and I told her what had happened to me in that basement and that the Lord wanted me back real bad. I also told her that we were going to start going to church."

Marty still remembers the tears in his wife's eyes as she listened to what her husband had to say, and how afterward she gratefully embraced him. That Easter Sunday—and every Sunday thereafter—found Marty and his entire family in church.

Marty states that there have been many trials in his life since that morning in his basement, adding that his renewed faith helped him survive those difficult moments.

In late 1991, while in the midst of prolonged and bitter litigation over the band's right to use the Shenandoah name, Marty received even more bad news when he learned that his mother had been diagnosed with cancer.

"I had gotten tired running from God and I think that was part of His ultimate plan. He had restored my faith to prepare me for the lawsuits over the name Shenandoah and for what I was going to go through with my mother."

While the trademark violations case involving Shenandoah was successfully resolved, his mother's health continued to deteriorate. Remembering that time, the superstar's voice cracks with emotion.

"We were at the foot of her bed—my two sisters and my brother and my aunt—and we were praying for my mother. And just all of a sudden, I mean, I never in my life ever felt such an awesomeness of God. I was on my knees at the foot of my mother's bed and I couldn't move to the left or the right.

"It was like I absolutely could not move. Everyone in the room felt that. I realized that the most important thing in my life—my mother—was being taken care of. That God was in control.

"I knew it was He that had my mother's day numbered. He knew when He was going to call her and He knew what was going to transpire.

"We prayed and told the Lord that she was a good mother, that we loved her and that she loved us. We told God that more than anything else in the world, she was homesick for heaven and that she wanted to be with Him.

"We said, 'If she could remain, she would, but she wouldn't want to remain in this condition because she wouldn't be who she once was to us.' It was the truth. Mother was homesick for heaven."

Marty chokes back tears before continuing. "I said, 'Lord, I ask you in Jesus' name to take her.' And just that very second the angels came and got her."

That faith sustained him through Shenandoah's legal battles as well—a struggle, he recalls, that eventually forced the band to file for bankruptcy.

"We had lots of faith in God that we would succeed, and we came shining through. We went through a lot then as a band, but through it all the Lord continued to bless us. And all the bad stuff actually helped solidify our relationship with each other.

"I spoke to the Lord and I told Him, 'Lord, I'm trusting in you through these lawsuits, whatever the outcome may be.' I thought that if God wanted Shenandoah to be we would win the case and continue. And if it wasn't, we'd get another name for the group and start over."

For the singer with the heart of a preacher, prayer and faith remain important components of his life. "I talk to the Lord every morning. I need to be reminded that there's nothing I'll face that day that He can't help me through.

"The first thing I do in the morning is pray. I say, 'Lord, I know more than anything else in the world that you've got plans. And, Lord, sometimes those plans may not be the plans that I like. But, Lord, they're your plans.

" 'If you'll teach me humbly to abide and bestow on me and in me what you'd have me do, Lord, I'll walk with you. I know you'll be with me right by my side and that you'll never leave me nor forsake me.'"

Marty suggests that anyone struggling to renew their own faith turn to prayer. "Prayer makes things happen. As you grow into saying those words, before you know it you will be using your faith here and there."

He also counsels reading the Bible, as well as observing nature. "Watch a sunrise or sunset and then try to convince yourself that God's handiwork is not involved in such natural wonders.

"Most of all, all you need to know is that the Holy Spirit is there to lead you to Him. If He could lead a hell-bound pagan like I was, as lost in sin as I was, then He can lead anybody."

Marty hopes that his music also inspires people who are lost to God to return to their Maker. "We don't try to trick people by getting them to a Shenandoah concert and preaching to them. We don't want to browbeat anybody.

"We just try to keep things good and positive and hope that serves as an inspiration. We don't promote beer or broken relationships or glorify other negative things. We've been doing positive music for ten years. I just believe that our music is successful because God is in it."

The year 1995 was a special one for Shenandoah and its lead vocalist. Not only did the band net the prestigious Country Music Association's award for Vocal Event of the Year, but Marty was also honored by the Christian Country Music Association as the Mainstream Country Artist of the Year.

That CCMA award is something Marty is particularly proud of, because it honored his first effort as a Gospel singer—an album which he released simply titled *Marty Raybon*. That album, he asserts, gave him his first real opportunity to sing songs born of his faith.

"I wanted this album to minister to people that were lost. I wanted it to contain songs that would lift up people who are Christians that may be in the ditch and need to be lifted up a little bit.

"I didn't intend to get into this as a Gospel album. I just honestly and truly wanted to share my heart with people. I wanted them to fall in love with Jesus like I did. I don't want to force it on anybody, but I want them to realize that what I have ahold of is real."

Marty, who seemingly has just begun to stretch his talent and his calling, says of his future plans: "I just want to be a vessel of God. I'd be lying if I said I didn't want my Gospel album to do well.

"But more than that, I want those who hear it to hear God talking to their hearts. That's the real kind of music—the only kind worth hearing . . ."

Toby Keith

Toby Keith, one of Country music's newest superstars, was approaching thirty and feeling thoroughly discouraged about the slow pace of his career.

Although the Oklahoma native aspired to become a recording artist, what he found, instead, were jobs performing at local honky-tonks for beers and tips.

So the singer and songwriter set himself a deadline, asking God to let him know by his thirtieth birthday whether or not he should continue pursuing his dream.

Much to his amazement, just a few days before he turned thirty, Toby received a very special birthday present—a record contract!

With his 1992 Mercury Records debut album totaling sales of close to a million copies, and a current contract with Polydor Records, Toby has become one of Nashville's hottest new performers. In the wake of his success, the entertainer has not forgotten who is responsible for it.

"I owe everything I have to my Creator. I always keep my feet on the ground and remember who is really responsible for my career."

Toby Keith comes by his credentials as a blue-collar poet honestly.

The thirty-six-year-old husky-voiced, curly-haired singer and songwriter, who grew up on a farm just outside of Oklahoma City, has worked as an oil rig roughneck and operational manager, a test rider of bulls and broncos during his summers in high school, and for two seasons as a semipro football player with a farm team for the now-defunct U.S. Football League.

He also cut his teeth on a string of one-night and one-week engagements in the honky-tonks of Oklahoma, Texas, and Louisiana, something that thanks to his current success he no longer needs to do to earn a living.

With the release of his second album, *Boomtown,* Toby is today considered one of Nashville's brightest talents. When the superstar reflects on his current success, it is with the same no-nonsense manner that characterized his approach to his previous jobs.

"It's a job that involves lots of hard work and pays well," he states. "I just don't let it go to my head. I didn't have it easy getting here, because any kind of success is going to be hard, but now that I'm here I'm not a superficial person—I still drive my pickup."

Toby recollects a period in his life when he doubted all his struggles as a performer would amount to anything. He was nearing his thirtieth birthday, and the band he was playing with seemed to be spending more time traveling than earning money.

"I mean, when me and the band first started out it was great because we were going to a new town every week. We were going to towns that I'd never been in and traveling. It was neat. But after you've been to all those towns two or three times, then it just gets to be where you're playing in another bar.

"So the closer I reached to thirty, the more I began to face reality and get in touch a little more with myself and my prayers. I just didn't want to spend the rest of my life six nights a week playing in bars and honky-tonks."

That rigorous road schedule, he recalls, was also keeping him apart too long from his wife and kids. Toby remembers missing his family and wanting to spend more time with them.

There was something else bothering him as well. Toby had been raised in a religious household—the oldest of three children—and playing gigs in South Oklahoma beer joints made him feel as if he was betraying those spiritual values.

"My parents were hardworking farm people who were always giving the Lord credit for everything they had. I've never heard them as much as even doubt God in any way. They always taught me that. They taught me about Jesus and that I should never doubt Him.

"That's why what I was doing bothered me. I've always had a tight one-on-one connection with my belief in God. And I've always believed that you have to answer to your Maker when it's all over.

"And I felt like what I was doing was wrong—playing bars all the time and the drinking that goes hand in hand with being in bars. And there was no money in it. I was a regional act. I was struggling along there for eight or nine years."

Although Toby recalls often giving serious thought to quitting, it was no easy decision for him to make. Performing music was something he had loved doing ever since he was a youngster.

"I'd been singing about the Lord in churches from Oklahoma to Arkansas since I was old enough to sit upright," he recollects. "I remember this little bitty church way up in the sticks where my great-grandfather was the singing leader, the music director, or whatever.

"This was in the mountains over in Arkansas. We lived in Fort Smith, Arkansas, when I was a baby and about a hundred people would come down from the mountains on Sundays to attend this church.

"I remember my great-grandfather would stand up there—they didn't have microphones or anything—and just belt out these Gospel songs. It was great. And he and my grandfather were real instrumental in getting me singing and being into Gospel music at a real early age.

"And as long as I was in school and as long as I can remember I was always part of a choir or something. At church I would get up and sing all the time. I guess Gospel songs were the first songs I ever sang. I've always looked at Gospel songs as music and considered them as hip as pop music."

There was another, more practical reason why Toby couldn't leave his band—he wasn't skilled at doing much else. "I didn't have any serious trade because I came right out of high school and went into the oil field business.

"My dad had been in it thirty-five years and it was booming bigger than ever back then. But now the oil field wasn't for me because it had died. I about went bankrupt over that.

"And so that was a bad time in my life. There was lots of strife there. Lots of trials. So I got back to the only thing I knew and that was taking my band and trying to go make a living."

Mention of the oil fields evokes painful memories for Toby. He recalls having just graduated from high school at the time, excited about the prospect of working in the Elk Town, Oklahoma, oil fields, where he was hired as a roughneck. Things went well for a while, but then the times got tough.

"Elk Town went from being Small Town U.S.A. to boomtown overnight. They brought in fifteen hundred oil rigs and started pumping. For six years, you had corporate people coming in from Houston and Saudi Arabia.

"They built a Hilton, put a bar on every corner—there was even prostitution. Everybody had money—even people who were living under overpasses because there wasn't enough housing for everybody.

"Then the wells ran dry. The rich people got rich by saving their money and the fools who got it and spent it went broke. Even the Hilton couldn't maintain itself, so it was sold for ten cents on the dollar and it's now a mom-and-pop hotel."

Toby remembers being handed his pink slip. It was a disaster for the twenty-six-year-old, who by now was married. So Toby returned to playing Country/rock in local bars and honky-tonks.

Even when his band, Easy Money, finally began to take off and break out of the competitive Texas-Oklahoma dance club circuit to play more lucrative gigs at bigger clubs, Toby remained dissatisfied.

So the singer and songwriter devised a plan. With the money that he had managed to save, Toby purchased a Silver Eagle bus and began making trips to Nashville. In Music City, he would pound the pavements along Music Row, handing out his demo tapes to anybody who promised to listen to them.

"I had been to Nashville a few times. I'd cut some demos and did some sides with some of the different labels trying to get them interested in me, but I couldn't get anybody interested in my songs or in me as an artist or anything.

"And I was still thinking that I didn't know what I was going to do, because nothing was happening and the last thing I wanted to do is play bars the rest of my life.

"That's when I started this prayer—it was probably when I was about twenty-six—and I said, 'Let me know God by the time I'm thirty if this is what I'm supposed to be doing. Give me some kind of sign.'

"I would always be talking to God through my prayers. I would always say, 'If I turn thirty and there's not a tunnel with a light at the end of it that I know I'm supposed to go down, let that be my sign. And I'll go do something else.'"

As his thirtieth birthday rapidly approached, Toby recollects feeling discouraged about ever succeeding as a recording artist. "I was coming up on my thirtieth birthday and I was putting God in a bind.

"I've prayed my whole life, but I never asked for anything this specific. I was saying, 'Hey, show me which way I do need to go by a certain time. Should I not be doing this music thing?'"

What happened shortly afterward still amazes Toby and convinces him to this very day that miracles can happen. "It was now less than three months before my thirtieth birthday and the vice president of Mercury Records called me from Nashville. A tape with a bunch of songs that I had written had landed on his desk. He wanted to know if they were my songs.

"At first I thought he was wanting to pitch them to somebody else. He said, 'Are you singing these?' I said, 'Yeah.' He said, 'Is this your band playing on it?' And I said, 'Yeah, it is.' And he said, 'Could I fly in to see you do a live show?' I said, 'Sure.'

"He flew in Friday night and we played the show for him. I had a record deal the very next morning. I considered it a miracle. It was too big of a coincidence not to be.

"I had prayed for three years for God to show me the way I

needed to go. I had even put Him in a bind by saying I wanted an answer by my thirtieth birthday. And he answered me just before that time.

"I was in a bad situation—already sick and tired with my life and fed up. I was in a declining situation and I probably would have kept declining until I could do something else. But God had this plan for me."

Toby doesn't recollect undergoing a renewal of faith as a result of this experience. What he does recall is feeling a strong sense of gratitude.

"I didn't have a renewal because I never lost my faith," he declares. "I never doubted there was a God and I've never doubted His word. And I've never doubted His existence ever. And I believe I was rewarded for that."

As a performer with strong religious convictions, Toby offers that he is trying to impart some of those convictions to his two daughters. "I try to explain to my kids how important prayer is and to keep God in their life.

"I'm not with them as much as I should be, but when I'm there I'm making sure that they are understanding what prayer is about, and what kind of relationship you have to have with God.

"That's probably the most important to me—more than success—it's to know what my relationship is and to make sure that my children have the opportunity to have the same relationship with God that I do."

Toby asserts that he practices what he preaches to his daughters. "I'm not near perfect and I'm far from being perfect, but for some reason He's shined a wonderful light on me. And I'm very thankful." An important element of his spiritual life is daily prayer.

Despite such strong faith, the Country music superstar admits that there have been occasions when his faith was challenged. One such moment took place in the aftermath of the Oklahoma City bombing.

"I was doing a live radio special in Nashville at the time, and I didn't seem to have a care in the world. Everything in my life was going great. Then a radio station employee walked into the studio during a commercial break with the bad news.

"He looked at me and he said, 'Don't you live in Oklahoma City?' I said, 'Yeah.' He said, 'A bomb just went off there and it blew something up.' " Toby remembers how his heart sank. His family lived in Oklahoma City and he was suddenly frightened for their safety.

Although his wife and children were not injured in that blast, Toby concedes that the disaster raised questions in his mind about why God would permit such a terrible thing to happen. But that lapse of faith, he insists, did not last for long.

"I know other artists that don't believe in God and that'll be the first thing they'll tell you. They'll say 'If God is there and He's supposed to be a loving God, then why do these bad things happen?'

"All I can say for that is He's got His reasons for it happening and I'm not the one to doubt. He's too powerful for me to doubt. He knows why it's happening and that's His deal and He has control of it."

As Toby's popularity as a performer continues to soar, the chart-topping singer and songwriter discloses that he would like to undertake a project which may not earn him a gold or platinum record, but would reap great personal rewards.

"I might head up a project with all the people who are my friends to sing a Gospel album or something. I mean, I don't know exactly what. I'll just know when it comes. I think once God has given you talent He doesn't want you to waste it.

"He's given me talent, a good clear head, and a heart filled with conviction. Success hasn't gone to my head and I'm as down-to-earth as anybody. If there's something He wants me to do that will be a positive reflection on Christianity, then I'll do it . . ."

Mark Collie

Mark Collie's road to success has been littered with obstacles, the most serious stumbling block being a battle with diabetes that on at least two occasions has brought him to the brink of death.

Despite such impediments, the popular forty-one-year-old singer and songwriter contends that all the ordeals he has had to face over the years have strengthened his faith rather than diminished it.

The Waynesboro, Tennessee, native, who with five hit albums to his credit is today considered one of Nashville's most successful songwriters, as well as one of its hottest new singing sensations, views misfortune as an opportunity to learn important spiritual lessons.

Such lessons are given to us in this lifetime to better prepare us for the next, the MCA/Nashville recording star declares. "It's God trying to talk to you. He's trying to get your attention.

"It's not necessary to lose faith or get angry at God if something goes wrong with your life, just understand that God needs us to feel these things . . ."

Among Mark Collie's earliest memories of growing up in Waynesboro, Tennessee, a city located midway between Memphis and Nashville, are those that have to do with his religious home life.

He recalls that no sooner were the dinner dishes cleared from the dining room table than the conversation would turn to religion.

"We were a very strong Christian family and we'd talk about the power of prayer, faith, miracles—even life after death. These were things my parents strongly believed in. I've carried those lessons about faith and prayer with me all my life."

In addition to such religious discussions at home, Mark and his four siblings were also regular churchgoers. "Each Sunday we as a family would attend the First Baptist church in Waynesboro. I also as a boy attended Bible school."

Besides such obvious religious zeal, Mark at a young age also enjoyed performing music. At age eight he was already playing the guitar and piano, and by his twelfth birthday was a member of a local band.

"I don't know where I developed that love from. My sister played piano in church, and I got some of it from her. And my older brother, Steve, played guitar and I learned to play on his guitar. As I grew older, I sang in church and we had a lot of singing. And I also sang in a Gospel quartet.

"I just loved music all my life, but I never really thought, 'Well, I'll grow up and become a singer-songwriter.' I mostly just grew up thinking about getting out of Waynesboro and about going into the military.

"My older brother, Steve, was the first guy in the family to get a guitar, and he told my brother John and me that if we ever touched the guitar, he'd kill us. I was eight at the time.

"So, of course, when he'd leave, the first thing we'd do was get the guitar out." He chuckles at that memory. "It was a good way to teach someone to play. Buy an instrument and say, 'Never touch this.' "

Mark always seemed to love a captive audience, and as he became more and more proficient with the guitar, he soon found himself in demand at family get-togethers in Waynesboro. He would also some-times-perform on the Gospel circuit with his sister's husband and current road manager, Clark Rose.

"When I was young Clark used to take me along to play shows with him—mostly revivals or decorations as we called them—because he used to be a well-known Gospel singer in the area.

"He helped me a lot. He helped to keep me focused on the music business when I was just out of high school. When I wasn't singing with him, then during the week I'd work for his daddy hauling hay."

To sharpen his performance skills, Mark remembers slipping off to the Tennessee-Alabama state line where on weekends he would play at beer joints and honky-tonks.

"It was more rock 'n' roll than it was Country music that I was playing in those days, because people in the bars and clubs weren't dancing to Country as much as they are now."

Although he liked working clubs, Mark recalls that his enjoyment was tempered by a sense of guilt. "Playing clubs was always a very difficult dilemma for me. You're faced with all your church learning and then you're going out and making a living playing in roadhouses and bars.

"It was very strange. I would be singing in the roadhouses on Saturday night and then playing the revivals on Sunday afternoon. Many a Sunday I felt like the preacher was speaking directly to me.

"I struggled with that some, but at the same time I believed that the music that I wrote and sang was a very powerful, heal-ing, and inspirational thing that as human beings we need. Music is something that's a necessity to us. It's a reflection of our innermost thoughts."

To this day, Mark continues to view music as a vital spiritual outlet. "It's a way for us to communicate and understand each other better. And it's a way for us to celebrate. It's a celebration of the spirit. Even sad songs make us feel better. They make us connect and they make us feel not alone."

At age eighteen Mark remembers deciding that he wanted to become a professional singer and songwriter. By then, his mother, a factory worker, and his father, a photographer who suffered from alcoholism, had been divorced.

With his family torn apart, there was nothing much to keep the teenager from hanging around town. Mark took off to seek his fortune as a musician.

"That was in the late seventies. I wasn't too crazy about what was going on in Nashville, so I went to Memphis looking for whatever it was that Carl Perkins and those guys at Sun Records had."

Now living in Memphis, Mark continued to perform in bars and honky-tonks throughout that city and the Southeast. He remembers still feeling somewhat guilty about doing so. "It wasn't the healthiest thing for a kid my age to be doing. But there was no other outlet for me to learn my craft and to develop it while making a living."

Mark also recalls trying not to lose complete contact with his religious roots. He would regularly attend church services and continued to perform at revival meetings, but that did not stop him from being criticized for his behavior.

"I think some of the folks who preached at churches and revivals thought that maybe I was losing my way. I never felt like God was against what I was doing. I felt my music was God's gift to me. I needed to use this gift and wherever I had to go to do that, I did so.

"I know that—even today—there might be some people who think that what I'm doing is not right. There are people who think God doesn't like Country music, but I tend to think He does. I'm sure God's just like everybody else. Some records He likes, some He doesn't. He's probably got a collection of records that He listens to."

Looking back at those days, what upsets Mark the most is that he succumbed to the temptations of alcohol and drugs despite his strict religious upbringing.

"I've been exposed to everything you can be exposed to. There's no way to avoid it in this business. But I didn't experiment with *every* drug out there because I saw people who did and they were destroying their lives, and that was obvious enough to me.

"And besides killing people and destroying lives, I knew it was illegal. So I never had that kind of attraction to drugs. Alcohol, on the other hand, I think most people who are going to be around it are tempted. You're going to indulge in it.

"I never had a drinking problem—probably because my father was an alcoholic and I saw alcohol destroy his life—but I drank some even though I was raised in a Christian family."

Mark states that he has nothing against people who drink, unless they abuse alcohol. "I don't think that God frowns on people who drink alcohol, but I think that we have to understand that we're not supposed to abuse ourselves—whether it's food, alcohol, money, or any of the other things that tend to give us great satisfaction.

"Self-indulgence is against the teachings of Jesus and against the teachings of any religion or philosophy. It results in human loss. If you do too much of anything you're going to destroy yourself or your life will be ruled by it."

Mark remembers eventually growing weary of his Memphis lifestyle. He had just turned twenty, and upon taking stock of his life was not pleased by the progress he was making with his career.

"I was just playing at the music game. I rarely recorded the songs that I wrote. Many I didn't even write down. I don't want to try to remember how many songs I wrote and forgot to record."

Anxious to make a change in his life, Mark decided to follow a family tradition and join the Air Force. First, however, he would visit his brother in Hawaii.

After living for two years on the island, where he supported himself playing music, Mark was ready to return to the mainland for his physical. Upon completing his physical, there was some disturbing news in store for him—Mark learned that he was suffering from diabetes, and that he would require daily insulin injections.

"I was depressed, but I didn't lose my faith. I did go through a thing of trying to figure it all out, asking myself 'Why me, Lord?'

"Everyone goes through that for a short period of time. Then I thought, 'Well if I do have this disease it's probably going to kill me anyway, so I'm going to have a lot of fun before it does.'

"It was a reckless point in my life and it was a rebellious time for me. I used the disease as an excuse to be that way. I went through this denial period and I didn't take very good care of myself and I really am fortunate that I did outgrow that and got through that."

Mark, who today heads up a foundation dedicated to finding a cure for diabetes, recalls many instances when his reckless behavior endangered his own life. He remembers even ignoring his doctor's orders to test his own urine in order to monitor its sugar level.

"I was still devastated and in a denial period. And I started to drink a lot. It never took a lot to get me intoxicated, but with not taking the insulin and not eating right, I put myself at some real high risk with my drinking.

"Now I know that God's hand was on me during that time because there were some very close calls—there were times when I probably should have been dead. I had these insulin reactions. But I didn't die. And I wasn't really thinking much about God at that time."

Although ineligible for the Air Force, the twenty-two-year-old musician still wanted to get as close to the action as possible. Mark joined the USO as an entertainer, where he found himself performing for American troops in Iran just before the overthrow of the Shah.

"It was a pretty dangerous time to be in that area, but it was exciting to me because I thought I was going to die anyway, so I liked going into places like that."

While on a military transport plane flying from one remote U.S. outpost in Iran to another, Mark finally did come close to dying, nearly succeeding in taking his own life.

"I got off an airplane and I had taken my insulin. But the plane route was very long and there was no food on the plane—it was a military transport plane." As a diabetic, Mark was required to eat at regular intervals after each insulin injection, but he had not taken any food along with him.

"I had a real bad insulin reaction and I went into a coma. They got me to a Dutch mission hospital out there in the desert and they were trying to inject pure glucose in my bloodstream to get my blood sugar level up. It had dropped to zero and there was no oxygen going to my brain.

"They kept sticking me and I kept jerking and I was having convulsions. I would jerk the IV out of my arm. I know that God intervened there, because even the doctors thought it was pretty miraculous that I had recovered.

"That was the most amazing thing—that I didn't have any brain damage even though I was out so long with no oxygen going to my brain."

When Mark finally emerged from his coma he was in for a shocking surprise. "I came out of it and I opened my eyes and one of the Dutch missionaries was giving me last rites, asking me if I knew Jesus Christ.

"I couldn't see all too well yet because my vision hadn't entirely come back. I could mostly just hear this voice. And I was trying to tell him, 'Yeah, I know Him very well.' I couldn't even figure out what I was doing there.

"When I finally could see clearly and the doctors came in, I saw that I was totally covered in blood and everybody in the operating room was covered with blood and I thought that the plane must have crashed."

When Mark learned what had happened, he remembers feeling grateful to God for being still alive. Yet despite his gratitude, there was no accompanying renewal of his spiritual life.

"I didn't think about that until later. I just felt that God wasn't ready for me to die, and that I should probably get my act together and take a little better care of my health in case I did have long to live."

Mark failed to honor that resolution. "I started to, but part of the problem was being a young kid and not knowing much about my disease. I was still kind of going through the denial stage.

"I just never really realized that not only could diabetes kill me, but if I took the wrong amount of medication—if I didn't keep it in balance—that could also take me out. I sort of had this James Dean syndrome, live fast, love hard, and die young."

There were other episodes where Mark nearly died because of his own negligence. "I had several of those, but I remember this one particular night in Memphis when I was driving home from a gig. I had an insulin reaction from drinking and I drove through a light and ended up in some guy's living room. I was in a coma.

"I was totally stiff with my eyes wide open, but I was blind and unable to speak or move. They rushed me to the emergency room and I was revived again."

Even after that close call, Mark continued to drink against the orders of his doctors. He remembers one morning waking up with a hangover that made him "feel like hell." Gazing at his reflection in a mirror, Mark recollects despising the face that stared back at him.

"I was twenty-five years old and I thought, well, it's possible I can live a long time but I don't want to feel like this my whole life. I realized what a foolish and ignorant way of life I was living and if I was going to be in the music business and write songs, I should be more serious about it."

He still might have continued to ignore his own best advice had it not been for meeting Anne, an attractive young Memphis artist, whom Mark fell in love with and married. It is Anne whom the multitalented performer credits the most for turning his life around.

"I met her in Memphis—we had been friends way back—and she probably helped save my life because she talked some sense into me. She helped me to chill out a little bit. She convinced me that I had talent and that I should work hard to make it in the music business."

Anne's concern for him and her unswerving faith in his talent touched him deeply, he recalls. "I decided then that I wanted to live, and that I wanted to live every day to its fullest. So I refocused my life.

"I thought, 'Well, I do have this ability to write songs and to make music, and I should focus whatever days I have left to doing that.' I really became committed to working as hard at that as I was at trying to kill myself. So that's what I started doing."

Mark also underwent another important change. For the first time in years, he began to pray. "Every time I would go home it wasn't only me who was praying to straighten my life out, but my wife, my mother, and everyone else in my family. We have some pretty strong prayer words in our family, and I'm sure it was all this prayer that ultimately helped me."

In 1982, Mark and Anne left Memphis for Nashville, where the young musician hoped to find work as a songwriter. "I knew that a lot of new talent was also being discovered there. Guys like Ricky Skaggs and Randy Travis were starting to make it in Nashville. So I thought I'd give it a shot."

Unable to find a job, Mark recalls becoming discouraged. A new addition to the family brought even more financial pressure to bear on him. "We had a child and I was writing bad songs, trying to write what I thought other people would want, and getting no place."

Adding to his family's financial difficulties, his son, Nathan, was born two months prematurely. Without any medical insurance, the young couple were barely able to pay for the cost of their infant's special medical treatment.

"I was really discouraged, but even to that very moment I never lost my faith. I just felt that He needed me to go through these things—things only He could understand. I just knew that my failures had nothing to do with God because He didn't care anything about the Country music business.

"It wasn't necessary for me to lose faith and get angry with God just because things were going wrong in my life. I know that everybody at some time or other has been a little bit ticked off at God—I had done that myself after I learned about my diabetes. But He is the last person you should blame. I just knew that He had some reason for me to feel and experience these things."

In the meantime, Mark had decided to quit the music business and look for steady work. But Anne wouldn't hear of it. "I told her I was going to give up the chase, but she told me that if I gave up music she was going to leave me. She didn't give me any choice. She was serious."

Anne also remembers that moment. "It wasn't a case of love being blind," she recollects. "I didn't want him to give up because I just knew that he had talent."

Mark recollects that Anne had another suggestion. She would get a steady job doing art work, while he continued to pursue his career as a songwriter.

Mark agreed, while also deciding on a new course of action. Instead of writing songs for other musicians, he would write his own music and perform it himself.

"I went back to writing the kind of songs that I liked to hear, that I didn't mind singing. I got my old band from Memphis back together, and we started playing around."

Nights would find Mark and his band performing at Nashville's Douglas Corner Café, where the audiences sometimes numbered fewer than twenty people.

But as word began to spread about the talented young entertainer, Mark soon found himself playing to standing-room-only crowds.

In 1989, Mark arranged a showcase, inviting record company executives and the press to hear him perform. Among those seated in the audience that evening were MCA/Nashville Records executives Tony Brown and Bruce Hinton. The record company executives were so impressed by what they heard that Mark was signed to a record contract the very next day.

His debut album hit the Top Sixty on the Country music charts, while his second album did even better. A song that Mark co-wrote with Don Cook called "Even the Man in the Moon Is Cryin' " went to the Top Five, and the Country rocker's days of scraping by were finally over.

Reflecting on his present-day success, Mark attributes it to his renewed commitment to God. "There's an inner voice in all of us and you have to listen to that voice. God is never far away," he asserts.

"But until you try to listen for His voice—until you really try to look for Him—you won't know He's there. If you listen, you'll hear God trying to talk to you. He's trying to get your attention.

"I listened to that voice when I went out and decided to start playing songs that were an honest expression of myself. And if you're also honest about what you're doing, then eventually you'll make good music or write good songs."

Speaking from his own experience, Mark suggests that anyone struggling with turmoil in their lives hold firm to their faith, as he has done. "Sometimes those are wonderful, joyous experiences that He gives us and sometimes they're the most tragic, devastating experiences that you can imagine.

"But when you see the tragic things happen, what you're actually seeing is God's work because He's trying to teach us something with this. When we lose a loved one or we find ourselves with a disease that's going to kill us, we start to wonder why. But we won't know why yet.

"We will understand it at some point. He wants us to be better and stronger and to have a strong spirit and to have understanding, and sometimes this is the way He works it.

"Just keep in mind that whatever is happening to you is only part of our life experience. We experience heartache and all these things because God needs for us to feel these things. He needs for us to understand these things. We can only know Him better through these experiences . . ."

Ricky Lynn Gregg

During a one-year period of time, singer and song-writer Ricky Lynn Gregg went through a painful divorce, his mother's heart attack, the death of a beloved pet, and two serious injuries that nearly ended his career.

The thirty-four-year-old Texas native and part Cherokee Indian emphasizes that through it all his faith sustained him. That faith came into play again when the Country music star helped a dying boyhood friend renew his connection to God.

Such experiences prompt the Liberty Records star, who has two albums, six videos, and more than seven singles to his credit, to testify that God is a daily part of his life. Ricky affirms that he will never make a life or career decision without first consulting Him . . .

The youngest of five brothers, Ricky Lynn Gregg grew up on his family's one-hundred-acre watermelon farm in Longview, Texas, where he can still recall an incident which early in life helped to shape his religious faith.

The soft-spoken, long-haired performer was a nine-year-old at the time, working in the field with his father. Ricky remembers reaching down to pick a watermelon, when a sharp pain shot through his hand.

"I can still see this big, black, furry spider biting me right on the middle of my finger. It scared me. My dad was out in the field plowing at the time, and I ran to him and I pulled him off the tractor.

"And this spider was black and it had a dot on the top of it. I thought for sure that it was something bad. And my dad he got down off his tractor and he knelt down with me and grabbed me by the hand and he prayed to God."

That scene remains indelibly etched in Ricky's mind—a profound and unforgettable memory of faith in action. "My dad prayed that whatever it was that bit me, that God would take care of it right there and then.

"And, you know, I'm walking back to the pickup truck wondering whether I'm going to be okay or not. But my dad, he just got back on his tractor and he believed without any doubt that I would.

"It turned out that it was a cotton spider, which is black and furry and it's got a white dot on it—not like a black widow, which is black and smooth with a red dot on it.

"Here I was, a nine-year-old boy, and I didn't know the difference. But it didn't matter what kind of spider it was to my dad, he just believed God would take care of it."

Ricky, who is one-eighth Cherokee on his father's side, was raised in both the Southern Baptist and Pentecostal churches, along with the unique spirituality known to Native Americans. He can recall other incidents in his life when prayer was also the answer to a family crisis.

"You see, my dad was a farmer and he didn't believe in the doctor too much or the dentist too much. And he didn't believe in taking me to a doctor until I had suffered for three or four days and it was obvious that I wasn't going to get over it. He was big into prayer—a very spiritual man—and that's the way we did it at home. We would pray for healing.

"My mother was the same way. She didn't take me to a dentist until I was thirteen years old. She not only gave me my life, but my strong morality as well. They both did. They were both strong role models."

Ricky recalls it was that kind of upbringing which led him to embrace religion at an early age. "There was a Trinity Baptist church down the street, and I used to go there a lot. I was drawn there. And I was almost six when something compelled me to go and give my life to Jesus, and I asked to be saved."

Besides religion, Ricky also recollects enjoying music. "I started singing in church when I was a kid. I remember standing on a chair at the pulpit next to my father and singing with the choir."

That love of music remained with him. Besides singing, the youngster became proficient at the guitar, bass, and harmonica. While still in high school, Ricky was already performing at local honky-tonks.

At age nineteen, after managing to save enough money, Ricky moved to Dallas/Fort Worth, where he began playing his high-octane brand of Country rock with a band named Savvy. It was Ricky who penned all the material for the band's first album, *Made in Texas.*

In 1983, his career got a major boost when the Texas Music Association presented him with multiple awards as Entertainer of the Year, Male Vocalist of the Year, and Musician of the Year.

After several years of fronting his own Ricky Lynn Project, he joined one of Texas's hottest bands, Head East, as lead singer and guitarist.

Ricky began making trips to Nashville to work with songwriters there, continuing to perform as well as write his own material. With his flashy, demonstrative stage style, the good-looking, six-foot-one entertainer quickly earned himself a solid concert following—and a record contract.

Recalling the years of struggle before he was signed, Ricky describes them as "turbulent" ones. "They were a roller-coaster ride. And although I had been a sinner—drinking, profanity, rudeness, chasing girls—I was never that awful.

"But I was one of those kids that even though I was saved and had God in the back of my mind, I would go out and get drunk. And every time I got drunk and threw up, I'd be sitting over a commode and telling God, 'I ain't gonna do this again.'

"I had a lot of guilt from doing some of the things that I did. I've done a lot of things that have been habitual, but I've never done anything that was addictive."

Ricky contends that although one of the biggest achievements was signing his record contract, that feeling did not surpass the one he had in 1994 when he was able to bring a dying friend back to God.

His soft-spoken voice takes on a solemn note as he reminisces about that experience. "Mike and I used to have the same interests when we hung out together. He was one of those guys, you know, who we never got on each other's nerves. We'd go to sporting events and have a great time and he enjoyed different things, not just music.

"He was thirty-six years old when he got cancer, and he only let a few people know about it. In the five weeks before he died he had no choice but to let other people take care of him. His mother was bedridden and living out East with his brother, so he was alone.

"I would see him in town before the cancer got really bad, and I'd bring him food and stay with him if I had the time. Then they called me in Baltimore and said he didn't have more than a week to live."

After hanging up the phone, Ricky recollects being enveloped by a feeling which he had never experienced before. "It was kind of miraculous—like I felt compelled by God to go to Mike."

That following morning he was at his friend's bedside. "I would begin to pray and cry and talk to him. This guy wasn't a spiritual person. And God put a heavy burden on my heart to make sure he was saved. He didn't grow up having religion in his life the way I did.

"I was praying to find a way to reach Mike spiritually, and I opened my Bible and I read where I opened it, hoping to get a sign. I landed on Second Corinthians, Chapter 5. And, of course, it's talking about going from the earthly body to the heavenly body.

"I talked to Mike about that and it opened the door for us to start being able to read the Bible together. He was still timid in a way, but we'd pray together. And he'd cry. I think he was filled with joy of the spirit.

"One night I was by his bed and he had fallen asleep. He woke up and he wanted to hug and wanted a good cry, and he repeatedly said, 'You pray with me.' "

It was a spiritual breakthrough that brought tears to Ricky's own eyes. Somehow, he had managed to instill into his best friend some of his own love of Jesus.

"My faith and spirituality are extremely strong," Ricky proclaims. "But at this moment in my life it was as if God had taken me over and used me as a tool to save this soul.

"And I was swept up by it all. I asked Mike, 'Are you ready to receive God in your heart? Jesus in your heart?' And he looked at me and said, 'Yes.'

"I told him to ask God to forgive his sins, and then I told him: 'Mike, you're going to heaven.' Those last days before he died he would tell people how jubilant he was that he'd been saved."

Ricky pauses for a moment to collect himself, still moved by the memory of those final moments with his dear friend. "It taught me a lot. It's taught me to appreciate things differently. All of a sudden, I wanted to be a giving person. And I wanted to change my own life. It took Mike's death to make me feel that way.

"I'd been a sinner, but I learned from Mike that it's never too late to accept God and change. It took Mike that eleventh hour to accept God, but I know he has a home in heaven."

Ricky now turns the clock back to 1992, when he recalls how faith and prayer helped him cope with a series of personal disasters that included a painful divorce, the death of a beloved family pet, serious hand and leg injuries that threatened his career, and his mother's heart attack.

"The divorce came about because we weren't getting along. And in the process of doing that I had to give up custody of my child. I'm telling you, the devil was drowning me in guilt to a point where I'm surprised I made it."

Ricky remembers how in the aftermath of that painful separation he fell down on his knees and prayed for strength to sustain him through his ordeal.

He believes those prayers were answered when one afternoon he received an unexpected visit from a former girlfriend. "She was my first girlfriend from high school—and she had become a very spiritual person. She had turned her life around at some point.

"And she showed up from out of nowhere and brought me a Bible prayer book. It was another miracle that all of a sudden she would come into my life and get me on the right track. It was kind of overwhelming evidence of the power of prayer and my faith that God would guide me."

Ricky recalls learning a technique from his friend which not only comforted him at the time, but one which he continues to utilize to this very day. "I found this way to thumb through the Bible, stop at a page, and find messages and passages that were comforting to me. I found myself doing this more and more.

"Doing this would help me understand what I was going through. I began that miracle of using the Bible that way, and it was overwhelming what came into my life as a result. All of a sudden I got a record contract. All of a sudden I had a hit song. All of a sudden I was out there doing everything that I had dreamed of doing.

"It was miraculous. Jesus came back into my life and people would come into my life who were spiritual and I could just tell that there was an army of faith that helped make things happen. That Bible was the start of my spiritual renewal."

Despite the good things that were beginning to take place in his life, more misfortune soon followed. Several months after his divorce, Ricky got into an automobile accident and suffered a serious hand injury which he worried might bring his career to a halt.

"I was on my way to a golf tournament at the time and I was stuck in heavy traffic. There was a blinding sun in my eyes and I became confused and I made a wrong turn and smashed into a car.

"I splintered my guitar-playing finger and I had to have surgery to put the thing back together. I thought for sure that my career was over."

Although Ricky was able to resume performing, more ill luck continued to plague him. Two weeks later, Ricky's mother suffered a serious heart attack. That was followed by an incident while performing onstage where he tripped and broke an ankle.

"It was a wet stage and I really had to keep the faith when that happened. My mother was in the hospital, I had just had surgery on my hand, and now, boom! I fell and broke my ankle.

"It was at that point that I made up my mind that this is when I needed to be the strongest with my faith—now that I was so down. And I believe that helped me heal faster. I was healed in about a month, which seemed like no time to me."

There was still more calamity to come. A beloved dog that Ricky had since he was a child suddenly became critically ill. "I cried my eyes out when I found out he was about to die.

"I sat there and I held him in my arms and I said, 'I don't care if it costs me a thousand dollars, you're gonna have one more good day in your life.' And I made sure that dog had two wonderful months before he died."

By this time, Ricky and members of his band were beginning to suspect that there was more than coincidence involved in this string of calamities.

"My band's very spiritual and theological in the sense that we've discussed the Bible on several occasions. This was one of those times where, you know, everybody was wondering what was going on.

"We had something good going for us and we believed that the devil wanted to ruin it. He wanted to smash what we had and make sure that things were agonizing for us."

Ricky remembers gathering his band together where a decision was made to fight back. "It was because we were spiritual people that we prayed as a group to fight this evil entity that we all agreed was after us. We joined hands and prayed together. We did this on a day-to-day basis, and the wonderful thing is that we won.

"My mother had a miraculous recovery and I got to release my second album and we continued to tour. We didn't miss one show during the time all this was happening. I think it was the sheer determination of the human spirit to defeat evil fueled by faith and heavenly spirit."

As a result of that experience, Ricky is convinced that "If you're not spiritually guided, then the devil will eventually find a way to really get to you." It is a lesson that the Country music star tries to share with others—but not too forcefully.

"Right now my light's shining brightly, but I don't want to blind people with it. I don't want to push what I know on people. It's just that I feel more zest for life and I feel more compassion for people than ever before.

"I feel people just need to be told that with faith, miracles can happen. I know they happen because I've seen them and experienced them. And I also know that with prayer, the devil can be defeated. I want people to know that we have choices.

"We can choose good over evil, we can go up or we can go down. God gives us crossroads. All we need to do is keep the Holy Spirit in our hearts to deal with these choices and the right ones will be made."

Ricky also wants people to understand that if they are searching for renewed faith in their own lives, "All they need to know is that Jesus is their only way. That's especially true if they're hurting and do not have peace of mind.

"And if they can't figure that out by themselves, they should go to someone who is in the ministry, or who is spiritual, and learn more about what comfort Jesus Christ has to offer. Ask a lot of questions and don't expect your faith to be renewed overnight. Just be patient."

Looking toward the future, Ricky states that he is leaving the direction of his career up to his Maker. "I know that you cannot push God's fate, so I'm looking to find out where He leads me. If God intends that I have a number-one hit, I'm sure it will happen.

"He'll make it happen because He knows I'm a spiritual person and that I would use my success in the right way. And if it doesn't happen I certainly won't be disappointed in God.

"I'll just know that there's a reason for that. And it also might be God's way of testing my faith. And I'm up for the challenge . . ."

Susie Luchsinger

Spousal abuse was the last thing on Christian Country star Susie Luchsinger's mind when she fell in love and married rodeo champ Paul Luchsinger in 1981.

But Susie soon discovered that her handsome new husband had a temperamental side to him which could turn as nasty as one of the steers that he wrestled.

Their marriage soon disintegrated into one that, for Susie, was at times a frightening nightmare of physical, verbal, and emotional abuse. For fourteen years Reba McEntire's baby sister lived life as a battered wife.

It would take a special church service, professional counseling, and what Susie ultimately learned was the most important ingredient of all—faith—to turn her marriage around and create a loving relationship . . .

It was at the 1980 National Rodeo Finals in Montana where Paul Luchsinger, a professional steer wrestler, first laid eyes on the pretty redhead from McAlester, Oklahoma.

At the time, Susie was attending the finals with her older sister, Reba, who was scheduled to open the competition by singing the national anthem. When Paul first saw Susie, she was collecting tickets for a dance following the championship event.

"I noticed right away he was pretty good-looking—you know, a hunk," Susie smiles. Mutual friends set them up and the young couple began dating.

Susie recalls that in some ways Paul was an odd sort to her. While she had grown up in the rodeo—her father was a world champion steer roper and her grandfather was a rodeo cowboy—Paul was a city boy from New Mexico whose father worked in construction.

And while her pursuits had always been creative ones—Susie loved to sing and had been performing with her brother and sister since age seven—Paul was a much more physical type. He had always been interested in becoming a professional football player or a wrestler.

Also, when they first began seeing each other their spiritual lives were entirely different. Paul had experienced a religious conversion in the late 1970s after becoming fed up and depressed with a lifestyle of too much drinking and partying. Susie, on the other hand, came from a family which did not place great emphasis on religion.

For Susie, who grew up in Atoka County, a small ranching community in southeastern Oklahoma, religion meant mostly attending church with her grandmother and occasionally taking Bible study classes.

Both her parents were hardworking people—her mother worked for the Superintendent of Schools, while her father was a rancher and rodeo cowboy—and didn't have much time to devote to religious instruction at home. So it was Susie's grandmother who became her main spiritual influence.

"My mama and my daddy went to church some, but I don't

remember going to church with them much. They used to say, 'Y'all go to church.' It was just a little ol' country church near where we lived. But it was my grandma who took us kids. She and my grandpa were a little Baptist, mostly Pentecostal.

"My grandma was the influence in my Christianity, but she didn't sit down and drill me about Christianity or anything. She mainly showed me the Lord by her actions. She was very patient, very kind. She worked very hard—she and my grandpa grew vegetables and stuff —but she was also a fun-loving woman."

The award-winning vocalist was age twelve when she recalls first embracing God. "I went to a Baptist church revival in Kiowa and walked down the aisle and accepted the Lord and was baptized. I knew that I needed the Lord. I knew that there was a void in my life from all the seeds that Grandma had planted in my life.

"But then life rocked on—the pressures of junior high, high school—and I turned my back on the Lord. I said, 'I want to do what I want to do.' And I was caught up in a lot of peer pressure to go out and party and drink and date boys.

"And so, by the time I got through college, I was pretty well fed up with my life. And I knew I was doing wrong—you know—going out and drinking and all that kind of stuff.

"But it was like Satan was feeding me a lie and saying, 'Well, you've already messed up anyway. Your God could surely not love you.' And that's exactly what I felt like he was saying to me. There was a war raging on the inside of me.

"And yet when I'd commit those sins, it was like God was saying, 'You don't need to do this.' And the devil was saying, 'Aw, you might as well go ahead because He doesn't love you anyway.' "

Upon graduating from Oklahoma State University in Stillwater, where she majored in Personnel Management and took a minor in Accounting, Susie accepted a job with an oil lease company in Oklahoma City.

"The Lord really wasn't dealing with me then. I continued doing what I wanted to do. I had a friend who also worked in the oil business and he would ask me to go to church with him.

"And he would look at me at times when we were going out and say, 'You know, you don't really need to do all the stuff that you're doing.' But I did it anyway."

When Reba asked her younger sister if she would be interested in working for her band as a backup singer, Susie eagerly agreed. "I went to work with Reba, but I was still pretty much running from the Lord. In the meantime, me and Paul met."

That meeting would gradually begin to change Susie's lifestyle. "When Paul came to see me he'd have the Bible open and the Christian radio station going in his car. And I'd think, 'Oh well, here he is, a Holy Roller,' " she laughs.

Only later did Susie realize that Paul was testing her. "He had become born again, and he was praying for a Christian wife. So what he was doing was putting the pressure on me—you know, 'What is she going to do? Is she a Christian or isn't she? She says she is, but she isn't living the life of a Christian.' "

Although Susie recalls initially resisting those pressures, eventually she began to surrender to her new boyfriend's influence. "Going out and partying wasn't as nice as it used to be after I met Paul. It just wasn't as neat."

Meanwhile, the young performer continued to pursue her singing career. Susie had always been drawn to music. It was an interest that dated back to the seventh grade when she began touring with her brother, Pake, and Reba, as the Singing McEntires.

Susie had learned to sing from her mother as the family traveled together on the rodeo circuit where her father worked as a cowboy. She recalls sometimes even singing in hotel lobbies where rodeo folk gathered to swap stories and songs.

Working as a backup singer for Reba gave Susie even more professional experience. She appeared with her sister's band on the "Grand Ole Opry" and the "Hee Haw" television show, as well as at concerts and fairs across the country.

As Susie's relationship with the handsome steer wrestler deepened, she remembers feeling more pressure to change her lifestyle.

"One night I was in my apartment and I was ironing some britches all by myself—nobody was there—and I didn't have any television show on or music or anything like that.

"And I was thinking about how fed up I was becoming with my lifestyle. I said, 'Lord, if you're still there, would you show me your love?'

"All of a sudden it was like He poured a warm oil from the top of my head to the bottom of my feet. It was like He showed me his love. I mean, I could feel the presence of the Lord—His love going all over my body."

Although it was a transformational moment in her life, Susie still chuckles at the image of herself receiving God while she was ironing some clothes. "Yeah," she laughs, "I was doing something as simple as that.

"The neat thing about it is that a lot of people classify being in tune with the Lord as you've got to be on your knees and you've got to pray for twenty minutes crying and shouting, and maybe you have to be in a church, or somebody has to be laying hands on you.

"But that moment proved to me that God heard me right where I was. And He knew where I was and He wanted me to be with him. I was so excited about it but I couldn't get anyone on the phone—I couldn't even reach Paul. But that was my personal coming back to the Lord."

On November 27, 1981, eleven months after meeting Paul, Susie married the good-looking rodeo performer. Although she cites her marriage as one of the happiest moments in her life, upon reflection Susie admits that neither she nor Paul was prepared for the commitment that marriage involved.

"Paul told me, 'You go ahead and do what you're doing and I'll continue doing what I'm doing.' So I continued on the road singing backup for Reba."

It was not an arrangement designed to bring two people closer together. Instead, the Christian Country music star describes her marriage as "two single people living in the same house. It was a license to sleep together, but there was not much more to it."

Even after the birth of her first child, she and her husband found themselves spending more time apart than together—each of them focused on their individual careers. The only thing that had really changed was that Susie was now performing with her brother, Pake, instead of with Reba.

It was the 1980s, an era when duets were trendy in Country music, and in 1981, Susie found herself working hard with Pake and their backup band to capitalize on that interest. She remembers taking little Eldon Paul, her baby boy, along with her wherever she performed.

By now, it had become obvious to both Susie and Paul that their marriage was not working. Quarrels between the young couple had escalated to the point of abuse.

"Paul was angry inside," Susie recalls. "You would never have thought that he would be an angry person because he was so jovial and happy-go-lucky. Everyone loved him and nothing ever bothered him.

"They even called him 'Lucky,' because everything always went well with him. I mean he was a natural at everything he did. But underneath it all he was a very angry and insecure person."

There was one morning just before Paul was leaving for a rodeo in Texas when he became particularly angry at his wife. "For some reason he got mad and went into the bedroom. And I was in the living room. And he slammed the door so hard that it went past the doorjamb. And he couldn't get out. So he had to bust the door down to get out."

Observing her husband's rage so frightened the young singer, that she recalls becoming fearful of her husband from that moment on. "That was the first time I'd ever experienced someone to be so mad at me. I mean, my dad had gotten mad at me, but never like this. I became afraid of him and I stayed afraid of him for a long time."

Although their marital problems continued to worsen, the young couple kept their domestic problem a dark secret. Susie remembers being too embarrassed to discuss what was going on in her life with anybody—even her closest friends.

"We came to a low point in our marriage and I thought it was going to end. There were power struggles and a lot of pride. We were walking on eggs all the time."

Worsening the situation, Susie remembers that Paul was growing increasingly jealous of members of Susie and Pake's backup band. This would also cause him to fly into fits of anger.

"I knew I wasn't going to cheat on my husband. But I'd be doing a show, and during the break Paul would come in and rake me over the coals. I'd be crying and upset, and then I'd have to get back up there and put on a cheerful face and sing."

If he was jealous of the men who surrounded her, Paul was also jealous of his wife's growing success. She was becoming a nationally known celebrity, while he worked in relative obscurity.

Susie remembers turning to her church for some answers, but those answers weren't quickly forthcoming. "We were going to church, but the church wasn't really showing us how to deal with our problems.

They would preach that we needed to be born again, and that we needed to rededicate our lives.

"But no one could tell me how to live with a person that seemed angry toward me all the time. There was no answer for me about how to deal with this. I continued to walk on eggs all the time."

Despite their misgivings that renewed faith could resolve their problems, Susie and Paul decided to listen to their pastor and give it a try. They would rededicate their lives to God. The couple also agreed to make their marriage—rather than their careers—the central focus of their lives.

"We rededicated our lives to the Lord in 1984. We went to the Day Spring Church in Atoka, Oklahoma. And I quit singing Country music with my brother. Paul and I now traveled together as a family. I'd say it was probably the first step in our healing because we needed to be together.

"The Lord told us that morning, He said, 'A house divided will not stand. I want you to go together as a family. You need to be together because this individual lifestyle is tearing your marriage apart.' If we hadn't gone to that service I don't know where we'd be today. I think it would have ended in divorce."

That rededication service would also have a major impact on Susie's career. She was abandoning a flourishing career as a Country music singer—one that she had worked long and hard to establish.

Although Susie recalls having some initial anxiety about doing so, when the time came to make that decision, it was not as difficult as she had expected it to be.

"I'd never been really happy singing Country music. So much of it was about turmoil and fear. God didn't want me to be singing in bars and honky-tonks to people too drunk to care what I was singing about. God wanted me for His service. He wanted my talents to be used for people's good, to get them into a relationship with Jesus Christ.

"Sure it was a step out in faith. A lot of people might have called it blind faith because I quit a career that was growing to sing Christian music. And I only knew two Christian country songs at the time. So to most people it would have seemed idiotic, but God told me to do this and I was going to follow Him.

"I mean it was plain and simple. I knew that God had spoken to us and had said, 'I want you to go together as a family and I want you to sing songs for me. I want you to sing my kind of music.' He also took it a step further. He said, 'As you sing, people will be turned to me and they will be healed.' "

Susie soon found herself performing Christian Country songs with a more positive message and enjoying it. She also liked traveling the rodeo circuit with Paul and booking dates along the way.

The couple would also attend cowboy chapel services together and, sometimes, even lend a hand to the rodeo preachers—an endeavor that some years later would lead to their own full-time rodeo ministry.

Their marriage seemed to be headed on the right track, although as things would turn out there was more healing that needed to be done.

"There were still some problems with anger, bitterness, and abuse in our lives," she recalls. "We were still fighting, still bickering, and there were still power struggles."

For the second time, their marriage began to untangle. Matters came to a head one evening when Paul became so physically abusive to her that friends had to separate them.

"We were with Marcy and Jim Scott, the guy that led Paul to the Lord. Paul got angry with me about something and he pushed me up against a wall.

"Jim got in Paul's face and said, 'Hey, brother, that's not the way marriage is supposed to be.' He said, 'I want to walk you through this thing and we're going to come out on the other side.' "

It was a tense moment. Susie feared that with Paul's temper, he would become enraged at his friend for interfering in his private business. Instead, her husband expressed remorse rather than anger.

"We stayed at their home and spent countless hours talking and hashing things out, hashing feelings out. Shortly after that we went to a seven-day program of counseling and healing in Idaho, and then we went to numerous retreats. We were starting to rely more and more on faith to get us through this period.

"It never came down to me being disappointed in God that we again had problems with our marriage, I just felt there was something wrong and that we needed to fix it. I cried out to God a lot, but I always felt that God was with me.

"I just had faith that God could heal this marriage. I knew that

God had put Paul and me together, and He just had to get us straightened out so we wouldn't kill each other."

For Susie and Paul, much has changed in their marriage since those days. "We're just like every other married couple," she declares. "Sure we have problems, but there's been a big change in the guy who used to holler at his wife and pound on doors. We feel we can testify that if you have faith in God, He can heal marriages."

That message is one which the couple try to bring across to their audiences wherever they are invited to speak. "I think we need to give back what God gave to us, so we minister mostly to the rodeo cowboys or western-type, farm-type people. We go to a lot of rural areas and we testify about our marriage."

Another way that Susie shares her message is through her music. In the more than nine albums that Susie has released since 1985, one can find songs that she has written like "Real Love," which talks about commitment, and "That's When the Real Love Starts," about couples loving each other through the hard times as well as the good ones.

Susie, who was voted Female Vocalist of the Year by the Christian Country Music Association both in 1994 and 1995, hopes to continue writing such positive lyrics.

"Paul and I had what the world said we needed: money, success, security. But we were still falling apart. Jesus healed our marriage and brought peace, love, and joy back into our lives. Through my music I want people to know that He can do the same thing for them . . . ."

Paul Overstreet

Grammy Award–winning singer and songwriter Paul Overstreet was an eighteen-year-old fresh-faced kid when he first arrived in Nashville with a guitar in hand, a couple of hundred dollars in his pocket, and a dream of someday making it as a Country music star.

Although he would eventually realize that dream, it came attached with a high price tag—a struggle with alcoholism.

When the forty-two-year-old Newton, Mississippi, native eventually wearied of that lifestyle, he turned to God to help deliver him from his alcohol dependency.

It was not a change which would come about overnight but

through a series of "small steps," which the Country music star compares to "tumblers" on a combination lock.

Since that day in 1985 when the combination finally clicked into place, the multifaceted entertainer, who has won more than a dozen major songwriting awards and has numerous hit records to his credit, has ceased his dependence on alcohol.

Paul is hopeful that through his music he can assist others struggling with an addiction to find the right combination which will open their hearts to God's changing powers . . .

Paul Overstreet's bedrock Country ballads portray a world where romance is always in bloom, love goes right, and the focus is on a happy family life.

The superstar of Country music songwriters leaves it to others to write lyrics about cheating hearts, Sunday morning hangovers, and breaking up.

It is his positive approach to songwriting which has earned him two Grammys for Best Country Song, ten Top Ten hits as a recording artist, and at least a dozen other major awards. He has also earned a solid reputation as one of the most important songwriters to emerge in Country music in the past decade.

"It's a lot harder to write positive songs than it is miserable, heartbreaking, cheating songs," he submits. "But I feel we should encourage people toward things that are good for them."

Paul's own life reads like one of those "hurtin' songs" he has tried to avoid writing. The talented singer and songwriter was six years old and the youngest of five children when his parents were divorced. Paul's father, a Baptist minister, took off for California, and the Overstreets' happy family life was forever shattered.

The singer and songwriter recalls that before his parents' divorce, religion played a primary role in his family life. "We'd go to church all the time, and when we didn't go it felt really strange to me.

"I felt like church was very important to me even at that early age. But the major religious impact in my life was later on when I became baptized when I was about nine."

Following his mother's second marriage—one which was also not destined to last—Paul recalls that there was a lessening of family religious life. His new stepfather turned out to be an alcoholic who seemed more interested in his next drink than in scripture.

"He had a lifestyle of drinking before he married my mom, and after he married he stopped for a while. And he went to church with us and stuff. But he wasn't the spiritual leader of our family—my mother was. Then he started drinking again, and hanging out at truck stops. That's when this marriage fell apart."

Although the house was always filled with his brothers and sisters, Paul remembers feeling lonely and missing his father. The disheartened teenager soon became a rebellious one.

"I was starting my teenage years and I felt like everyone was against me—that the world was against me. I didn't like my stepfather because he had been in the military and he had all these rules and regulations. We had a real strange relationship."

Paul believes he would have continued behaving rebelliously had it not been for a missionary couple who one day arrived in town. "They really spent time working with the kids in the church. They had children so they understood things that kids liked to do.

"We started doing some fun things with them. Whenever I was looking for some guidance they were there to help me. Knowing that was real pleasing. It was a pleasant time when God was working in my life."

Paul recollects that the atmosphere at home was always a tense one due to his stepfather's drinking. At age sixteen, while a junior in high school, the teenager decided he had had enough. Paul took off to live with his brother in nearby Prentiss, Mississippi.

He remembers enjoying life in Prentiss for about two years—playing some football and graduating from the local high school—before deciding to visit another brother who lived in Waco, Texas.

"I went out there for a while and got a job as a mechanic's helper with the Young Brothers Construction Company. And I saw a concert one night in one of the nightclubs with Tanya Tucker and Johnny Rodriguez.

"I saw what they did. They came out onstage and sang their songs and I thought, 'Man, I think I can do that.' I'd been playing in a band in high school. I had even made a record when I was in high school and had sold it in my hometown.

"One thing led to another and the record got some attention

from a guy in Nashville. So I left shortly after that and went to Nashville."

Paul was eighteen at the time. He remembers arriving in Nashville with a couple of hundred dollars in his pocket, a dream of becoming a Country music star, and the notion that his money would last him until he attained that dream.

"I thought it would happen quickly because performing was something that had always been a part of what I did—even before the high school band. As a kid, about eight years old, I was playing and singing at family gatherings, ice cream suppers, and so on.

"Throughout junior high and high school I entered talent contests every opportunity that came around. I guess if I really stopped to think about it, I probably wrote songs to have something to sing."

Although he was armed with the cocky confidence of a teenager ready to set the world on fire, Paul remembers that his spiritual life was on the back burner. "I kind of had walked away from faith back then. I just kind of wandered away from it. I don't know where it was then."

When his money finally ran out, Paul found work welding the bottoms of hot water heaters and working as a carpenter. Things improved for him a few months later when the struggling young musician landed a twenty-five-dollar-a-night job performing two nights a week in a club located in Nashville's Printers Alley. That led to more club work, and soon Paul was able to devote full time to playing Country music.

As the months passed, Paul began to feel that he was not making much headway with his career. "I just kind of ran into brick walls wherever I turned. One thing led to another and I got a little more heavily into drinking. I started hanging out in bars and I started playing clubs. I was there six nights a week in clubs.

"I was drinking every night because I really couldn't stand to be in those places unless I was drunk. At first I was having fun, but after years of it, it started to be a habit. And then marijuana became a daily part of my life for a while."

For the next five years, Paul continued to play bass, drums, and guitar in clubs and on the road with a variety of bands. There was one evening, just before he was scheduled to go onstage in a club somewhere in Columbus, Georgia, that Paul remembers feeling completely fed up with his lifestyle.

"It was around 1978. I just started realizing that I was going nowhere and could rot in these clubs. Everything just started kind of getting old. I remember that this club owner had come up to me and she said, 'You drink too much.' She was even concerned about me.

"It was all these little bitty things that started to make me realize that I was going nowhere. I also realized I wasn't going to be able to quit drinking as long as I was playing in these clubs.

"So I prayed that night. I had prayed a little before, but never about something like this. I said, 'God, if you'll get me out of these clubs I'll quit drinking and smoking.' "

It was not long afterward that Paul received an answer to his prayers. "I got a phone call from someone from a music publishing company who was interested in listening to my songs. They had tracked me down on the road, which is really unusual. So I saw him and I wound up getting a job at a publishing company writing songs."

Although impressed at how quickly his prayers had been answered, Paul sadly recalls that he failed to keep his word to God. "I kind of let the promise go to stop drinking and smoking. I just had so many things going on in my life—I felt trapped, you know."

Several more years would pass before Paul again became determined to straighten out his life. "It was 1984 and I just got *really* sick of everything. I didn't like me and I didn't like music anymore. I didn't like what I was doing writing these songs I didn't believe in.

"But I was afraid to quit. I was afraid I'd end up doing some boring job again—that I would be living some boring life. That's what really kept me from surrendering to God.

"I also thought that if I surrendered to God He would make me repent by sending me to preach in some small country church or in Africa someplace," he chuckles.

"I thought one or the other was going to happen to me, because that's what I had seen happen with people who had repented when I was growing up. Little did I know that when I finally did surrender to God it would be the most exciting life that I could imagine."

In the meantime, Paul began taking steps to turn his life around. He even began staying home at night to study the Bible. "I'd stay home as much as I could because I knew that if I went out I'd get drunk."

One evening while at home reading the Bible, Paul remembers turning on the television set and tuning into a program where Billy

Graham was conducting one of his crusades. He recalls becoming transfixed by what he saw.

"When the broadcast was over I called the show—there was a number that came up on the screen. A lady answered the phone and I had her pray for me.

"She prayed for me and told me things like she knew me. I just couldn't believe she would even know about some of the things that she was praying about for me.

"It was just really incredible and it had a major impact on me. I believe to this day that her prayers for me were heard and answered, because a lot of the things she prayed for happened."

Paul believes watching that television program was the second "tumbler" on the combination lock which, when it finally clicked into place, would renew his spiritual life. "My spiritual renewal was like little tumblers on a combination lock. Every little tumbler meant something.

"At that point I had realized that I was powerless over some of the things that had me in bondage—the alcohol and the lifestyle. Now I had surrendered to God—surrendered my life—and I was getting closer to that door opening and I would be freed."

In the months to come that door would open even wider when he met and fell in love with a young woman named Julie, whom Paul would eventually marry.

"I wasn't looking for someone to make me happy. I was looking for someone to share what was happening in my life. I wanted someone to share God with and someone to share the nights and days and seasons of my life with—not someone who I could lean on."

Paul remembers being elated when he learned that his future wife shared the same goals. "I think that's why it was real incredible when Julie and I met because we were both kind of looking for the same thing. We started growing together."

By New Year's Day 1985, Paul had not only quit drinking, but he had also joined a Bible study fellowship, vowing to devote himself to God and his wife.

Paul states that joining the fellowship was the final click of the combination lock which would open his heart to God. And he remains grateful for that religious conversion.

"God was so faithful to me, even though I had been in a bad place. He heard my prayers because He can see through all that. And now He started blessing me with songs being recorded and stuff like that. Most of my success came after that."

Today, keeping pace with Paul's achievements isn't easy. His *Sowin' Love* album, which he recorded for RCA, yielded a string of hit singles for Paul and went on to sell more than 250,000 copies. It also inspired two critically acclaimed music videos.

"There was a time when I'd pick up my guitar to sit down and write and I would try to think of something really sad and miserable to say about myself," he reflects. "That's what Country was to me—just a lot of sad, miserable songs. The sadder and more miserable, the bigger the hit.

"And then I read in Scriptures and in some other literature that what we tell ourselves our subconscious believes. I mean, our subconscious doesn't really know if it's true or not. And if we tell it bad things about ourselves long enough, we may believe it and we may act it out.

"And so I started writing things that only had positive things to say. I was trying to change my own way of thinking. And then all of a sudden I started feeling better about myself. It was having an impact on my life.

"I started believing good things about myself and I started seeing them happen in my life. And I just went, 'Man!' and for me that's enough reason to keep writing that way."

With his smooth, persuasive vocal delivery and obvious delight in the subject that he is singing about, Paul sweeps the listener away with his storytelling skills and positive lyrics. "I feel very strongly about positive messages such as love, forgiveness, hope, sharing, and caring," he declares.

The award-winning singer and songwriter utilizes the same positive approach in his personal life. "I deal with challenges in my life by thinking positively, and then getting on my knees to pray to God and tell Him that I believe in Him."

Paul encourages anyone facing challenges in their own lives to follow his example. "Tell Him that you believe there is a Supreme Creator that created all of this—heaven and earth. And that you want Him to reveal Himself to you.

"And look out! I'm telling you. That's all you've got to do. Just ask Him. He doesn't want anyone to perish. So just ask Him to reveal Himself and He will."

Although acknowledging that many people consider themselves unworthy to be loved by God, Paul believes such thinking is often inspired by the devil. "It's a trick of our spiritual adversary to make you believe that. If you start believing that you'll never get over your hurdle —whatever it is.

"There were so many times I used to say to myself, 'Golly, how can I pray right now the way I'm acting?' But that's the very time I needed to pray. That's why I say pray no matter where you're at, because when you do, it has an impact."

The Grammy Award–winning songwriter, who in 1991 made history when BMI Nashville named him its top songwriter for the fifth year in a row, offers that his favorite prayer is "The Lord's Prayer," and that he recites it daily while meditating upon its words.

"I dissect that prayer line by line and really try to expound on what it's saying. By the time I get to the end, I've covered a lot of material."

Although he often prays on his knees, Paul adds that his hectic schedule sometimes prevents him from doing so. "Most of the time when I'm in my room I do it that way.

"But if I'm sitting on an airplane or some other public place I pray and talk to God without getting on my knees. It's always different. Each day brings with it a different prayer—a different concern."

In many ways, Paul Overstreet views himself as the prodigal son. "I foolishly went out on my own and blew everything away in the process. Now I've come back to Him and He doesn't hate me for it. All the angels in heaven rejoice when a sinner comes home.

"So if you've been a sinner, read that Scripture in the Bible. You can be in the worst place and He can see through all that. Just have faith that He loves you no matter where you are . . ."

Ken Holloway

Some ministers deliver their message from a pulpit, while others use books, tracts, or cable TV to share God's word. Christian Country music star Ken Holloway, an ordained minister, spreads his message about the power of faith and prayer using simpler tools—a resonant voice, a guitar, and a host of great Country songs.

Once a featured attraction in the bars and honky-tonks of his native Lafayette, Louisiana, Ken, who in 1995 was named Entertainer of the Year by the Christian Country Music Association, eventually wearied of that lifestyle, yet was unable to walk away from it.

It would take a prayer and a most unusual response to that

prayer—a barroom brawl—to open his eyes and finally make him see the light.

Since then, the thirty-four-year-old performer, who for two consecutive years was voted Male Vocalist of the Year by the International Country Gospel Music Association, has been playing an entirely different tune.

Nowadays Ken is no longer performing songs about cheating hearts, false starts, and lost weekends. Instead, he is bringing to his audiences a more healing message—one which uses the power of Country music to touch peoples' hearts and lives . . .

At age twenty, Ken Holloway was already earning himself a reputation in his hometown of Lafayette, Louisiana, as a talented acoustic guitar player.

The youngest of four children, it was a talent which came to him naturally. Ken remembers always being surrounded by music, proudly noting that his father was even something of a locally well-known musician himself.

"They offered my daddy a record deal when he was in his early twenties. They drove down from New York to meet with him. This was before I was even born.

"He told them no. He said, 'I'm just a little ole Cajun down here. All I want to be is a family man and I'm not interested in being a star.' But he always loved music and he taught me and my brothers and sisters the little tricks of the trade."

The award-winning performer with the Cajun roots recalls being a bit shy, at first, about singing in public. He slowly gained confidence performing weekends at bars, dance halls, and honky-tonks where "people couldn't care less about a ballad that was really a tearjerker. They just wanted songs that they could dance to."

His reputation as an exceptional musician eventually grew to a point that when Country music star Sammy Kershaw arrived in Lafayette to give a concert, it was Ken whom he hired to back up his act.

It was an important career boost for Ken, removing him from the category of local talent. The young musician now had the sheen of a celebrity about him—after all, he had been up on that stage with none other than recording star Sammy Kershaw.

"All of a sudden I got a lot of notoriety and everybody wanted me to play and do this and do that. Things started to steamroll and my career was starting to take off."

Ken recalls there was a harsh price to be paid for his newfound recognition. Success brought with it a lifestyle much different from the one in which he had been raised—a strict moral upbringing where he had been taught early in life the difference between right and wrong.

"There wasn't really any spiritual background in my upbringing, but we grew up with great morals. My dad was a jack-of-all-trades and he did a lot of work on cars and stuff, and my mother was the kind of person who worked hard and stayed home with me and two older brothers and an older sister.

"It was my dad who drilled into our heads about having great morals and stuff, and about being hardworking. His number-one priority in life was teaching us how to work and demanding that we respect him and my mother.

"My mother would always teach us about trust. She would tell us, 'I know you're going out with your friends, but I trust you. You're going to be okay.' Those words rang in my head all the time. These two people were not only my parents, but they were also my friends.

"They both came from families that worked really hard and they passed that down to us. Even after I became a Christian they said, 'Listen, you may be a Christian, but God's not going to deliver everything to your front door. You're going to have to get out there and work for it.'

"More than anything else it was a good, clean upbringing—you know, don't steal, don't rob, and try not to lie as much as possible. It was that kind of thing. But now I was doing things that I knew would make my mom and dad feel ashamed.

"I remember the first year I started playing I couldn't sing while I was drinking a beer. I mean, if I was drinking at any time I would stop, knowing I had to sing.

"Well, toward the end I couldn't really sing well unless I was drunk. I mean the tables began to reverse and the drugs came in and that kind of stuff."

Although he had succumbed to such temptations, Ken recollects that he was never quite comfortable with his new lifestyle. "Deep inside

I knew it was wrong. And I knew that I had to get away from all this, but I just couldn't."

In 1984, the six-foot, 190-pound long-haired performer fell in love with and married Connie Robin, a pretty local girl, who came from a religious family. Like her parents, she also frowned upon drug and alcohol usage.

Ken recalls that the marriage made him feel guiltier than ever about the lifestyle he was leading. "My mind and my flesh kept telling me that I wasn't running around or cheating on Connie—I mean I would just play my music and go home to her.

"But the drinking was starting to destroy our marriage. It was falling apart because I was drinking so much and staying out so late all the time.

"When Connie became pregnant and didn't want to come out with me, I said, 'Well, I'm going out. I don't care. Do whatever you want to do.' Things were falling apart and she knew it and I knew it."

There is still a trace of regret in Ken's voice as he recalls those days when he would be out all night performing cheating-heart songs and getting high, while unknown to him Connie would be at home praying that he mend his ways.

"She had met the Lord already and she knew that prayer and faith could change things. She told me later that every night that I would go out and play and carry on she was on her knees for me."

Back then, however, Ken paid little attention to his wife's expectations for him. He recollects being too busy chasing his dream of Country music stardom. And to satisfy that dream, he would do whatever was necessary to get ahead.

"For as long as I can remember—as far back as five and six years old—I was this kid who would be strumming a stick behind the house and saying, 'Hey, I don't want to be a farmer and I don't want to be a cop. I don't want to be none of those things.

" 'I want to be a Country music singer. And if I don't become a Country singer some time in my life and make it big, I'm going to be disappointed the rest of my life.'

"It wasn't for the money, it was for the music that I did what I did. I wanted to play music so bad that my biggest fear was that now that I'm finally starting to get popular, really starting to have a career, what am I going to do? Become a Christian?

"If I became a Christian, then I'd never play music again. Musicians like myself are some of the hardest guys to reach spiritually because we feel way deep down inside that we've worked all our lives to get where we're at, and we're not going to give it up to become a Christian.

"You know, I've had some great job offers. I was even offered the job of vice president at the company where my brother works. I said to him, 'Man, if I do it, my heart won't be in it. Music is what I live and breathe.'"

By now Ken's drinking had gotten so out of hand, that even some of his closest friends were urging him to slow down. He remembers paying little attention to their advice. "I just figured that if it was really wrong, God needed to show me."

Ken recalls one particular morning when he returned home to his wife after a night of heavy drinking. "I was stone drunk that night and crawled into bed hoping that Connie wouldn't wake up and see me in that condition. But as soon as I did she rolled over, took one look at me, and began to pray for me."

As drunk as he was, Ken remembers how affected he was by his wife's prayers for him. "No one had ever done that for me before. The impact was incredible. Two weeks later I gave my life to the Lord at a revival meeting. It happened at a time when I was at the lowest point of my life with all my drinking and the other stuff.

"There was like a big old empty hole in me. And I just knew I had to become a Christian in order to make it to heaven. That night I ran up to the altar. I wanted all that God had for me."

Despite his religious conversion, Ken still found himself unable to resist the temptations of drugs and alcohol. "When I became a Christian I said, 'I don't want to drink anymore. I don't want to do any more drugs.' I prayed to God to just let me sing.

"But every night that I would go to play in a club I would struggle with my decision to do that. I was praying, but in all honesty I wasn't praying that hard for God to show me how to quit, because I still really didn't want to.

"I knew that if I continued to play in the clubs I'd continue to be subjected to temptation. And I often was. I just knew that there was no way I could continue to play those clubs and live a Christian life. I knew it, my friends knew it, God knew it, and my wife knew it ahead of all of us, I think, other than God."

Ken recollects that despite his guilt, his alcohol and drug dependency continued. The singer and songwriter remembers one evening when he literally exploded at his wife for daring to tell him what deep inside himself he already knew—that he could not continue to live both in the world of spirit and in honky-tonks.

"Connie kept telling me that after giving my life to the Lord, the first thing I needed to do was leave the clubs. And I said, 'Well, I don't think there's anything wrong with it. I don't find anything wrong. I'm not doing anything wrong.' "

Looking back, Ken says he now realizes what an outlandish self-deception that was. At the time, however, he simply wanted to believe it was true. He continued to fear that if he quit the club circuit, all the professional momentum he had built would be lost.

"I still just wanted to be a singer. Meanwhile, my wife continued to pray and have faith that God would show me what I was doing was wrong.

"So now I was going to church on Sundays, and smelling from the smoke and the beer from the night before. But I didn't think anything of it. I thought, 'Hey, I'm here in church. I'm a Christian now and that means that I'm serving God.' "

Ken is convinced that his wife's prayers—and his own—were finally answered one evening as he was preparing to go on stage at a local club called Cowgirls. As Ken reached for his guitar, he remembers uttering a small prayer.

"I said, 'God, if it's wrong for me to be playing here, you can just show me. And if you show me, I'll quit.' And I'm telling you, I was just sitting there on that stage and playing when a fight broke out at the bottom of the stage.

"When I looked down at that scene I suddenly saw some of the things that I was doing in my own life. I saw this guy in the corner who was doing a couple of lines of cocaine. And I looked at this guy sitting in another corner who was an alcoholic and who probably had a family waiting for him at home. He was just sitting there stone drunk.

"And I thought, 'Man, I don't want this. I don't want this.' It was as if God had suddenly snapped His finger and took all the desire for this kind of lifestyle out of my heart. I looked at all this and I said this is who I'm entertaining and I don't want to do this anymore.

"I was just blown away. And this fight is going on around me and some of my best friends are involved in it. I just looked around at all this like I had never noticed it before.

"And then I see this drunk sitting in the corner waving me on and yelling at me to keep singing. 'I love your voice,' he says to me, 'give me another beer,' and then he's yelling at me to sing another song about cheating.

"I thought, 'No, no, I don't want to do this anymore.' I stood up, put the mike on the stand, and I just walked off the stage. The band just kept playing and they were looking at me. I'm sure they were thinking that I really needed to use the rest room real bad, because I'd never done anything like that before.

"I just walked off the stage and walked out of the place and never looked back. I never went back and I told the owner of the club that I would never play Country music ever again in a place like that. I walked away and I've kept my promise ever since."

Ken remembers debating what to do next, when Connie offered him a suggestion. "She said, 'Maybe you can be the one to bring Country music into the Christian market.' And I said, 'Those people aren't waiting for me.'

"Back then I kept saying 'I don't even like Christian music, so why should I want to sing it? I think it's boring. I don't think there's anything out there unless it's Country.' "

Still, without much else to do, Ken decided to give it a try, performing at revival meetings and just about anywhere else that Christian music was being listened to.

His preconversion career as a honky-tonk crooner transferred well into his growing reputation as a purveyor of Christian Country music. Ken developed an anecdotal, sometimes storytelling style, and a large following as well.

It did not take long before he was approached by the Ransom/Brentwood label and offered a recording contract. For Ken, it was the beginning of his dream come true—in the most unexpected way.

"I look back and I'm actually honored that God had enough faith in me to take me out of those clubs and away from the things that went on there. He actually put me in the forefront of Christian Country music.

"My wife and I just talked about this a couple of days ago. I said it all seems weird because a few years ago people couldn't care less what I had to say, and now people want to know what I have to say.

"Knowing that God would trust enough in me to do something like this really blows me away. Just knowing that God called me to sing Christian Country music and positive Country music, and to minister to my family, and to minister to folks who don't know me—it's a humbling experience for me."

Ken confides that ever since that night when he walked off the stage at Cowgirls, he has been trying to make amends for his former way of life. Becoming a minister was one way for him to do so.

"One day after I was doing a concert at a church, and after I finished the show, the pastor said, 'Man, you need to get a license.' I said, 'Why?' He said, 'If you get ordained and get a license, it will just open more doors in the ministry for you.' He told me that I was already doing ministerial work during my shows."

Ken remembers accepting the minister's advice, and how difficult it sometimes was to walk that path. "It was a real struggle for me to pursue this ministry. Sometimes I felt like I was falling to pieces and I got angry at God. But I didn't fall to pieces. I fell to my knees. God led me through those difficult times and He never let me down."

When he is performing onstage, Ken declares that he is not up there saying, 'Hey, look at me, I'm a Christian and I've got a perfect life and everything is normal.' No, I battle with everything normal folks do.

"I'm trying to show folks that if we're human, and that if we care, there will be big successes in our lives. I try to explain to people that we all make mistakes, that we all fall short, but that God will take you just the way you are—not the way you think you need to be.

"What I'm trying to do is reach out with love through my songs and try to bridge the gaps between people, and between the world and the church."

He also likes to remind his audiences that he considers himself more of a spiritual person than a religious one. "I just knew that I had to become a Christian in order to make it to heaven. When they began to show me the Bible, I thought, 'Wow, how could I not have known about all this before?' It literally changed my life.

"But when people say to me, 'You're one of those religious singers,' I can't stand it. I say, 'Man, I'm the furthest person you'll ever find from being a religious singer. I sing in jeans and belt buckles and stuff. But I've got a relationship with God and that's what separated me from my past.'

"I mean, there's a lot of people who walk around and who talk the talk but don't walk the walk. My family and I, we're regular churchgoers when I'm in town and not on tour, and we serve God the best way I know.

"I try to live a Christian life as close as I possibly can, but I'm not going to get in front of people and become someone else just to make me look good and to have them think, 'Oh, he must be a very religious person.'

"I'm not going to run around and say things that I don't mean and do things that I don't mean. When I say something or do something, I mean it. There's a lot of people who walk around and point their finger at everybody else and say if you don't come to my church, or if you don't worship God my way, you're not saved.

"I'm just not like that. When I do something or say something it's not for show. Besides, I figure I've got enough problems keeping myself straight—much less somebody else."

Having now firmly established himself as one of the top-ranked stars in the Christian Country music field, Ken offers that he is eager to perform more secular Country music without compromising any of his spiritual values.

"I've just got signed by this label—B&G—which means they're taking me into the mainstream market. This same label offered me a record deal five years ago. They wanted me to sing cheating songs and I said no.

"I've turned down three or four offers with record companies that wanted me to do that. And with this company I fought long and hard to not let them make me compromise with the lyrics.

"Now they've come back and they've picked me up as an artist and I'm still going to be able to do what I want to do—which is really, really rare in the music industry.

"I'm going to be able to sing songs about faith and God and about a wife and husband either struggling to stay together or happily staying together or whatever. Songs about family. That's really my niche. That's really where God's called me to be."

Ken's best advice to anyone interested in renewing their faith is to read the Bible. "That's the first thing that I would recommend. It was an unknown thing to me until I became a Christian. Now I pray whenever I have the opportunity.

"Next I would find a good church to go to and start a relationship with a pastor who can help and guide you to become a Christian. That's what I did. I would go to revival meetings with my wife, and there was that one night that it changed my life.

"And if you feel shy about praying, then just have a conversation with God. You don't have to fall down on your knees. Just talk to Him. Think of Him as a really good friend. I guess that's the best way to describe it . . ."

Kent Humphrey
(MidSouth)

In 1987, when a band he was performing with split up, Kent Humphrey, now lead vocalist with Bobby Bowen of Mid-South, found himself suddenly out of work.

The thirty-three-year-old Kentucky-born singer and songwriter prayed for his career to get back on track, but it would take almost four years and a near loss of faith before those prayers were finally answered.

That experience taught the Warner Alliance artist an important lesson about the nature of answered prayers, and the value of having patience when it comes to God's timetable.

"We often want things to happen right now when we pray, but God doesn't always work that way," Kent declares. "It's just when we say to ourselves, 'What's the use?' that we have to put our faith in the Lord . . ."

Kent Humphrey was raised in a family where his father and grandfather were both preachers.

It was the kind of upbringing where if he and his two younger brothers weren't in a Methodist or Baptist church listening to one family member or another preach, they were usually there singing with their folks as part of a Southern Gospel quartet.

"We were the kind of family where every time the church door was open we were there," he laughs. "Church has always been a big part of our lives and singing is also something our family has always done.

"I can't recall a time in our lives when someone in our family wasn't performing music, somehow. Even, today, my mother still sings with my dad.

"I remember that as soon as I was old enough to be traveling with my dad on the weekends and singing, that's what I was doing. It's just one of those things that kind of got bred into me, I was doing it at such an early age."

Even as he grew older, Kent recalls that religion and music continued to remain part of his life. "I sang Gospel music with my father and my brother and friends with different local Gospel groups up and through my high school years. I did that until I got my first paying job on the road when I was seventeen."

The Paducah, Kentucky, native offers that while his family grew up materially poor, they were wealthy in the kind of respect that they received from their neighbors.

"Going to church with my parents and grandparents, I saw the esteem that they had in the community for the lives that they lived. Religion wasn't just a Sunday kind of commitment for them, it was an all week long one.

"People knew that they lived what they talked about. That really left a lasting impression on me growing up about how you can live your life and be respected for it."

Another lasting impression that Kent has of life in Paducah comes from the stories he heard as a youngster about townsfolk who had strayed from the spiritual path only to later turn back to God's fold.

To this day, the Country music artist remains grateful for never having had to undergo such an ordeal. "I've heard some people with some great testimonies about how they came out of some terrible things in their lives.

"Although I feel for those people—and I don't want to slight anybody who has gone through hard times, or has been into things that got them into a lot of trouble but now have made a change in their lives, because that's a great testimony to have—for me I was just blessed that I didn't have to.

"I'm just thankful that I was blessed to have a Christian family all the way around me—from grandparents to aunts and uncles. It was a different world for me.

"I just got involved in the things of the church and that kept me busy and I enjoyed them. For me that was a great comfort. I didn't have to go through a lot of things that I saw people around me going through. I learned that you could avoid them if you really try and keep your faith."

Despite having been raised on such solid spiritual footing, Kent concedes there have been tests of faith in his life, and he is not certain that he always passed them.

"There are periods still when I go through hard times and my faith has been challenged. It's easy to sound like a super spiritual guy, but we all go through the same struggles on a day-to-day basis.

"At times when problems get overwhelming, there's a tendency for me to think, 'What's the use?' But that's when we have to put our faith into the Lord, and place things back into His hands."

Kent recalls that his toughest test of faith took place back in 1987, when the North Carolina band he and his brother were performing with split up. Kent remembers worrying how he would support himself and his wife.

When no other opportunity to perform presented itself, the unemployed singer recalls reluctantly accepting a job which he detested—as a delivery driver in Philadelphia, a city where his wife's family lived.

"I was performing a little music here and there, but nothing like I had done as a professional musician for seven years. So I was very unhappy and saying, 'I don't really understand you, God; you gave me talent to sing and I've been able to use it and things have been going great, but all of a sudden it's done. Now I'm doing something that I'm not happy with.'

"It was a real hard time for me. In the beginning I thought, 'Well, you know, this will last a few months and I'll get back into the music thing.' It didn't. I stayed out of performing for almost four years.

"That was probably the time my faith was tested the most. I knew what the desires of my heart were, what I wanted to do, yet they weren't happening."

Although he prayed regularly, Kent recollects that the years passed with no opportunity presenting itself for him to perform with another band.

"I was trying to be faithful to where God had me at that particular time in my life. I would say, 'I know, God, that you're going to have me here for a little while. And I can live with that. I just want to do what you want me to do.'

"But as the days went on and the months went on, it got a little harder to pray and believe that God had everything under control when you knew what you wanted to do, yet I was feeling so frustrated."

Kent is convinced he would have completely lost his faith had it not been for his wife Marie's encouragement. "She was so supportive that she lifted me up. She was always that way. She told me to continue believing that God would change things."

Her words proved to be prophetic when Kent received a phone call one evening. By the time the conversation was finished, his prayers had finally been answered—Kent had just been invited to join Mid-South, one of the hottest groups on the Southern Gospel concert circuit.

It was a band that Kent had become friendly with during his own days of performing on the road, and over the years he had stayed in touch with the group.

He had even once filled in for a band member who became injured during a scuba diving accident. Now he was being invited to become a full-time partner in that band. His days as a delivery driver were finally over.

"Things changed for me overnight. This just came out of the blue. God opened a door for this to happen with MidSouth, for me to come in and be a partner. It was an answer to my prayers and it was just great."

Sweetening the deal, Kent would again be performing with his brother, Darren, who only a few months earlier had also joined Mid-South.

"My brother and I had played together in our first band in North Carolina. And when that disbanded we thought we'd never get to play together again.

"So this was a dream come true for a lot of reasons. One of them being that we were actually going to get a chance to travel the country together again.

"It did take quite some time for this to happen, but it was absolutely an answer to my prayers. And I was able to learn and draw from my experience. Through the situation that I found myself in—the people that I met as a deliveryman—I was able to see things that other people in the world are going through.

"As a musician, I knew those things existed in some cases but I had never dealt with it. So it's helped me where I am right now to be able to write and relate to people who are having difficult times."

More importantly, Kent offers that he also learned a valuable lesson about God's unique timetable. "We always want answers to our prayers to be right now. And sometimes it is—it's immediate and overnight.

"But sometimes it's not, like in my own case. It takes time because there are some lessons to be learned. I think I definitely learned some lessons through my tough time that I can fall back on—and one of those lessons is patience."

Prayer continues to be a mainstay of his life, Kent asserts. "When I pray I always start off thanking God for what I have, for my family and their safety, and for the opportunity to do what I've always dreamed about doing—to be able to play music for a living and to be used by God."

He adds that because of his busy schedule, his prayer sessions are sometimes shorter than he would prefer them to be. "Traveling by bus on the road sometimes makes it difficult to pray at any length, especially when you're with a lot of other guys on the bus, which gets pretty small after a while.

"You don't always have time to get alone too often to pray. You find yourself praying through the day or I may have a second here or a second there where I can slip away.

"I always try to find some time during the day to spend some time with prayer, but most of my praying comes at night when everything has kind of died down and everybody's kind of hitting the hay."

For anyone waiting to have their own prayers answered, Kent suggests that in the meantime they reach out to other people for comfort and assistance.

"I know that I couldn't have made it without the encouragement of my wife and my friends, and without God's help. Christianity is set up so that we do have brothers and sisters to reach out to. God set it up so that we can lean on each other when we go through tough times.

"He ultimately wants us to lean on Him—to have complete faith in Him—but he also set it up to have people to counsel us as a friend. It just sometimes eases the pain and the pressure—whatever it is that we may be going through.

"Remember that there's probably someone else who has gone through what you're going through, and made it because they were patient and kept their faith."

Kent acknowledges that it is not always easy to hold on to one's faith. "It does get hard at times to pray and to really have the faith to pray, but I think that's when God gives us an extra measure of faith. God's not going to turn His back on anyone because maybe they don't have all the faith they need.

"He's always there to come to, no matter what you've been through or how you've acted. He'll be there when you do realize that maybe there is no way you can make it without Him. He'll reach out and take you back and love you the way He always has.

"So no matter how far away from God you may seem and no matter how tough times may get—and maybe you even feel like you've really blown it—you don't have to be ashamed to go back and say, 'You know, God, I've messed up. I didn't do the right thing. I'm sorry.' Thank God and He'll be there."

Looking toward the future, Kent looks forward to having Mid-South, a primarily Christian Country band, which, in 1995 won both the Christian Country Music Association's Song of the Year award, and the CCMA's Vocal Group of the Year award, make a transition to secular Country music.

"We're stepping out in faith on this," he declares, "but MidSouth has done this before. At the time the band started recording Christian Country music there was nobody doing it.

"This was in 1984 and Christian Country simply didn't exist. There was no radio marketplace for it—it hadn't been developed. We helped to put it on the musical map and pioneer the Christian Country sound. It was a very big step of faith for us then as it is now.

"I think what we're trying to do right now is exactly where God wants us to be. Our last couple of albums have a modern Country sound, and we're able to deal not only with Christian issues, but also with every other kind of issue.

"So we're real happy to be where we are. We're trying to hit head-on issues that people face every day in their lives. Our new album deals a lot with relationships, families—just things that people are going through now. It's about how to live an everyday life from a Christian perspective.

"We're doing a lot of positive and encouraging songs about how to handle those situations. And that includes a lot of faith and a lot of prayer. It's a real breakthrough for us, but we're not going to abandon our spiritual roots.

"We want to be true to who we are, say what God wants us to say, and let our music fall into whatever market it may. It's another test of our faith . . ."

$Jim\ Rice$
$(Brush\ Arbor)$

I n the aftermath of his father's death in an automobile accident at age forty-seven, Jim Rice, co-founder and lead vocalist of Brush Arbor, a band which helped to pioneer the Country Christian sound, turned his back on God.

Grief-stricken by his loss, the forty-six-year-old California native questioned why God would permit a man of such great faith to suffer such an untimely death.

Although he never received an answer to that question, the talented singer and songwriter did experience a vision—one which not only restored his faith but also made him realize the importance of a strong family life . . .

. . .

Whenever he is asked about his religious upbringing, Christian Country music artist Jim Rice likes to refer to a Gospel song he wrote called "Swingin' Bridge."

That ballad, which topped the Christian Country music charts, is an endearing reminiscence of Jim's and his brother Joe's spiritual roots in Clarksville, Tennessee.

"It's one of my favorite songs because if you listen to it, it's the story of our family, which is the most dear thing on the earth for me. Line for line the words of that song are true."

Jim's voice resonates with warmth as he recites a couple of lyrics from the song, which is set outside his grandparents' home in the Cumberland Hills of rural Tennessee.

"I was just a young boy playing on
that swing, out at Grandpappy
Nesbitt's home through the creek
and over the ridge,
laughin' out loud on that old bridge,
us kids could sure make it swing.

And we could hear, comin' from
the house the old folks as they'd
sing, on that swingin' bridge.

Throwin' rocks to the water below,
I could hear 'Amazing Grace' and
I could picture Grandpappy sing as
tears rolled down his face.

He'd call us kids together, knowin'
that we'd rather play, but there's
no way he'd see us leave without
some time to pray. Swingin' bridge."

"Somehow deep inside my soul all I am and all I know traces back to the day of that swingin' bridge," Jim asserts. "My parents and grandparents played a crucial role in my spiritual formation.

"Every summer we would go visit Grandpappy Nesbitt. We'd have to cross a creek and climb a hill to get to his log cabin. And we would go up there and he would pray over us.

"We even have tapes of him praying over us that God would use us to build His kingdom. He prayed and my parents prayed that we would grow up to serve the Lord, and those prayers have been answered."

Whenever he listens to that song, which appears on the band's recently released album, *Brush Arbor,* Jim professes that he feels blessed to have such a heritage of God-fearing people in his family—including several ministers.

"We go back six or seven generations in that area. Our relatives homesteaded that part of the country when Tennessee was still a part of North Carolina. The oldest grave site there is dated 1776, and we still own the farm.

"I've been to family reunions and on both my mom's and father's sides many of our people were involved in lay ministry. That's true even today. I'm the middle of three boys and one younger sister and we're all four in the ministry."

Although Jim and his brother, Joe, had not been back to the old homestead for many years, Jim recalls that they recently decided to do so, hoping to recapture some old memories.

When they arrived, Jim remembers being disappointed not to find a single trace of the cabin. "Then we ran into a man who said, 'Follow me.' He took us over to the Montgomery County Museum. Joe went in and when he came back out he was crying and weeping. The cabin was standing there inside the museum.

"They had disassembled the log cabin and reassembled it inside the museum. Joe said, 'Do you realize that God has blessed our family because of the prayers of Grandpappy Nesbitt there in that cabin?'"

Jim remembers how much he agreed with that statement. "I absolutely believe that. Grandpappy prayed that God would use us to build His kingdom, and Brush Arbor is a musical ministry.

"The power of our music and its ability to affect people's lives never ceases to amaze us. A lot of the songs I've written have been written just out of response to God in my life and out of worship to Him.

"And the letters we get from people who have been touched and encouraged and even transformed by this band make me weep. We're just going to continue in His sovereignty and let Him move us wherever He wants to move us."

Although his parents and older brother were born and raised in Clarksville, Tennessee, Jim was born in Southern California where the Rice family relocated after World War II.

Jim relates that the family arrived out West in an old car that contained nothing more than a cedar chest stuffed with children's clothing.

John Foster Rice, who died in 1973, was a builder, and after the war California was seeking people with construction skills. The elder Rice went on to establish his own construction company—Foster Construction—a firm that Jim and his brothers continue to operate to this very day.

Jim fondly recalls that his father had three loves—family, church, and the construction business, and that he often donated his skills to build churches in the Ventura County area.

His mother, he remembers, mostly stayed at home. "She was a homebody. She kept the house and raised us four children. My father owned a lot of real estate, so she kind of kept track of the paperwork."

As a young boy praying in the local Church of the Nazarine, Jim can still recall how proud he felt that this was a house of worship which his father had helped to construct.

"He wasn't a pastor, he was just a dedicated Christian committed to seeing the church grow in each community we lived in. His strong religious foundation saved his family countless heartbreaks down the road."

Jim remembers becoming attracted to religion at a young age. "I was eight years old when I received Christ. I was in church and the preacher asked 'How many of you want to receive God's provision to redeem your life from what Satan would like to do with it as opposed to what God would like to do with it?' " Jim's was the first hand to be raised.

In 1973, while Jim and his brothers were attending San Diego

State University, he received some shocking news. His father had been killed in an automobile accident.

Jim recalls that one of his first reactions was feeling disillusioned with God. "I was nineteen years old at the time and my father was only forty-seven years old. I was in complete turmoil and I did not understand why bad things happen to good people.

"My father was number one in the Christian community. He built churches, he built the office for Youth for Christ and gave them free rent for many, many years. What happened to him made me reevaluate my entire faith. I remember being more disillusioned than angry at God. My family still had faith but I didn't."

Jim further recalls that he engaged in a long period of grieving, during which he tried to escape his grief by busying himself in any type of frantic activity. But his sadness would not depart.

One evening, while feeling drowned by sorrow over the loss of his father, Jim experienced a vision which would ultimately change his life. "I don't know if I was asleep or awake or what because I was in such turmoil.

"I was weeping and crying. And then I had this vision. I saw my father before God. And he's before God and God says to him, 'Well done, my good and faithful servant.'

"And God is pointing—it's like slow motion—and I look to see where God is pointing, thinking that He's pointing at all the ministries my dad was involved in—he gave a lot of money to Billy Graham and everything else.

"And when I looked to where God is pointing, He's pointing to us four kids, and my mom's standing there. And I realized then that the most important thing in my life is my family.

"And that's my number-one ministry because I think family life is something that we've lost in America. And I also saw that I had to make the faith that my family never lost my own. Really mine.

"It demanded a recommitment to God, and I did that. And the vision also demanded a recommitment to family life. And I did that. I went and got married and I've been married to the same woman for twenty-five years."

After first meeting Daryl, Jim recollects that he had some reservations about continuing to see the attractive young French woman. "I dated her and on that first night I came home and I got on my knees and I said, 'Lord, I'm afraid I'm in love with her, but I will not marry her unless she's a believer.'

"And I said, 'Lord, I'm not going to tell her how I feel about you because I need to know that she is the woman that you've selected for me.' The very next day she called me and asked me if she could go to church with me.

"It was incredible. I hadn't said anything to her about how I felt. And the next day I went to church with her and she received the Lord. It was unbelievable. She was the first one down to the altar."

Jim's strong commitment to his marriage is reflected in a story he enjoys telling about a night when he and his brother were asleep in a motel room.

"One night this lady was bangin' on our motel door after a concert until four o'clock in the morning," Jim laughs. "Finally, Joe got up and let her out.

"We joke about that because we're very, very serious about our marriages. Our Christianity begins in our home. If I'm not a godly man to my wife and my daughter, I'm not a godly man to anybody."

Returning to the subject of his father's death, Jim now views it as a time in his life when God tested his faith. "I think just like Christ on the cross, sometimes God withdraws from us or makes us withdraw from Him to test our faith. God withdrew from me to test my faith and to see what I was made of.

"Just like he tested Job, I went through a testing period. Nowadays, when I have dark times or when conflict comes into my life, I realize it's just another test.

"Satan is the tempter. God does not tempt. But God is the tester and He will allow those temptations to become a test for you.

"And I always say, 'Lord, help me to learn through the little things so that you don't have to slam me with the big ones. I know you love me so much that you're going to continue to bring me to the image of Christ.'

"I want to be victorious in these tests, so that when I walk through the pearly gates I can hear the words, 'Well done, my good and faithful servant.' "

Jim also submits that his father's death taught him that sometimes tragedy can serve as a catalyst to renew one's faith. He expresses that point of view in a song which he wrote, "Unbroken Communion."

"I believe that God, somewhere in everyone's walk, breaks us. I raise horses, and there's a parallel there. Horses aren't worth anything until they're broken and realize the best thing for them is to do what their rider instructs them to.

"That's what happened to me after my father's death. As a result, now the only thing I really want in this life is to have unbroken communion with Jesus Christ. But that promise of deliverance comes with a side result, which is to be broken before God so you can be led through the trials of life on a light halter."

Faith, family, and music are the backbone of Brush Arbor. Their love of music dates back to a time when "as youngsters we would often sing at family gatherings."

That love of music continued through college, when in 1973 the Rice brothers formed Brush Arbor as a bluegrass trio while attending San Diego State University.

As new members were added to the band, the group took on a more contemporary Country flavor, although its message remained solidly spiritual.

Soon Brush Arbor was a popular attraction at bluegrass festivals as well as in church services and at Christian youth events. Jim recalls that the band's first big break came when, "just for laughs," he, Joe, and his brother Wayne auditioned for a local radio station western talent contest. To their amazement they won the contest.

"We got a chance to appear at the Grand Ole Opry. Then we got a contract with Capitol Records, and within two years we were voted Country Vocal Group of the Year."

Brush Arbor, now performing without Wayne, soon found themselves touring and performing on national television with some of the biggest names in Country music.

Even when the big time beckoned, Jim and his brother approached their success with a solid grip on the other realities of their lives.

"We finished our educations, maintained a close family life, and continued to operate the family construction business. We didn't get into drinking or smoking or anything in that kind of lifestyle. We didn't fall into the same potholes that other performers did. We just realized that for the grace of God, there go I."

Over the years, Brush Arbor has changed record labels, styles of music, and addresses, but one thing which has not changed is the band's awareness of its spiritual roots.

When after a long run in the world of secular Country music, Brush Arbor decided to commit all its energy and efforts to Christian music, Jim recollects it was the band's religious grounding which helped ease the transition to Gospel music.

"We wanted the values that we gained from being raised in Christian homes to be reflected in our music. We had seen our parents give big parts of their lives to the Gospel, and we wanted to share the extraordinary message of the Gospel of Jesus Christ through our music."

It wasn't long after signing with a major Gospel label that the band underwent yet another transition—a switch to a Christian Country music format.

Jim recalls that the decision was made at a time when the genre had not even been invented, leading the group to its current home at Benson Records and Brush Arbor's current popularity as one of the leading Christian Country bands.

"It was another decision which required that we step out in faith. It was also a decision prompted by concern about what was happening to other secular Country music acts like the Gatlin Brothers, who were into drug and alcohol abuse.

"I've seen some acts over the years trying to get hit records and I saw what happened to them. We didn't want that to happen to us. I'm grateful I never had to go through alcohol and drugs or take my wife through that.

"I've always prayed, 'Lord, if any music or any hit of any kind, whether it be in business or in music, takes me one speck away from you, please don't give it to me.'

"And I'm convinced our switch to Christian Country is why we never had some of the hits that other people had. I watched Larry Gatlin and his brothers get hits back when we were also trying to get hits. And I saw what happened to them and I'm so grateful it didn't happen to us."

There is more to Jim Rice than just a beautiful singing voice. The talented entertainer, who also has a master's degree in theology, is also kept quite busy as a guest lecturer.

"I try to use humor and I use stories. God most often speaks to me through His word. When my wife's not around, I also tell people that God secondly most often speaks to me through my wife. But I don't tell her that," he quips.

During his lectures, Jim often encourages those in his audience who are experiencing turmoil in their lives not to neglect their faith.

"God's preparing you for His use," he reminds them. "He's allowing all those bad events in your life to bring you to the perfect place that you would want to be if you could see it. Take one step toward God and He will walk a mile for us. That's what needs to be done during such times. Take that step."

Although a deeply devout Christian, Jim concedes that there is much room for improvement in his own spiritual life. "Sometimes I say something I wish I hadn't said, or I think something I shouldn't be thinking—whether it's jealousy or greed or envy or strife.

"I realize that these are words that were born out of my human, carnal nature—not God's words. I have these setbacks daily. I come home and sometimes I say, 'You know, I wish I'd done that a little differently. I'm going to work on that tomorrow.' I want my life to be more Christ-like."

At such times, Jim states that he consoles himself by turning to prayer. "I forgive myself and I ask for God's forgiveness. Prayer helps me fine-tune my life.

"I love doing what I'm doing and I love life. And every day I pray constantly, 'Thank you, Lord, for health. Thank you for this day. Thank you for this person. Thank you for this.' I do this throughout the day.

"I pray when I get out of bed in the morning and even when I'm in the shower. I'm just saying, 'Lord, thank you for this day. Thank you for my wife. Thank you for letting me feel great.' "

Brush Arbor's lead vocalist believes he has come far in his spiritual life since those painful days after his father's death when he became disillusioned with God.

"I'm a pilgrim continuing to make progress," he testifies. "Do I have setbacks? All the time. But if you look at where I was years ago and where I am now, I'm on a graph headed up. I'm working harder and harder to please God every day of my life.

"I started this life with nothing, and I'm going to end this life with nothing when it comes to material things. But the only thing that's going to count is what I've done for Christ while I've been here . . ."

Joy Lynn White

Joy Lynn White dreamed of becoming a Country music star ever since she was a young girl singing Gospel music with her family in church and at revival meetings.

When after years of struggle, success finally beckoned for the flaming-red-haired Arkansas beauty, the one person whom she most wanted to share her accomplishment with—her father—was suddenly taken from her.

Although Joy Lynn's faith was briefly shaken by her loss, the Columbia Records artist, with two albums to her credit, did not remain estranged from God for too long a period of time.

With her usual positive outlook, what she came to realize is that everything which happens in life—whether it be good or bad—is all part of God's sovereign plan.

"Sometimes it's really hard to figure it all out because you feel so darn bad that you don't want to think that this happened for a reason," she asserts. "But I've learned that things do happen for a reason . . ."

Born in the small farming town of Turrel, Arkansas, and raised in Mishawaka, Indiana, not far from the big-city lights of South Bend, Joy Lynn grew up in a musical family where singing came as naturally as eating and sleeping.

The hillbilly beauty learned to talk at the age of ten months while listening to Country radio, and her exuberance spilled over into her music.

"Singing is like a fix for me," she proclaims with an infectious laugh. "While other kids were playing outdoors, I would go home and sing along with my albums. My major musical influences were Emmylou Harris, Linda Ronstadt, and Jimmie Rodgers."

The youngest of three children, Joy Lynn is proud of her "hillbilly" roots. "My dad was born and raised in Arkansas and my mother was born and raised in East Tennessee. They moved up to Indiana in the sixties for work.

"There was a lot of factory work available in the Midwest at that time, so my dad went to work at one of those factories and my mom mostly stayed home to raise her three babies. Sometimes she'd work odd jobs."

Joy Lynn's roots are steeped in religion as well as music. "I was brought up around a religious family, but not so religious that we didn't have a good time. I went to church all my life—it was the Baptist church in Osceola, Indiana. That's where I started singing. My first singing live came from there.

"I would sing Gospel music in that church and then I went on to work with my whole family—my brother, my sister, my dad, and my uncle. They were Gospel singers who performed at revivals. I was about five years old at the time and in kindergarten.

"We did radio shows and revivals all the way through Indiana and Michigan. I was singing Gospel songs before I could read—I memorized the stuff. We were called the 'Singing White Family featuring Little Lynn White.' Everybody in my family calls me Lynn."

Joy Lynn reflects back upon those years with fond memories, remembering all the love and encouragement that she received from her parents. "My mom and dad were really unique. They supported me a lot and they made me understand that what I had was a gift from God. They would tell me that everyone has a gift and mine happened to be music.

"They would tell me to respect my gift, but not feel that I was any better than anyone else because I had it. That was always really instilled in me—not to think that I was such hot stuff.

"My mother would really instill that in me and she would tell me when I sang good and when I didn't, so I had a lot of constructive criticism from the very beginning."

While still in high school, Joy Lynn put together her first band. She then found work singing jingles for radio commercials. It wasn't much in the way of professional credits, but the young singer nonetheless felt ready to tackle her dream of being a Country music star.

At age nineteen she left for Nashville, arriving in Music City in an old beat-up Gremlin, with two hundred dollars in her pocket, and a lot of expectations.

"I believe my whole career is a gift from God because I had no business sense at all when I moved to Nashville in 1982. I was still a teenager when I moved here and pretty immature.

"All I could do was sing and have faith in my ability to sing. I always just felt that was what I would do. And that's really all I ever have done."

Despite such faith, the only work Joy Lynn could find was a job shining shoes. Meanwhile, she began to pursue demo and studio work, soon becoming one of the most in-demand demo singers in town.

Her vibrant voice captured the attention of recording star Marty Stuart, who became her sponsor and introduced the talented young singer to various music executives. She would eventually go on to sign with Columbia Records.

At the moment, however, Joy Lynn found herself doing demo work and not making much progress toward her goal. "That was a period when my faith was temporarily challenged," she recalls.

"I would say, 'God why would you give me all my talent and not make it to where I can use it? How much longer do I have to keep building character?'

"I would feel that way, but most of the time I would keep my faith or else I don't think I would have stayed in this town and tried to do this. If you really believe—and I really always believed that I was doing what I was supposed to be doing—things will happen.

"Faith is about focusing and believing with all your heart in whatever goal you're trying to do. It means just being real strong and faith keeps you that way. It keeps you focused and going in that direction, whatever it might be."

During those moments when she felt discouraged, Joy Lynn remembers turning to nature to boost her sinking spirits. "There were long periods of time when nothing would be happening for me and I would go out in the woods, go for long walks, and pray to God.

"I would say, 'Hey, there's lots of other things that I would like to do, too, so if this is not what you want me to do, then you open the doors for me to go somewhere else.' And that's how I would look at life.

"And most of the times after really getting down and having these conversations, the doors would always open and something new would happen. A phone call would come and something new would happen which would keep moving me into that direction to where I am today."

Joy Lynn remembers that it was shortly after one such talk in the woods with God that she received one of the most important breaks in her career. "I was doing a lot of demos for singers and I was doing a little bit of writing. In the meantime, I was working at a hotel here in Nashville in the banquet department. And I was really getting tired of struggling.

"So I was seriously thinking about trying to get into a whole different field—a different lifestyle that wouldn't involve music as a business. I would always sing and be into music for personal enjoyment, but I was going to try to do something else with my life that would involve some kind of work with animals.

"And I really was getting into all this gorilla research. I was reading books by Diane Fosse—this lady who had done all the mountain gorilla research in Africa. And I was even talking to friends all the time about doing that kind of work.

"It was one of those times that I went out to the woods to pray, and I told God that 'If being a performer is not what you want me to do, please let me know.' That's when stuff started happening with Tree Publishing."

Upon returning home, Joy Lynn received a phone call from the music publishing house offering her a job as a songwriter. "This all of a sudden put me back into the heart of the music business just when I was thinking about leaving it."

Joy Lynn remembers being ecstatic about the job offer, but not all that surprised that it came so swiftly after asking God to point her in the right direction. "I always felt when I really got down to the nitty-gritty with prayer, that I'd get some kind of an answer.

"I wouldn't dwell on it after I prayed. I'd go and do it—kind of like getting something off your chest—and then I would just go on with life for a while and see what happened."

Even, today, prayer continues to be an important part of her everyday life. "I pray to be a stronger person, to go with the flow and accept it. To accept my career. I don't really pray for success. I pray to be happy and to get by.

"I'd rather be happy in this life than to be success, success, successful—you know what I mean? I want to be happy and, of course, I want to make money to keep the roof over my head. I'm not looking for the jet-set and the Cadillac-in-the-driveway kind of lifestyle.

"I pray almost anytime. I can be washing the dishes and something will come to my mind and I'll pray. And I always do a small prayer every time I go up in front of an audience to sing.

"I wear my mother's little wedding band that she wore all her life. I wear it on my right hand. She gave it to me when my dad died five years ago. She gave it to me at Christmas.

"I always wear that ring and touch it and say a little prayer like 'Bless my voice, bless my band, bless me.' I can't really remember a time since my mother gave me the ring when I haven't done that."

Even today, the mention of her father brings an echo of sadness to her voice. "I was very much a Daddy's girl," she confesses.

"I would talk to him on the phone maybe four, five times a

week. And whenever I felt bad the phone would ring and it would be him. He would know. We had that kind of telepathic relationship.

"His death was a challenge to my faith. There was a temporary loss of faith. There's been a temporary loss of faith on and off in my life, but mostly I'd keep my faith. I don't think I'd stay here in this town and try to do this if I didn't keep my faith.

"But losing my dad was the worst thing that ever happened to me, and going through that I wasn't a very strong person. I had worked all those years to do something that my dad had only dreamed about doing himself in life but he was never able to do. And he was taken away before he could see any of it.

"So I was angry and hurt and feeling kind of left out like 'What the heck did I do all this for?' But I wasn't angry at God. I've never been angry at God. I would never say, 'Why did you do that?'

"I guess it's because I've always been brought up to know that God is good. He didn't cause the bad things. I was just angry at all the forces around me. Then, after a while, I began to realize that I did do a lot of this work for myself, too.

"I've always said that things happen for a reason and I believe to this day that they do. So I really couldn't blame God for anything. Sometimes it's really hard to try to figure it all out because you feel so darn bad that you don't want to think that this happened for a reason. But it does."

Despite the grief she felt at her father's death, Joy recollects trying to put that tragedy into perspective. "I think that losing my dad made me grow up and made me much more of a stronger person for myself. I've never been married and I don't have anybody to take care of me.

"And I can't call my dad anymore to tell him about a situation I'm having. So I've had to go ahead and take care of things all on my own. So although my faith was shaken, it was later revealed to me that maybe some good came out of what happened."

Joy Lynn acknowledges that after losing a loved one it is often difficult to separate from the grieving process. She believes, however, that it is important to try. "You just have to realize that people do die and that God didn't take that parent away to try to hurt you or them."

With her signature good looks—flaming red hair and red lips— and her signature sound, which has been described by one critic as a "sassy voice and a hint of bad-girl spunk," Joy Lynn admits that people are often surprised to learn that behind that show-business facade there lurks a deeply spiritual woman.

"It might surprise some people who don't know me that sometimes I even walk around every room in my house and thank God for this house. I think it would surprise them that I sometimes even go to the basement and say, 'Thank you, Jesus, thank you for this basement.'

"My house has been a blessing to me. From day one that I slept in the bedroom I've slept like a rock. I think you should remember to be thankful for what you get.

"I keep in mind that things could be a lot worse and I could be going through what I was going through a couple of years ago. I was lost and found myself kind of wandering around after my father's death. But if you have faith you can always bounce back . . ."

Red Steagall

Western recording artist Red Steagall was a teenager when he contracted polio—two years before Dr. Jonas Salk introduced the lifesaving vaccine.

Instead of bemoaning his fate, the fifteen-year-old turned this devastating experience into something beneficial. Red learned how to play the guitar and mandolin to help rehabilitate his disabled arm, and thus began a lifelong love affair with music.

Today, the deeply spiritual sixty-year-old Texan, whose music is a celebration of cowboy lifestyles in West Texas, has more than a dozen albums and twenty-six consecutive hit records to his credit.

Red also has a dream—to share his positive outlook with as many people as possible who may be challenged by illness. "Take what you have and do the best with it that you can," the award-winning singer and songwriter counsels. "Keep a positive attitude and always have faith . . ."

Red Steagall is a man of varied accomplishments. Not only has he had popular success as a singer and songwriter, but he is also a gifted poet, actor, record and movie producer, entrepreneur, and former bull rider.

The Western music recording star is also a nurturer of talent. He is the person credited with discovering and encouraging the career of Country music superstar Reba McEntire, whom Red first heard when she sang the national anthem at the 1974 National Rodeo Finals in Oklahoma City.

At the time Red remembers being so impressed with her voice that he brought Reba to Nashville, helped her make her first demo tape, and as her career took off, continued to offer advice and guidance.

A longtime lover of cowboy tradition, Red has always felt intimately connected to the West Texas countryside where he was raised. It is the stark, vast beauty of this landscape which inspires much of his music and poetry.

"When you get to stand up on a rise in the morning just before the sun comes up, and all of a sudden you see the prairie come alive and you see all of God's handiwork in the creatures, the canyons and the colors, and the sky, it would be awful tough to stand up on that hill and say there was no such thing as God. That's not the kind of person I'd want to ride the prairie with."

Born in Gainesville—now Dallas—Texas, Red was raised in the small ranching community of Sanford, a few miles north of Amarillo.

There he was surrounded by cowboy life—not the celluloid images of cowboys galloping across movie screens, but real-life cowboys whom as a youngster he always admired.

"When I was growing up, those cowboys in the area were the finest guys in the world," the popular performer with the bushy white beard and cowboy hat recalls. "They were my real heroes. They were the people I looked up to, and I looked up to them because they were the right kind of people."

He remembers not only admiring cowboys but dreaming of becoming one himself when he grew older. "They had the skills I really wanted to have. I really wanted to ride a horse, I really wanted to rope, I really wanted to get up in the morning and push those cattle out of those drawers and work the cattle in the pen—that's what I really wanted to do. So naturally I looked up to those people.

"I also grew up in the oil fields, but I really had no desire to be a roughneck. Cowboys are all about faith and values. It was their spiritual values that attracted me to them as a kid and it still does."

Red's own upbringing was filled with faith and values. It was his parents as well as his church pastor who instilled in him his spiritual lessons early in life.

"I was brought up in the Methodist Church and I was exposed to the teachings of Jesus as a youngster. I always wanted to go to church. I always wanted to be a part of that happening down at that building. I wanted to associate with those people every day.

"The person I looked up to more than anybody else in the world except for my mother and daddy was our pastor. I looked up to him kind of the way I would look up to a doctor. Whatever he said was right."

While in college, Red's zeal for religion eventually led him to become a lay minister in the Methodist Church. But he soon discovered another calling as well. "I realized one day when I was in the pulpit that what I was getting out of preaching was the show-business aspect of it.

"I discovered that I had the power at that point to hold people's attention, and I enjoyed that. I also began to question whether I did believe every single thing I was saying doctrinal-wise. So I decided not to go into the ministry.

"I questioned my motives and I didn't think I was worthy of it. My faith was not shaken at all—it never has been—just my motives.

"I just had trouble with doctrine. I grew up in the Methodist Church but I didn't believe that its doctrine is any more right than the doctrine of the Baptist Church or any of the other denominations. To me the utopian situation would be for all of us to belong to the same church and worship God the same way."

It was a career as a singer and songwriter that Red now decided he wanted to pursue. "I knew what my Lord wanted me to do. I knew which direction He wanted me to take in my life. He had given me a talent and He wanted me to use it. I didn't need to go find any other answers."

Red's passion for music was developed while recuperating from a bout with polio at age fifteen. It continued through his college years when he formed his first Country music band while attending West Texas State University.

Turning the clock back to that time when he was stricken with polio, Red recollects that it was music and some words of advice from a family friend which most helped him cope with that harrowing experience.

"My mother's best friend then was the janitor at the school where she was a schoolteacher," he recalls. "He was also my best friend. Lou Steen had been the first settler in our little town. He came there in 1901 as a government wolf trapper.

"And he had his whole barn full of traps, and he knew where all the old Indian burial grounds were and where their campfires were and where you'd find arrowheads.

"And he became my confidant and my teacher and my mentor. I spent lots of time out in the river country and out on the prairie with Lou trapping coyotes and bobcats and learning how to set traps. So Lou was my hero.

"One time—I guess I was about twelve years old—I had a paper route. I was able to buy a new bicycle with the money I earned. I had that bicycle one day, and my dad came home a little under the weather and ran over that new bicycle. I was devastated.

"Lou was over our house having coffee with Mother—this was after school—and Daddy went on to bed. And I was just heartbroken over my bike and I was sitting down on the stoop.

"And Lou came out and he put his arm around me and he said, 'Son, remember, the good things that happen to you are to make life enjoyable today. The bad things that happen to you are toughening you up for tomorrow.' I never forgot that."

Three years later, while lying in a Plainview, Texas, hospital room, diagnosed with polio, it was Lou's words of advice that continuously played through the teenager's head.

"I remember going to the hospital and I, of course, was just devastated. And then after the fever was gone and I was rational again, my left arm was just like a rope. I had lost the use of it—and just when I was starting in with an all-state football team.

"They sent me down to Plainview, Texas, which was the foremost polio clinic at that time in America. They didn't have room for me so they put me in a ward with iron-lung patients. And there were fourteen kids there who couldn't breathe on their own.

"And I remember lying there in that bed, and all of a sudden something that Lou said to me after I got polio flashed through my mind: 'Hey, you're not so bad off. You can still walk. You still got one good arm. You still got your lungs, and your eyes, and your ears, and your nose. Get out of this bed and go do something with what you got left.' That was a turning point in my life."

From that moment on, Red remembers becoming fiercely determined not to allow his useless arm ruin his enjoyment of life. With activities such as football and bull riding during the summer no longer possible for him to participate in, Red turned to music.

"We had a lady in our town named Mrs. Miller. She lived about three miles from town. I would ride my bicycle over to her house and she had a little mandolin. Mother bought that mandolin from her for ten dollars and paid it out a dollar a month. And I took mandolin lessons and my fingers wouldn't even work.

"And so I would sit down and it took days to concentrate hard enough to make one finger hold down the strings. I worked for weeks and weeks and weeks until I gained enough strength in those fingers to make chords on the mandolin.

"Then when I felt my hand was strong enough to play the mandolin, I went to the guitar. And Mother and I together with money I earned from my paper route bought me a new guitar. That was my senior year in high school.

"Through all of this, never once after I had made that decision in the hospital have I ever said one time in my life, 'Poor me.' I have never said, 'Why me?' I have always felt that I have total control of my destiny.

"And I felt that if I had faith enough in God, and if I did the things that He knew I was supposed to do, that whatever happened to me was going to be the right thing.

"And I can honestly tell you that I wake up every morning knowing that it is going to be a good day. I have control whether it's going to be beneficial or detrimental."

In 1965, after earning his degree in animal science and agronomy from West Texas State University, Red relocated to California. There he began to perform in folk clubs in the Los Angeles area.

He also began to write music, gaining recognition as a talented songwriter in 1967 when Ray Charles recorded one of his songs— "Here We Go Again." The song hit the charts and, two years later, was rerecorded by Nancy Sinatra. Based on that song's success, Dot Records hired Red as a songwriter in 1969. Three years later he moved to the Capitol Records label.

Now Red not only found himself writing hit songs that were being recorded by some of the most popular performers of the day— including Country music superstar George Strait—but by the late 1970s he had launched his own recording career.

As Red wound down his connection with the Nashville music business after 1980, he returned to his small ranch in West Texas where today he keeps himself busy maintaining a heavy touring schedule. He is also frequently in demand at rodeos, fairs, and concerts.

In addition, he hosts his own hour-long nationally syndicated radio show, "Cowboy Corner," which celebrates the lifestyle of the American West through poems, songs, and stories.

The Country Western star is so knowledgeable about the subject of cowboy lore, that in 1991 Red was named Cowboy Poet of Texas by the Texas Legislature.

One of Red's strongest interests is the spiritual life of the American cowboy. "A cowboy sees the Lord in all different kinds of places," he states. "He appreciates the Lord's handiwork. The cowboy may not drop down on his knees and tell the Lord about it right then, but he still has those strong beliefs."

This theme is explored in Red's recent Warner Western album release, *Faith and Values*. On the album, the entertainer uses songs and poems drawn from cowboy music rather than Gospel music to illustrate the spiritual history of the American cowboy.

"In the early days of the cow business when it was all open range there weren't any fences and there weren't any headquarters," Red explains. "They used what they called line riders to keep the cattle of a particular owner pushed back into the area that he called his home range.

"Those line riders would ride in a big circle and they'd meet another line rider from another ranch coming in the other direction. And they became the pipeline for information for the cow country.

"And all the information about what was happening in town was passed along that line to the far-reaching cow camps—these camps may have been seven hundred miles away from where the event took place. As a result, if a guy was a liar, a thief, or a cheat, his reputation would precede him to that next cow camp.

"And as the law of the range dictated, they fed him, they allowed him to roll his bed out, but the next morning he was expected to leave because they wouldn't give him a job—he wasn't the right kind of guy. So eventually he would weed himself out of that society.

"So we were left with a group of people who were very dedicated to their way of life, very strongly convicted about their belief in God, and dedicated to family. They were hardworking, honest people who believed a day's pay is worth a day's work—and that was different than believing in a day's work for a day's pay.

"And those kind of people are still operating the ranches of the West. They passed that on down to their children and grandchildren. You go out to the ranches now and you talk to the young people who are coming up in that industry, and you'll find that nearly every single one of them grew up with those values."

When not busy performing, Red spends much of his time working on other cowboy music projects.

"The goal of my music is to express my thoughts so hopefully somebody else will like them, and to try to perpetuate and preserve the image of the lifestyle of the American cowboy.

"Faith is a part of that, which is why I recorded the *Faith and Values* album. I feel that faith is a very important part of the lifestyle of the American cowboy."

Another pet project which keeps him busy is the annual Red Steagall Cowboy Gathering and Western Swing Festival. Each summer the event draws more than thirty thousand people to the area for a weekend-long, family-style celebration of the heritage and lifestyle of the cowboy.

When it comes to his personal religious beliefs, the singer and songwriter states that "I am strongly convicted about my belief in God. I feel the need to live the kind of life that would be exemplary of the life in the Bible.

"To me that's not preaching to anyone or telling them how to live. It's witnessing—not being vocal—but treating people the way I was taught to treat people, by a mother who was very strongly convicted also.

"I don't want to preach to anyone, or tell them how to live. I don't want to say that my way is the only way to look at it. All I want to do is express my feelings through my music about my Maker and how He appears to me."

One way Red nourishes his spiritual side is by enjoying the natural beauty of the West Texas landscape where he was raised. It was that landscape, he notes, which inspired him to write the *Faith and Values* album.

"I was seated on this rise with a cowboy friend [John Gaither] watching the cattle come off a hill toward their pen on Gaither's ranch.

"John said to me, 'If a man can sit here and say there's no God, he sure needs to be somewhere else.' The line stuck and eventually resulted in the collection of songs that make up the album."

Red agrees with his friend's words, submitting that whenever he rides alone through the prairie, he thinks about "What a lucky human being I am to be able to experience all this and be alive this morning. That's also the very first thing I think about when I get up—about how fortunate I am to be able to experience these things."

His life is also filled with prayer. "There's no specific prayers or specific times that I pray, and most of the time when I pray it's only in thanks.

"The things I ask God for are to help me be strong, to realize my shortcomings, to keep my family safe—those are the kind of things I pray for. I don't say, 'Help me win the lottery.' I don't ask for material things—I never have."

As someone who survived a near fatal bout with polio, Red has words of advice for anyone stricken by disease. "Take what you have and do the best you can with it. You've just got to take the good out of the bad things that happen to us.

"We've got to realize that the good part is what we're supposed to have. My faith in God is that He is a loving God. I don't believe He wants to harm me. I believe that He loves me and that He wants the best for me. People should feel the same way about themselves.

"I don't hide my head in the sand. I've traveled all over the world, so I've seen people in all walks of life. I realize that life is not perfect, that the world is not perfect, and my life is not perfect. But, by golly, it's as good as I can make it. I just wish that everybody could have a positive attitude whether they believe in God or not . . ."

Lisa Stewart

Getting involved with a religious cult was the last thing in the world that Country music recording artist and television talent Lisa Stewart expected when she accepted an invitation to attend a Bible study class.

By the time the twenty-nine-year-old Louisville, Mississippi, native realized what she had stumbled into, the cult had so manipulated her mind that for nearly two years the singer and songwriter avoided attending any church.

Lisa eventually resumed worship, although she still bears the emotional scars of that disturbing encounter.

Today, the rising young star who in 1994 became known to

millions of Country music fans when she regularly appeared on TNN's "Music City Tonight," warns anyone who is approached by members of a church with whom they are not familiar to beware.

She asserts that faith is much too precious a commodity to risk losing, as she nearly did . . .

Lisa Stewart laughingly recalls that she didn't have much of a choice in the type of music which she listened to as a young girl in the small town of Louisville, Mississippi.

"We lived a few hundred yards from the radio tower, and the signal was so strong that Country music was all we could get on the radio.

"It even came through our television and the speakers of our church," she chuckles. "The preacher would be in the middle of a sermon, and we'd hear, 'Don't come home drinkin' with lovin' on your mind.' "

The strawberry blond beauty acknowledges that her current career was influenced by the songs of Patsy Cline, Jim Reeves, and other Country singers that she used to listen to on that one-station radio.

"I remember when I was three, I used to run around the house singing 'Delta Dawn,' and I always watched the 'Glen Campbell Show' and the 'Mac Davis Show.' I guess I can't remember not wanting to be in music."

Lisa's interest in music led the young girl to give her first performance at age six. "We'd have soloists singing in our church. I remember that I wanted to be up there so badly to sing a song. Finally, I got my chance."

It was an impressive debut, and word quickly spread that this youngster could sing. Soon other congregations were clamoring for her to appear before them. "They called me 'the little girl with the big voice,' because I sounded pretty much then like I do now."

Religion also had an important influence on her early in life. Lisa's mother was the church organist at the local Southern Baptist church, while her father, a potter, was also a devout churchgoer.

"Church was a big part of my growing up, and I've been going to church ever since I can remember. I grew up in a Southern Baptist church that was walking distance from our house—it's called the East Louisville Baptist Church.

"And also ever since I can remember I was part of the church's children's activities and the choir—me and my family were there all the time. I just loved religion—and I still do—it was sort of instilled in me."

Besides singing with the choir, Lisa also appeared on local TV shows, in nursing homes and before civic clubs, and sang with other church groups. At age eleven, a demo tape which she had sent to the promoters of Nashville's Fan Fair so impressed its sponsors that Lisa was invited to perform at the event's tent show.

The young girl progressed from there to performing in local theater, playing first-chair saxophone in the school jazz band, and becoming a school drum majorette.

At eighteen, Lisa left Louisville for Columbus, Mississippi, where she attended Mississippi University for Women on a scholarship. She then won a Roy Acuff Vocal Scholarship at Nashville's Belmont University, where she took classical voice training.

"My only complaint about Nashville is that I couldn't find a church where I felt like I was really at home." Instead of settling into one church, Lisa would drop in at various churches to attend Sunday services.

Little did she realize at the time where this search would lead her —to an involvement with a religious cult that nearly destroyed her love of religion.

"It all began when I was working at Opryland USA as a singer/ dancer in one of the shows. It was about six years ago. One of the cast members and I had become really good friends, and she asked me if I was going to church anywhere.

"I said no, and told her that I hadn't really found a church that I was really settled into. And she said, 'Listen, I go to this great church and we have Bible studies and if you want you can come to some of the Bible studies and kind of meet some of the people and see if you like it.' "

Lisa recollects eagerly accepting the invitation, hoping that this would turn out to be the church she could call home. "I started going to their Bible studies. And right from the beginning I thought it was really strange that the Bible studies were really late at night.

"They would start at nine-thirty or ten. I just thought that was a little bit odd, but I understood it, too. I mean, we worked pretty late. Before I knew it, I had gone to several of these Bible studies and then I went to a church service.

"It was a strange thing that when I showed up everybody there knew who I was. People came up to me saying, 'Hi, Lisa, we heard you were coming today, it's so nice to have you here.' And I was like, wow, these people are super-nice."

Still, something bothered her about these overfriendly people. "It made me feel uncomfortable that everyone knew all about me." She also became annoyed at how insistent church members were that she not miss a single Bible study class.

"They kept saying, 'We'll see you next Sunday,' and we'll see you this night and that night. I'm the type of person that if I'm pushed into a corner, I start kicking. I don't want to go. I'm not happy being pushed into a corner. And I just kept feeling that there was something strange about this."

Her disenchantment increased when she began receiving phone calls at home each time she missed a class. "They would call me and say, 'Why weren't you there?' I would tell them that I had to work late or I had a final tomorrow and I had to study.

"They would say, 'You know, Lisa, if you don't show that you love the Lord by coming to worship Him and learn about Him, then you love your work more than you love God.' "

For Lisa, that was the final straw. "I told one of them who said that, 'Hey, wait a minute! That's not true. There are just things I have to do.' And when I started going back to my hometown church on weekends, they started telling me that I shouldn't do that.

"They would say, 'What are you doing this weekend?' And I would tell them that I'm going home to visit my family. And they would ask if I was going to the church where I grew up. I said, 'Yeah, I'm going to sing as a matter of fact.' And they said, 'No, Lisa, that's the wrong thing to do.' "

Angered at the implication that singing in her hometown church was not spiritually correct, Lisa remembers confronting group members about their attitude. "They said I was condoning what my church believed in, which was wrong. I said, 'What do you mean it's wrong?

They're Christians.' This cult believed that no one was going to heaven but them."

Lisa recalls with a shudder how persuasive the sect was, nearly convincing her not to sing in her hometown church. "They almost had me believing that my people were not dedicated to God like they were. And that was when the final flag went up. I said, 'Wait just a minute. These are people who have loved me my entire life and these are the people who led me to Christ.

" 'They have fed me, nurtured me spiritually through my childhood and teenage years, and you're telling me that they're not righteous people?'

"Anyway, basically that's when I left. And I had to change my phone number because these people kept calling me. I ended up doing some research on this particular church. They were formed in Boston and they're a branch of the Church of Christ, but they're not the Church of Christ.

"The people who started it once belonged to the Church of Christ. And it turns out that during my research—I was digging through library newspapers—I found out that they are considered a cult. They're called the Nashville Church."

By now, Lisa's experience with the cult had so dampened her enthusiasm about religion that she wanted nothing more to do with worship services. "My head was a little bit messed up by these people and I really got away from religion.

"For about a year and a half I wanted no part of it. I got so tired of these people telling me that I didn't love God because I missed a Bible study. I mean, they even wanted me to break up with my boyfriend because he wasn't in their church. They only wanted me to date people that were in their church. I got so fed up with religion after that that I needed to get away from the church for a while.

"I got involved in some wild times and through that I was looking for a different outlet for my spirituality. That experience just hurt me deeply and I was looking for something else.

"I don't think what happened to me totally destroyed my faith in God, but I was very cynical for a while and it took me a while to get back to where I could go back to church. I did a lot of praying, but it was just God and me. I would not step foot in any church to pray."

It was in the aftermath of a "wild party" in her Nashville condominium that Lisa began to reconnect with her spiritual core. "I had fallen asleep, and when I woke up and walked down the stairs into the living room what I saw was a room full of people who were passed out on the floor.

"Seeing that, it was like God had pulled me back to reality. It was like I woke up and God opened my eyes to the fact that it was my party and I was encouraging that sort of behavior. I was not being a good example to these friends of mine that I was supposed to love and care for.

"I just thought, 'I can't let this happen to my friends and I can't let this happen to me. They're going downhill and I'm going with them.' It just all became clear to me after a wild, crazy night. I was encouraging them to hurt themselves. I realized that this had been an evil time in my life, but now I saw an opening and I was going to take it."

The following morning, the first thing that Lisa recalls doing is getting dressed and searching for something she thought she no longer wanted anything to do with—a church to pray in.

"I needed God and I thank Him to this day for helping me find this church in Franklin, Tennessee—Christ Community Church. It's about twenty miles from where I live now, and it's a wonderful nondenominational church."

From the moment that she first stepped foot into the tiny church, Lisa recollects feeling suddenly engulfed with love for God. "I prayed that day that God would help me. I felt like I had somehow led some people astray.

"So I just prayed for forgiveness and for strength. I still had a lot of people hanging around me who it would be very easy to get into trouble with. So mostly I just prayed for strength not to get into trouble."

Those prayers, she believes, were answered. "These days I'll have a glass of wine here and there, but I don't get smashed or anything like that anymore. The worst time of my life is over."

Lisa also credits her renewed faith with helping her through many of life's trials. "I've been through some terrible times—times when my label dropped me and my management and I split, and record deals fell through, and I broke up with my boyfriend—and all I could do was reach up to God and say, 'Can you please help me?' "

She recalls one particular time in Nashville when, like so many other struggling young musicians, Lisa found herself singing on demos, recording jingles, and performing with various local Country music groups.

After nearly four years of this type of work, the sheer level of competition led her to think about giving up. "When I told my parents, they said, 'Make sure you think long and hard about this. Music has been your whole life. Are you sure you want to give it up?'

"I thought it over and stayed. A few months later I had a record deal. Every time I thought I was at the end of my rope, God kind of came and swept me up."

Although her first album slipped into what she describes as a "void," another break soon came her way. Lisa received an offer to host "#1 Country," a video countdown show seen in 130 markets.

A few months later, she was asked to join the cast of TNN's Music City Tonight, where she performed two or three nights a week singing Country standards by artists like Patsy Cline, Jeannie Seely, Roy Orbison, and the Everly Brothers. The show offered the young star much needed exposure to millions of viewers across the nation.

"I was on the show for six months, and I felt like it was another gift from God. Music is a very powerful thing. Its lyrics say things that we feel but can't seem to put into words. I'm glad I can be the messenger."

Although she has suffered some ups and downs in her career since then, Lisa continues to remain grateful to God for all that He has brought her.

"When I pray I thank Him for what He's done and praise Him. Some days I just praise God and other times I do have things that I need help with and I need His guidance.

"I talk to God like He's my friend. Sometimes I'm just walking through the woods, sometimes before I go to bed, and sometimes I do get down on my knees with my face to the floor. It's not always that dramatic. A lot of time I pray to God while driving around Nashville."

Lisa believes anyone can have opportunities present themselves if they just open themselves to God. "I used to get very stressed out and I tried to take control of everything. I was a real control freak. There was a time when I think I would have even sold my soul to be a superstar. But not anymore.

"I've turned my life over to Him. I've given it up to Him. I do all the legwork—I don't just sit around and wait for things to happen—but knowing that my career is in God's hands is such a comfort to me.

"I think the hardest thing about giving up control is a lack of faith that God's going to take care of you. You know the story about how when God was sending the manna and the people wanted to hoard it— they worried about what if He forgets to send us food tomorrow.

"We just have to have faith that God will not forget to send that nourishment, and that He will take care of us and provide us with abundance. I know that because He has certainly taken care of me."

Today, besides being a much in demand singer, Lisa has also been doing some acting. She recently landed a small part in Sidney Sheldon's CBS mini-series, *Nothing Lasts Forever*.

At quiet moments, Lisa admits that she is still sometimes haunted by memories of her frightful experience with the religious cult.

During such times, the entertainer tries to put a positive spin on what happened to her. She views her ordeal, for example, as a learning experience about tolerance.

"Those people seemed to think that they were the only people who were right. They condemned other Christians. I learned from this never to condemn anybody's belief because it will just totally push them away from religion the way it pushed me away.

"I guess I learned not to judge people. It's better to be helpful and maybe disagree and say, 'This is the way I see it.' But never say, 'Well, you're damned because you don't believe this.' Never, never, never.

"That's not the way to handle it at all. I pray for those people because they have a lot of hatred in their hearts for other people, and that's not right."

Looking ahead, Lisa hopes to add to the two albums she has already recorded, although one of her major goals is to try and lead an exemplary Christian life.

"Hopefully people will see God in me by me being a good example of Christ's love. God has given me a lot of strength, and I don't get pulled down anymore.

"I want to share this strength with people. God has opened doors for me so that I'm able to talk to people about Him. And I do so without making anyone feel uncomfortable. I just tell them to love God and if they have faith in Him, He will take care of His children . . ."

Brian Barrett

Christian Country star Brian Barrett's career almost took a different path after he decided to follow in his father's footsteps and become an airline pilot.

But those plans were grounded when the twenty-nine-year-old singer and songwriter with Tennessee roots and a minister's heart experienced a religious conversion while videotaping a revival meeting where his father was preaching.

That experience would change his life and lead him in a different direction. Instead of flying solo at thirty-five thousand feet, Brian decided to turn the controls over to his co-pilot and see where he landed.

Today, Brian, who sees himself as a minister first and a performer second, is still flying high—but not in the cockpit of an airplane. Instead, he remains on a steady course of performing, writing, and communicating the Gospel through his music . . .

Brian Barrett still can recall as a small boy walking down a country road with his grandfather to buy ice cream at his uncle's general store.

For the good-looking and talented performer, it's an image that captures the essence of life in the rural middle Tennessee hamlet of Mona, where he was raised. It was there, surrounded by relatives, that Brian, the youngest of three brothers, learned his early lessons about faith and the importance of family values.

"Mona's really not even a town, just sort of a cross at the road," he quips. "It's located about thirty miles east of Nashville, and when I was growing up there were mostly milk farmers, dairy and corn farmers there.

"There were also some schoolteachers and other professionals—like my mom, who was a nurse, and my dad who was a pilot—who lived just outside the city. And a lot of my neighbors were family members."

Both of Brian's parents were religious people, although the Christian Country star with bluish-green eyes and boyish good looks gives most of the credit to his father for his love for religion.

"He taught me all about family values and about Christian faith. He's an airline pilot, but he's also a lay minister. He can preach with the best of them. Mostly he just shared Christ with his life. He showed there was really and truly a God by the way he lived his life."

Brian remembers how at an early age he was impressed by the spiritual example which his father set. "Oftentimes religion is a word used to mean a devotion to a tradition—a way of thinking and a way of being and a lot of ceremony.

"But both my parents—especially my dad—imparted the fact that God could be real in your life. Religion became more than just a ceremony. I learned that there could be a real relationship with Christ. A real relationship with God."

Brian learned something else from his father besides his zest for religion—a love of music as well. He recalls getting guitar lessons from his father on his eleventh birthday—on the same guitar which the popular performer uses today.

"It's an instrument that my father hauled all over the world during his stint in the Navy—a 1955 Gibson J-45. It's the one I learned on. It's an heirloom, a vintage piece. It's beat up and comfortable.

"It's a guitar that carries scars like all of us. It doesn't hide them. And when it plays, it sounds all the better because of those scars."

Even before he started to play the guitar, Brian recollects being attracted to music. "I started performing when I was eight years old. I remember being in a musical in school. That was my first public performance."

Much like that old guitar, Brian discloses that his spiritual life sometimes needed more tuning as he grew older—and wilder. "I was thirteen when my father was transferred by the airline he worked for to the Dallas/Fort Worth metroplex area, so we relocated there.

"It was definitely an adventure. It was also kind of a shock to me. I wasn't used to having a neighbor within half a mile. I lacked direction and I lacked knowing who I was. I was a little wild and going off on the wrong path."

Brian recalls turning to music to help him adjust to a new school and a strangely different lifestyle. He first joined his high school band, but seeking a more creative form of expression, with a few friends he soon formed one of his own.

It wasn't songs about faith or his experiences as a young Christian trying to keep his balance in an ever-changing world that Brian remembers singing about back then, but 1950s and 1960s rock 'n' roll—the kind of music he had grown up listening to when the lines between Country and rock weren't as distinguishable.

"They'd be songs that I heard from my father's record collection which included everything from Chuck Berry to Hank Snow."

Brian continued performing with his band through college, leaning more toward following in his father's footsteps and becoming an airline pilot than pursuing a musical career. He had already obtained his pilot's license and was getting ready to join the Air Force in order to gain flying experience.

"I was definitely planning on a life of flying airplanes and giving up on being a communicator with music. And when I got out of the Air Force I was going to settle for the dollar."

Brian did not know it at the time, but that flight plan was about to be revised. "What happened is that my father was going to sing at a revival, and he asked me if I would come along and tape it. So I wound up at this little revival service."

One moment Brian recalls peering through the lens of his video camera, and, in the next, finding himself in the midst of a life-transforming religious experience. "I started to hear this still, small voice. All of a sudden I started to realize that God was speaking to me.

"He was wanting to show me who I was. He was giving me a plan for my life that had to do with music and communicating for Christ. And He was cluing me in on everything. He said, 'I love you. I love who you are and I've got some wonderful things for you.'

"I understood that night that while I might know all about Christianity and religion—all about the Church—I still knew very little about the Author who made all those things possible and who made me.

"That's what was happening to me. I began to realize that the only way to get to God was to accept Christ. I began to talk to Jesus. I said, 'I don't know you. I know all about you but I don't really know who you are personally. I want to know you, so please come into my life. Forgive me for all the things I've done.'"

Brian cannot remember how long this experience lasted. All he can recall is suddenly snapping out of it and feeling astonished by what had just transpired. "I felt like a new creation. I felt brand new. The Bible calls it being born again. I realized that all my past had been forgiven and that I had a bright new future.

"There weren't any great sins I needed forgiving for. It was an average kid's life doing wild stuff, but I realized that even the most minuscule things came between me and God.

"I also felt like I had been rebelling against the truth—knowing what's right but not doing it. That I had wasted time and wasted effort were things that hurt the most.

"The people I had affected and influenced I had often influenced the wrong way. I looked back and said, 'Wow, why was I influencing someone that way? I could have been influencing them for eternal values.'"

When Brian caught up with his father and excitedly related the events of the evening, he remembers how his father's face was filled with sheer delight.

"Parents aren't dumb. They know where their kids are spiritually and even physically. They know what their kids are going through. So he was very elated and relieved and we both prayed and thanked God for what He had done."

While his religious conversion was joyfully greeted at home, at college Brian received a different reaction from his friends. Brian, after all, was known as cool rock-'n'-roller.

But now Brian was trying to explain to his friends that he had suddenly become more interested in the writings of John the Baptist than John Lennon.

Brian shrugs his shoulders at the memory of the cool reception that he received. "A lot of them were surprised, especially when I went back to my college and began sharing Christ with people. Some of them were even shocked. But that's what happens with life-changing experiences."

He also remembers that the best part of his religious conversion was no longer feeling confused about what direction his life should take. No longer was it all so complicated. All he needed to do was leave it up to God's will.

It soon became apparent that Brian's Maker was not interested in having him fly planes for a living. "God had different plans for me. The minute I said yes to Him he began putting things in motion that would ensure me a path that He would carve out for me.

"A week after I turned my life over to Christ at that revival service I met a friend who took me under his wing. He worked for a record company and said, 'This is what goes into a good song.'

"So I began writing songs and learning what goes into a good song. I wanted to communicate about God entering my life and I was now able to put it in music."

In 1992, after a Christian record company had heard some of his songs, Brian was hired to write with some of their songwriters. They also suggested he enter the Gospel Music Association's New Artist Showcase.

He was one of twelve entrants chosen from more than three hundred entries to perform live during Gospel Music Week, and he won the competition. "When we're truly living for God and wanting His best, when we have faith in Him and want to give Him the glory He deserves, he puts people in positions that make Him look good," Brian proclaims.

As his career continued to progress, and he found himself in much demand as a performer, Brian soon became touted as the top new unsigned Christian act.

Several record contract offers followed, but it was the Christian-oriented Star Song label that Brian decided upon. Shortly afterward, his debut album was released.

The album not only went on to win critical praise, but the most popular track on the album seemed to reflect God's ironic sense of humor—it was a song Brian had written called "A Wing and A Prayer."

Brian's voice brims with warmth as he recalls another blessing that came into his life after his spiritual renewal. "I was feeling particularly lonely at the time. I was single and I said, 'Lord, here I am following you and I'm still single. I have to deal with loneliness, too, because I'm still a human being.' "

Brian had hoped for an immediate response to his plea for companionship, but that was not to be the case. "It was a challenge to my faith to patiently wait on God and his timing to change my situation.

"And while I was waiting for an answer to my prayers I wrote a song called 'In Time'—it's about being a Christian and being single. Meanwhile, I continued to pray that God would send me a wife.

"I prayed, 'Lord, wherever my wife is, please send her my way and put her right in front of me.' It turned out that about a month later I came home from a concert—my roommate was having a barbecue get-together—and there was this young lady sitting on my couch."

It didn't take long for Brian and Katrina's friendship to blossom into wedding bells, with the young couple actually tying the knot in a surprise ceremony at their own engagement party barbecue.

It is a story which Brian is fond of relating, hoping that it will inspire other singles not to abandon hope of finding a mate. "God works for us and prayer is a powerful thing. So keep praying because He's just waiting to listen and to answer."

Despite his strong religious faith, Brian candidly admits that there have been moments while onstage when doubt has set in about his ability to communicate God's message. He considers those times to be tests of his faith.

"Sure there have been moments when I'm thinking, 'Lord, am I getting through? I feel like I'm not connecting.' And that's where the faith really comes in. You have to trust that even when you're at your worst—when your best is your worst—that you are doing what you have to do.

"Not knowing at a concert if you've really connected with your audience is really discouraging for an artist. Sometimes you want to connect by hearing applause—that's always a good meter to judge things. But that's not always the case with this type of music because my lyrics don't always mean everything to everyone.

"That has happened. And then someone who was at that concert will write me a letter and say that I really touched their heart. That's encouraging to me that God has answered someone's prayer once again. You think you've failed—and maybe you have—but you've done the best that you could. And then God does something like that and it keeps reviving you.

"People have also come up to me after a concert and said, 'I really want to know this person, Jesus, that you're singing about.' In those moments I feel blessed to have a real opportunity to share my faith with people and have them ask for Christ to come into their lives and make them a new creation."

Brian believes that the only answer for someone seeking a closer relationship with their Maker is to have faith. "That faith comes by hearing—listening to the word of God—listening to people who speak God's words out of the Bible. The Bible's not just a historic book to blow dust off, but it's very applicable to everyday life."

Prayer, he emphasizes, also is a powerful tool for getting God's ear. "Usually I pray when I get up early in the morning because there are no distractions yet. Before the phone starts ringing I ask, 'Lord, what would you have me do today?'

"I also thank Him and praise Him for giving me life for another day. I'll say, 'Lord, inspire me and energize me today. Help me be aware when you're speaking to me and when you want me to speak to people.'

"That's what I pray in the mornings—all the time. I pray for my family and other people, because praying for others is very important for me. After that I'll pray for anything really."

Living the life of a servant of God and communicating the joy of God's truth are the passions that drive Brian and make his music so unique. "I want so much to communicate the Gospel in a way that will be a beacon to a world that really needs a savior.

"It encourages me so much that people are listening—not just to the music, but to the message. I see myself as a minister first and a performer second. I'm really making it my goal in the future to figure out some sort of concert situation that may have to last two or three days, so that you further the kingdom by actually making disciples.

"I don't just want to sing a song and hope that somebody grabs a piece of that and loves God more. I really want to invest in their lives . . ."